Play On!

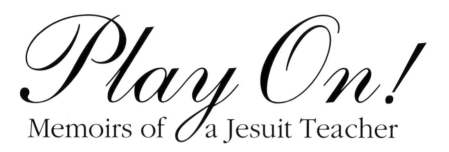

Play On!

Memoirs of a Jesuit Teacher

C. J. McNaspy, S.J.

Foreword by Louis A. Poché, S.J.

an imprint of
LOYOLA PRESS
Chicago

Special thanks to the following who contributed photographs for these memoirs—Thomas Clancy, S.J., archivist of the New Orleans Province; Eugene Geinzer, S.J., chair of the art department at Loyola University Chicago; my nephew and *tocayo,* Judge Clement Kennington; Arthur Stern, director of university relations at Loyola University New Orleans; Harry A. Tucker; Sidney J. Pivecka for the still life designs; T. Frank Kennedy, S.J.; and Jim Hietter of the University of New Orleans, friend and former student, for suggesting the quotations from Shakespeare and Keats that provided the title for the memoirs.

 an imprint of

LOYOLA PRESS

3441 North Ashland Avenue

Chicago, Illinois 60657

Cover and interior design by Anne Marie Mastandrea

Cover photograph by Sidney J. Pivecka

McNaspy, C.J. (Clement J.), 1915-95

    Play on! : Memoirs of a Jesuit teacher/C.J. McNaspy

        p.   cm.

    Includes bibliographical references.

    ISBN 0-8294-0867-3 (alk. paper)

    1. McNaspy, C.J. (Clement J.), 1915- . 2. Jesuits—Bibliography.

I. Title.

BX4705.M47657M37   1996

271'.5302—dc20   95-37834

[b]   CIP

Heard melodies are sweet, but those unheard
Are sweeter; therefore, ye soft pipes, play on;
Not to the sensual ear, but, more endeared,
Pipe to the spirit ditties of no tone . . .

John Keats, "Ode on a Grecian Urn"

If music be the food of love, play on . . .

William Shakespeare, *Twelfth Night*

Contents

Foreword

C. J. McNaspy had already moved to the Jesuit retirement home in New Orleans when he was asked to consider adding a final chapter that would take an overall view of the story of his life. It was obvious to us, however, that C. J., who had suffered a stroke in June 1994, was not up to the task physically. My ready suggestion to him at the time—"Let us write the last chapter for you"—was said with the same ease and spontaneity that might have prompted me to say fifty years earlier at Grand Coteau, "Let me carry those boxes over to the library for you." The plan seemed simple enough, and C. J., reluctantly at first, began to mention a few names.

Before C. J. died on February 3, 1995, he had the satisfaction of knowing that his last book was ready for publication. He had, in fact, actually drafted a letter to the editor a few days earlier, stating that the manuscript was on its way, but both manuscript and letter were still on his desk when the end came. Those who contributed to chapter 19, and his other friends as well, can take consolation in knowing that C. J. spent some of his last hours reading the chapter and sharing it gratefully with a few select visitors and family members. That he was finally granted this moment to allow others to express themselves about him certainly stands, in my mind, as fitting closure to the extraordinary life of one who was himself always ready to say "Thank you" and to encourage others, usually with compliments, and to move on to whatever came next. C. J. was characteristically concerned that none of his friends should seem to have been overlooked in his memoirs and hoped that everyone would see the contributions to chapter 19 as merely representative and certainly not exclusive in any sense.

The very title of this last book suggests the unfinished nature of much of what C. J. McNaspy stood for and taught. It will also be a constant reminder that something of his genius and great spirit can live on and that his memory will always bring out the best in the many scores of people whose lives he touched.

Read on!

Louis A. Poché, S.J.

Preface

Fact or Fiction?

Because friends were kind enough to encourage and even urge me to undertake this project, and later to offer help in transcribing and proofreading, I decided to go ahead with the present memoirs. Not that I feel endowed to memorialize anything especially important, but many memories suggest daily the many blessings God has given me to be thankful for.

Since almost all of these memories involve the special people I have been fortunate enough to know and the extraordinary friends that I have made, I would be pleased if these memoirs made it clear how grateful I am for all their kindnesses. For those who do not know me, but may be attracted to the story I tell, I would hope to convey this message above all: God in his mercy has created us and given us life in a world of inexhaustible riches. In short, my purpose is captured in the immortal words of Gerard Manley Hopkins in his poem, "Pied Beauty," written at St. Beuno's, Wales, in the summer of 1877:

> He fathers-forth whose beauty is past change:
>> Praise him.

Years ago, when I was not late, but even early for an appointment with my mother, she muttered fretfully to a friend: "That kid!"—referring to me then about age sixty—"If I should ever write his biography, the librarian wouldn't know whether to file it under fact or fiction." That struck me as an apt title for this preface and even perhaps for the memoir itself, especially one as unlikely and bizarre as mine.

Someone whimsically suggested that I start by describing some of the things in my room in Thomas Hall, the Jesuit residence at Loyola University, New Orleans, where I am currently living. To anyone who knows my room, such a beginning must seem impossible, or at least Herculean. But one has to start somewhere.

The most treasured object in my room is titled quite simply:

Certificate of Baptism

PARISH OF ST. JOHN THE EVANGELIST LAFAYETTE, LOUISIANA

The Rev. W. J. Teurlings, Rector

This is to Certify that Clement James McNaspy, Jr.

Child of Clement James McNaspy and Agnes Aimée Thibodaux

born on the 22nd day of March, 1915,

was baptized on the 9th day of April, 1915,

According to the Rite of the Roman Catholic Church

by the Rev. W. J. Teurlings,

the Sponsors being Emmet Blanchet McNaspy and Alyce Thibodaux Ernst

---

Just below this certificate hangs another one, given to me and signed by "The Honorable Kenny Bowen":

Proclamation by Order of the Mayor of Lafayette

Metropolis of the Cajun Country:

Rev. C. J. McNaspy

has officially been proclaimed an

Honorary Cajun, with all the rights and privileges

and joie de vivre thereby accruing

Done this 27th day of September, 1973.

The certificate goes on to affirm: "Cajuns dislike people who don't laugh enough or enjoy enough of all the good things God has given to the Cajun country." I have no scruple about not laughing enough, though I've never learned to fish anything more exciting or perilous than the lowly crawfish. This concession on my part grants that I can't claim to fulfill all the requirements of a perfect Cajun. My mother, Agnes Thibodaux, was only half Cajun, her mother, Celestina Dellucchi, being Genoese. That complication, I suppose, leaves me a sort of "sesqui-Cajun"—full

Cajun in the honorary sense, plus half Cajun, adding up to a Cajun-and-a-half or "sesqui-Cajun."

Also greatly treasured is a little crucifix hanging on the door of my room—the "vow crucifix" given to Father John LaFarge, one of our top American Jesuits, when he pronounced his vows as a Jesuit. How did I get this treasure? Since I was the one who discovered Father LaFarge's body just after he died, the Jesuit superior of the *America* community in New York, where we both worked, thought it appropriate to offer it to me.

I was preparing to introduce a younger Jesuit friend from the New Orleans Province, Charlie Coyle, who was understandably excited at the prospect of meeting such a venerable person as Father LaFarge. He had left his door open while reading, so we walked by his room quietly and looked in. He seemed to be taking a siesta. An hour or so later, we looked in again to find him in the same position. This scared me. So I tiptoed into the room, whispering "Uncle John, Uncle John!" (Since no one of such dignity could be called by a simple first name, we called him "Uncle John," not just John. All of us on the *America* staff felt the same way about him.) It was clear, even before we reached the bed, that Uncle John had already died. This was, in fact, two days after John Kennedy's assassination, which I knew Uncle John had felt profoundly. He, too, attended Harvard and was very proud of Kennedy; indeed, the last article Uncle John published was addressed to J. F. K. as a fellow Harvard man.

Immediately I ran out into the hall, calling out as loud as I could: "Uncle John is dead! Uncle John is dead!" Only two or three of us members of the *America* staff were home that Sunday afternoon. Because New York law required that we immediately notify the police, we did our best. I recall being a bit amused by the fact that the officers who came didn't realize that Jesuits had no personal property. They kept asking where he kept his money, and we kept replying, "He doesn't have any money." Their incredulity helped combine an element of comedy with our sadness. Our staff historian, Robert Graham, sat down near Uncle John's bed and went to work using his address book to notify his best friends; meantime, I contacted the media, since Thurston Davis, our editor-in-chief, was away. The national attention was still entirely on Kennedy's death, but recalling how quickly one forgets, I sat at my typewriter and wrote down everything I could remember of that day touching on Father LaFarge.

That very morning Uncle John had asked me, with a certain sadness, if I might show the ambassador to the United Nations from Upper Volta (today called Burkina Faso) around the city. He explained, "You speak French, and he speaks only French. I don't feel equal to it today." This was the last time I was to chat with Father LaFarge, and I was delighted to be of some small help. The ambassador had a chauffeured limousine, which made it easy for us to see various parts of New York at leisure. In any case, this was one of those monumental days in one's life when you tend to remember everything.

"Uncle John" LaFarge—why was I so fascinated by this man? In a word, because he seemed to be everything that one would like to be, dream of being, if one were ambitious enough—sort of the ideal Jesuit, "a man for all seasons," dedicated to all the finest causes. He was preeminently a leader in all justice movements, especially interracial causes. He was no less a leader in the entire liturgical movement, notably liturgical arts, ecumenism, and anything that dealt with the important happenings in the world and church of that epoch.

There were so many interesting people of all races and professions, all friends of Father LaFarge, who seemed eager to share friendships through him. On one occasion, when I was just about to leave for Israel for the very first time, Marc Tannenbaum, Uncle John's great rabbi friend, came to see me to offer contacts with interesting people in the Holy Land. I had hoped to meet Martin Buber, coincidentally the very day that was to be the day of his death. Later I had the opportunity to plant a tree in Israel in memory of Father LaFarge. This was under the auspices of B'nai B'rith, the Israeli government, and other movements throughout the Jewish world. I was particularly moved when the rabbi in charge of tree-planting proclaimed that Father LaFarge was and long had been one of the Lamed Vav—the thirty-six people so virtuous that as long as one of them survived God would not allow the world to collapse. Even as I write this, I notice in retrospect that, by yet another coincidence, C. S. Lewis died on November 22, 1963, the day of Kennedy's assassination and two days before Father LaFarge's death. Lewis, surely one of the Lamed Vav, will appear elsewhere in these memoirs, another major influence in my life.

What else is in the room here? There's a curious photo of a photo of Pope Paul VI, chatting with the patriarch of Constantinople, Athenagoras, certainly one of the most gracious persons that I've ever met, again through the instrumentality of Father LaFarge. The moment being photographed occurred when I was invited to visit the patriarch, and the very picture of him with Pope Paul VI was hanging on the wall. Father Elmo Romagosa, then editor of the New Orleans archdiocesan newspaper, who was with me at the time, wittily took a second picture—a picture of the picture—with me standing near the spot where Paul VI had been standing, while Athenagoras was where he was in the other picture. A whimsical and very delightful picture to keep, embracing several wonderful memories: Father LaFarge, the liturgical, ecumenical, interfaith movements, and the like.

Outside the door of my room hang two tiny flags: one of Paraguay, where I spent nine joyous years doing mission work of varying descriptions, and, the other the Cajun flag—more properly, the "Acadian flag"—which is hardly known among non-Cajuns and thus may bear some exegesis, though its symbolism would be self-explanatory to those familiar with Cajun history. It suggests the two principal nationalities of the Acadians' background: the castles of Castile, reflecting the Spanish charge from 1760 to 1803; and the fleur-de-lis, symbolizing France, from which the Cajuns come, by various routes.

A close observer will note the presence of a golden star adorning the white spaces of my wall. In religious heraldry the golden star commonly stands for the feast of Mary's Assumption into heaven. By happy coincidence this feast fits both Cajuns and Paraguayans: the former for their day of arrival and the latter for the founding of their capital city, Asunción (obviously Spanish for Assumption).

Another memento on the wall of my room requires a more round-about introduction. Among my close friends, my forgetfulness has become legendary and never surprises me, however much it may embarrass me. A day or so before my final departure from Paraguay my absent-mindedness went beyond all bounds. A good friend (whose name I can't recall) had invited me to have lunch with him. I did remember the day and the hour, but neither the place nor the person's name. How does one get out of such a predicament?

I vaguely recalled that my friend usually had lunch not far from the offices of Paraguay's leading newspaper, *ABC-Color.* So allowing an extra hour, in order to stop and say good-bye to other friends, I took the bus toward the Centro, stopped for a minute at the Franciscan church, where the remains of Roque González's Franciscan friend Fray Luis de Bolaños are venerated, then crossed the street to Radio Caritas. My friends there invited me to have a final lunch with them, but I had to say, "Sorry, I have another engagement." "Where?" they asked. "I can't remember," I replied, blushing. "How will you get there?" they wondered aloud. "I don't know," I had to answer, "but I believe I'll find the place if I keep walking." Not surprised, my friends burst into laughter and wished me luck.

I walked on to *ABC-Color,* recently allowed to reopen following Dictator Alfredo Stroessner's expulsion, and asked to see several of my friends there. When I told them that I was leaving Paraguay, they too wanted me to have a farewell lunch. I gave the same apology and unsatisfactory explanation. They were not surprised either, but had a good laugh that I joined in.

It was beginning to drizzle as I left the office and started off in what I hoped was the right direction. I stopped at several bars, described my friend as clearly as I could, but faced the same unhappy "I don't know him" again and again. At length something struck me as familiar, the Hotel Excelsior. So I went in and asked the concierge if he remembered anyone answering my friend's description. Meantime it became clear that I had given a talk, some eight years earlier, in the very hotel I had entered. "Does anyone remember such a talk?" I asked. "Maybe the man standing over there. He's worked here for years," someone replied. I approached him with the description of my friend. His face lit up immediately, as he gave my friend's name and place of work: "You mean the Strangers' Club of Asunción? It's right next door. I'll show you."

It was still a few minutes before noon, and my host greeted me with that good news. Lucky for me, he had invited some dozen of my closest friends in Asunción for this surprise lunch. Every time I look at the lovely plaque presented to me on that festive occasion I feel a blend of thankfulness and shame.

Yet another treasured souvenir hanging in my room—the last of those that I shall mention—was a collective gift from all sixteen of the religious orders whose seminarians or young religious I was teaching at the time of my departure from Paraguay. These included—in addition to Jesuits—Franciscans, Redemptorists, Dominicans, Marists, Vincentians, and others. The warmth of their send-off, if not all their names, I shall never forget.

These mementos seem especially significant from this vantage point in my life because they indicate, quite obviously, the frames within which most of my active life as a sesqui-Cajun and as a Jesuit priest-missioner has transpired.

Chapter One

At age six, with my sister Mary Agnes.

With More Than a Little Help from Friends

Lafayette, Louisiana, 1915–31

As mentioned in the preface, my mother was a Thibodaux, and her mother a Dellucchi. The latter name, being Genoese, was better known in Louisiana in the gallicized form of Dellucky. Mama (as I always called mother) was born the day after Christmas, 1881, in Bayou Boeuf, Louisiana.

Years ago, on my first visit to Europe, I stopped in Genoa, hoping to meet at least a few of my maternal relatives, not yet realizing the Dellucchis were no rarer in Genoa than Moutons, Broussards, or Leblancs in Lafayette, Louisiana. I have no idea whether we are related to Columbus, but I can imagine some of our relatives wanting to claim such aristocracy, as do those Hispanics who claim Columbus as Catalonian, Valencian, or Majorcan. I do remember my grandmother, Celestina, assuring me that when her family journeyed to Louisiana, they came as merchants, like most Genoese.

Finding the voyage to America unendurable, the family never ventured back to Genoa. They arrived safe—if not sound—in a state near starvation. I can't remember the year, however, and have no way of discovering it, since in the last century, there were so many immigrant entries into New Orleans from Europe. In any case, the Ursuline nuns came to my family's rescue, taking them in and saving them from an untimely demise. In consequence, our family has always felt especially grateful to the Ursulines of New Orleans.

Other nuns remembered always as special friends of my mother's family are the Religious of the Sacred Heart, whose founder was St. Madeline Sophie Barat. The convent for which the Louisiana town of Convent is named was founded by the other great pioneer of that order, the recently canonized—in

1989—Saint Philippine Duchesne. This convent was where my mother and godmother, Aunt Alyce, both went to school. Some years ago it was disestablished, and the bricks and other structural elements were brought over to Grand Coteau, a few miles from Lafayette. The new convent is now the earliest foundation of that distinguished order in continuous operation in the entire world. Grand Coteau, especially St. Charles College, the Jesuit seminary there, is only about a mile from Sacred Heart Convent and is the spot where I've spent more years than any other place thus far in my life—my first four years as a Jesuit and eleven others as a young priest teaching younger confreres.

A curious datum about South Louisiana that is unfamiliar to many non-Cajuns and non-Creoles is the frequency of German family names here, my godmother's husband's name being Ernst, from the Baden family that settled in Louisiana to escape Bismarck's influence. So did many other German Catholic immigrants like the Bahlingers, Fabachers, Kellers, Hymels, Wagespacks, Freys, Otts, Speyrers (the last three names being those of Louisiana bishops). Most of these names belong to French-speaking Louisianians, who use French at least as a second language.

My father's father, born in Baltimore, left school when the Civil War broke out, joined the Southern army as a teenager, and fought in the Battle of Bull Run, during which he assumed command when his captain was shot down. Following the Civil War, Grandpa never returned to Baltimore, but went to the Midwest; there he married Anne Blanchet, of a well-known French-Canadian family, which included the first two Roman Catholic bishops of the U.S. Northwest and the first Anglican missionaries to Japan, after one of whom my dad and I were named Clement. I shall have more to say about these people in the next chapter.

My father, after whom directly I was named and whom I always called simply Dad, had been born in Herington, Kansas, on April 20, 1882. He became a versatile, skilled athlete, who entered the University of Kansas in Lawrence, but was "drafted" by Louisiana State University for its undefeated football team of 1905. True, they played only three games, but when they beat Tulane (the "Goats" at that time) 5–0, Tulane officials brought charges against LSU for recruiting irregularities related to five players, including Dad, saying that he had played at a college "out west." The protest went nowhere, though, and the victory stood.

My father and mother met in Milton, Louisiana, where Dad became school principal; they were to be married in New Orleans on September 1, 1909, at St. Teresa of Avila Church. Very near this church stands an imposing marble statue, said to be the first in the United States erected to a woman and bearing the simple inscription "Margaret"—a memorial to Margaret Gaffney Haughery. She was an Irish-born widow who operated a bakery and won the hearts of New Orleanians with her gifts to the poor and her works on behalf of sufferers during the yellow fever epidemics of the nineteenth century. When Margaret died in 1882 (as historian Charles L. Dufour relates), "governors and mayors and distinguished citizens followed her cortege." My grandmother and aunt initiated my sister and me early in life with admiration of the famed Margaret.

Shortly after my parents' marriage, they moved to Lafayette, where Dad filled several posts at the University of Southwestern Louisiana (then Southwestern Louisiana Industrial Institute). In addition to coaching football, basketball, baseball, and track, he was a revered teacher of physics and chemistry and inaugurated the Newman Club, together with Miss Edith Dupre, professor of English and one of Mama's closest friends for the rest of their lives. The first stadium at Southwestern was named "McNaspy Stadium" and the library was named "Edith Dupre Library."

Apropos of the stadium named for my father, a surprising incident occurred on July 4, 1976, during my first visit to Brazil and to the Jesuit missioners working there in the state of São Paulo. Brother Tony Coco invited me to go with him to the bicentennial celebration of U.S. independence being held near the city of Americana, not far from Campinas. Few U.S. citizens recall that Americana was founded by ex-Confederates at the end of our Civil War, who were invited there by Brazilian Emperor Don Pedro to help modernize Brazilian agriculture. While some four thousand made the venture, only about half remained. Even today their descendants gather several times a year at the cemetery and church just outside Americana; they were particularly happy to have two extra U.S. southerners for the special bicentennial celebration.

The "grand dame" of the group, octogenarian Mrs. McKnight Jones, received us graciously, especially when I showed her my grandfather's photograph, taken in Baltimore in 1860, in his

Confederate uniform. I referred to it as my "Confederate passport." She smiled sweetly and exclaimed in an uncontaminated Northern Alabama accent: "Why, Reverend, I do declare, my own grandpappy looked just like that!"

We gathered in the little church for a nonsectarian commemorative service. The visiting pastor, Reverend Cicero Sathler, invited me to participate by reading something from the Bible in Portuguese—English being almost entirely forgotten by these third-generation ex-Confederates. Reverend Sathler was particularly delighted at this first ecumenical service ever in the American cemetery and presented me as "the Reverend McNaspy from Louisiana." After the service, a young lady ran to me excitedly and exclaimed: "Are you Father McNaspy from Lafayette, Louisiana?" "Yes, indeed," I replied, "but how do you happen to know of me?" She explained happily: "Because I go to Southwestern, where the stadium-dormitory is named after your father! My name is Toni Black, and I'm from Franklin."

As is clear from my baptismal certificate, I was born in Lafayette, Louisiana, on March 22, 1915, and lived there until I entered the Jesuit novitiate at Grand Coteau on July 20, 1931. The day I was born, the first president of Southwestern, Dr. Edwin Lewis Stephens, presented me with my first birthday gift. It was a baseball bat, child-sized, which suggests a strange reverse omen. Evidently Dr. Stephens assumed that the bawling baby before him would some day become a great athlete like his father, coach of the team playing that day against the visiting Cincinnati Reds. The baseball bat, however well intended, simply didn't "take"! I never mastered baseball, or any other sport, for that matter.

Why does this story mean so much to me? Because it tells me so much about my father. Instead of trying to make me over into his image and likeness, as so many parents might, Dad decided to let me have at least some say as to what I was to become. And when he discovered that I would never have the talent or the strength, or whatever else was required, to be a competent athlete, he was (or certainly gave me the impression he was) content to allow me to be what I seemed inclined to be. For example, when he found that, in addition to studies, I had a fondness and some aptitude for music, he gave me the opportunity to learn as much as I could. Fortunately, Lafayette's Mount

Carmel School could boast a splendid music teacher, Sister Emmanuel (whose surname I never learned—in those days it was assumed that nuns had no family names). Any success I later achieved in music should largely be credited to this great teacher and to my parents' eagerness to help me develop what I seemed likely to succeed in. Many years later, while working in Paraguay, I was invited to write an article for the review *Educar* on who were my best teachers. Since almost everything good that happened to me was largely thanks to my parents, the article seemed almost inevitable in its outline.

If my parents were to be disappointed at the athletic ineptitude of their only son, their wonderful daughter, my sister, Mary Agnes, would more than compensate, being excellent in just about every sport and destined (as Mrs. Henry Kennington) to be blessed with five children, all to inherit their grandfather's athletic genes. Mary Agnes (born May 13, 1917) started school with the Mount Carmel Sisters in Lafayette in 1922, when our parents judged that I was ready to enter third grade with the Christian Brothers at what was then called Cathedral High.

Why didn't they send me to Mount Carmel for something other than music? I'm not sure, but it may have had something to do with the fact that Mama had taught grade school before she was married and I came along. It was probably more economical for her to teach both of us children at home until we were ready for school and she could return to her professional teaching. She would teach second grade at Lafayette Central School until her retirement at the age of seventy in 1951. Her success in this position led to continuing contacts and comforting visits from former students and their families. When she died in 1973, among the first to sign the guest book at the funeral home were four mayors who had been her students.

My first teacher among the Christian Brothers was an inspiring young person named Brother Emile. I don't know whether he was born in France or Mexico, since most of the Brothers teaching in Lafayette at that time were refugees from one or the other, both countries brandishing vigorous anti-Catholic laws.

After finishing grammar and high school with the Brothers, I did not see Brother Emile again for thirty years. Then one day in the Houston train station I spotted a person dressed in Christian Brothers' garb. I went up to him and spoke with the confidence

"Old Brother's boys" always have, whether in Europe, North or South America, or anywhere, and asked whether he were a Christian Brother. He replied with a laugh, "Yes, and you're C. J. McNaspy from Lafayette, Louisiana. I taught you at Cathedral back in 1922 and 1923." "Then," I calculated half aloud, "you must be Brother Emile!" It all seemed so typical of teaching brothers, dedicating their entire lives to their students. Every Jesuit I know who was taught by the Brothers seems to feel the same way about them.

One admirable feature about the Brothers' educational system is that it is (or at least was) unabashedly Christian. Bells rang often, always a signal for prayer: "Let us remember that we are in the holy presence of God," the leader for the day would proclaim. Whether everyone prayed or not, at least that moment of silence offered the opportunity. If we alumni are not all saints today, it's surely not the Brothers' fault.

Over the years I've kept in touch with a number of Christian Brothers, especially a former classmate who was until recently working in Africa, Brother Cyril (formerly O. J. Ory), a very genuine, brilliant person. He was kind enough to invite me to celebrate the Mass of his departure for Africa and to have dinner with the other Brothers, plus his own flesh-and-blood brother Sidney, before he left for the missions.

A special buddy of mine among the slightly younger Christian Brothers is Alexis Gonzales, who came to Loyola in New Orleans after a brilliant career as dean of a college in the Philippines and considerable national fame, leading to a four-page article about his work in *Life* magazine's January 31, 1969, issue. Alexis is from the Santa Fe area but loves New Orleans (and the whole world, I believe) and has been an exceptional jewel in Loyola's crown, no less than a glory of his own congregation. I find him one of the great educators here and a person who has helped Jesuit artists to an eminent degree. It was thanks largely to Brother Alexis that our international Jesuit Institute for the Arts became a reality.

Among the Christian Brothers who taught me, I was fortunate to know a number of inspiring men who introduced me not only to academic subjects but also to such interests as chess. Though I was never to become an outstanding chess player, during my school years it remained a favorite game, thanks to several brothers. I also tried to play basketball, since we were all expected to participate in some team sport. In the early 1920s our school didn't have the facilities for American football. Soccer would have been a more suitable and more universal game, but we hardly knew of its existence. I had the dubious distinction of being equally incompetent in basketball and baseball and would probably have been even worse, if possible, in soccer. (While reading over the above paragraph, my colleague Father Ben Wren reminded me: "What about the time you shot twenty-one free throws from the foul line?" This spectacular exception, as I reminded Ben, was only just that, and when I tried it again twenty years later, the rule of course replaced the exception.)

This almost total failure in athletics may have provided a paradoxical blessing: since I was a good student and musician, and loved the arts, I might have seemed insufferably snobbish if I had been even a decent athlete too. This lack may be one reason why no one in my class ever seemed obliged to give me a sound thrashing.

It was not long before I had the strong ambition to enter the Boy Scouts. Tenderfoot and Second Class were not too taxing, but then a large hurdle presented itself before I could become a First Class Scout: I could not learn to swim, not even the fifty yards required for First Class. Try as he might, my dad somehow couldn't get me to learn, probably because I was afraid of the water. So he came up with a great idea: to ask a young athlete whom I admired, Johnny Morris, to teach me. Johnny was then winning about every medal one could win in track, and later would become an All-American, coming out almost first in the Olympic games as a high-hurdler.

I admired Johnny so much (and still do, though I haven't seen him in some sixty years) that I was delighted at the idea of his teaching me to swim. We went to the college pool. Johnny stood at one end and I at the other. "Don't be afraid, C. J.," he exhorted me. "Just dive in when I tell you and keep swimming until you get to me. Don't call for help unless you have to. I'll save you if you do need help." So, I followed instructions and must have been too proud to admit I needed help. I swam to the other side and received Johnny's coveted accolade: "Good work, C. J.!" My dad was as delighted as Johnny and I. Swimming the fifty yards opened the possibility of a series of merit badges—from astronomy to music, from leathercraft to hiking, almost any merit badge I wanted except athletics, which remained forever a closed door.

An enormous help given to me by a colleague of Dad's at Southwestern was in learning to type expertly, even before I had finished grammar school. The professor of typing realized that no special intellectual skills were prerequisite: only willingness to endure a certain discipline and sufficiently large fingers to fit the keyboard. One technique that seemed her specialty was that of learning rhythm through the use of music. Our teacher had a machine that could play at different speeds. So, we started typing rhythmically but very slowly, gradually increasing the speed as we could do so while retaining perfect correctness. For this she used various rhythmic compositions, especially the Toreador Chorus from the opera *Carmen*.

While in the course of time I personally found these musical masterpieces a bit boring, I also recognized that it was worth the sacrifice of appreciation to achieve total accuracy in typing. The Underwood Method involved frequent tests of words-per-minute at five strokes perfectly made; as an incentive to accuracy we were penalized fifty strokes for every single mistake and could easily end up typing minus–thirty-five words per minute, or worse, unless we typed perfectly. Before going to high school, I was able to average one hundred words per minute. No single skill ever saved me so much time, given the fact that many thousands of pages had to be typed perfectly during all of high school, college, university, and postgraduate studies. Again, this was owing to my parents' foresight.

A more specialized study, again offered through our family's contacts with Southwestern, was an early introduction to the history of visual arts. At that time two splendid art teachers were available, graduates from Newcomb College in New Orleans who produced important art admired all over the country—the Misses Emily Huger and Harriet Joor. Both had done advanced work at the Art Institute of Chicago under Helen Gardner, whose *Art Through the Ages* has gone through many editions, becoming the classic introduction to Western and non-Western art, and a healthy remedy against ethnocentricity in taste. Once, when I asked Miss Joor to describe the Paris "Holy Chapel" for me, she responded without hesitating: "C. J., entering the Holy Chapel is like entering an amethyst!" How right she was I would later discover for myself.

My interest in the riches of the world of art came largely from the presence of these fine teachers and their willingness to help even a youngster. It meant, too, that when I finally got to the Art Institute of Chicago, a truly great museum, thanks to them I was at home with most of the masterpieces displayed. It often happened that my visits to Chicago allowed only a few hours at a time, giving me the chance to visit this world-class museum between trains.

There are, of course, many other superlative museums in the United States, Canada, and Latin America. Here in New Orleans I came to know the excellent Middle American Museum at Tulane University, which was founded by Oliver LaFarge (nephew of Father LaFarge) and Franz Blom, both eminent scholars of Mayan culture. These scholars were as modest as they were generous, receiving a twelve-year-old as though he were someone of their stature. Thanks to them, years later when I was able to visit in person Yucatán, Guatemala, and other centers of Mesoamerican art, I already felt at home.

Mama and Dad were quite ready to encourage any interest or enthusiasm that seemed worthwhile. During the first decade of my life, I suppose my main one was amateur astronomy. It became a neighborhood standing joke that "C. J. was always stargazing." In fact, Dad's students—we lived only a block and a half away from the college—enjoyed the curiosity of coming and learning a thing or two about the stars from a mere child. I would prepare my telescope and give the students a chance to look at the moon and planets and several galaxies, objects that proved interesting even with a small telescope. Regardless of age, one does communicate one's enthusiasms.

On one occasion, when Professor Stokes, the astronomy teacher, (whom we lovingly called "Daddy Stokes"), was unwell and had to get a substitute for some elementary classes of astronomy, my father, his close friend, offered to help out. This gave me the chance to line things up using ordinary textbooks and my own telescope. I typed the lectures out, given my new "toreador" skills. This minor success enhanced my enthusiasm, and when I reached the age of twelve, I wrote a miniscule book called *The Junior Astronomer* for the edification of my sister and her friends.

Only one copy was typed, dedicated to Henry Voorhies, Bill Broussard, Bobby Latiolais, Lucile DeBlanc, and Lucile's sister Aline. In any case, someone misplaced the treasured volume. Many years later, when my widowed mother was emptying a family cedar chest before changing residences, she discovered the original lost manuscript and gave it to me when I was teaching in our seminary at Grand Coteau. I enjoyed showing it to the seminarians and joined in their gut laughter. It was dated August 12, 1927, and the preface started in this stately tone:

> I have written this book just to give you an idea of the wonderful universe that our earth is in, and to give you some acquaintance of the stars, who are the friends of everyone who knows them. This book is arranged to give you ways of finding north, south, east, and west at night, and to learn the names and all about the stars that twinkle like so many jewels of different colors.

How condescending can a twelve-year-old boy get? But there is worse to come:

> A long time ago, people thought that the earth was flat and that it was floating in an endless ocean, and the sun was a ball of fire that rose in the east and plunged into the ocean in the evenings. But people could not tell how the sun kept coming up every morning and how it fell into the ocean, so they said that a god made a large boat, and every morning he would throw the sun so hard that it would keep on going until it reached the other side of the ocean, and there was a boat, ready to receive it, and all night the god paddled his boat until he reached the place to throw the sun up, as on the morning before, and all this was believed when people didn't know any better, and now we know the real truth.

Apparently I was overcoming a tendency to make my sentences too short by going to the opposite extreme. At least something can be said for my high level of confidence, if not arrogance!

My interest in astronomy, starting at a very young age, carried over into a general interest in geography and other spatial matters. I was fascinated during World War I, when I was not quite four years old, by the fact that the "great war" was going on "in the East." I'd asked Dad where the East was—it was where our back porch opened out on the garden—but that never did satisfy me, since I'd gone out a number of nights and had been disappointed at the lack of visible fireworks. I felt that war should display many such marvels and had expected to see them. I should have had a better notion of distances as well as directions. In any case, I certainly didn't realize how far things could be. Still, it was a valuable experience.

Another enthusiasm of my childhood was foreign languages. In school I was generally the poorest in French (the only foreign language taught then in Lafayette), since I was also the only one in my year who came from a family where French was not spoken as readily as English. Again the kindness of Southwestern's teachers came to my rescue, in the person of Miss Lottie Montague, who allowed me to attend her summer classes in French. The next year, thanks to her, I not only moved out of the lowest position at school, but even won the top prize offered by the French government. This unexpected success opened other doors and later encouraged me to do some elementary French teaching after I entered the Jesuit novitiate.

Eventually I reached France, and once, while riding in a train, I started chatting with a French family. After a while they inquired, "Are you from the South?" I replied, "Yes, can you guess where?" They took stabs at several towns in southern France. "No," I replied to their delight and mine: "I'm from Louisiana, the town of Lafayette, in fact!" Apparently I didn't speak the way I was expected to as an American. Something had rubbed off from my time with Miss Montague, and again I could thank my parents.

Another language interest came along about that time. I had been vaguely thinking of the possibility of becoming a priest. This was probably in part because I knew some very fine priests in our church, the Cathedral of Lafayette: Father Teurlings, who baptized me, Father Kemp, and Father Louis Boudreaux, whom I looked up to as role models. Father Boudreaux was from Louisiana, but had been chosen to study theology in Rome, and in Latin, as was common enough in those days. I recall that, at some point, I asked him if he would introduce me to Latin, since no school in Lafayette then taught it. Latin had become my own dream, and since it was in no way imposed on me, I became fairly proficient in it. When in fact I entered the Jesuit novitiate at Grand Coteau, I was reckoned a rather good Latinist, even though I'd never had a formal class. Of course, I would have been far behind many boys lucky enough to have gone to the Jesuit school in New Orleans, or any other school where they studied Latin quite seriously. In one sense, I never studied it, but had learned it—shall we say—lovingly, simply because I wanted to and enjoyed it almost as a hobby.

I recall reading something about Esperanto and then finding a grammar text, which proved fairly simple. I have not kept it up and don't think it really proved useful to me, but it did stimulate me to learn something about language in general and even to make up my own Esperanto, simpler and hence—even if I dare say so—"better" than the Esperanto of Zamenhof, with its needless inflections. I must add that Interlingua, with its more modest expectations, seems far better than either. In any case, playing with such languages proved to be fun and the path to the riches of our Indo-European family of languages.

This slight, fairly superficial learning got me into some embarrassment when I used the word *Romany* as though it were a synonym for *Roman*. While the occasion was quite trivial, I recall it clearly: in 1930, on some anniversary of the Roman poet Virgil, a contest was sponsored by the New Orleans *Times-Picayune*. Any high school student in the state could enter, provided the work could be authenticated as done by the student. It involved an essay about the *Roman* poet. I somehow had seen the word *Romany* and, without bothering to look it up in a dictionary, assumed it was roughly the same as *Roman* and alluded to New Orleans as a city with "Romany" roots. Only later did I see the word used correctly, meaning "Gypsy," and I recalled my ostentatious error. Though no one humiliated me publicly for the gaffe, I felt ashamed, especially when the judges awarded me third place; it made me almost wonder about the linguistic competence of the judges themselves.

Another language that fascinated me, but which I barely scratched the surface of, was Japanese. Meeting someone who had worked in the U.S. Embassy in Japan, I asked him to teach me how to count in Japanese. After a few lessons I learned and still remember how to count from one to one hundred in the language. Even today, when Japanese observe this slight exploit, they smile politely as if to show they recognize that I'm trying.

Today I very much wish I had learned the names of all the U.S. presidents, back at an age when it was easy to memorize names. I did learn the names of all the Jesuit superiors general from Ignatius Loyola to Ledachowski (and since have added Janssens, Arrupe, and Kolvenbach), not because I was obliged to, but simply because such a list hung on the wall in the room where we, the novices, waited for a daily conference, in silence. Rather than endure the boredom of silence, I started repeating the generals' names time after time, day after day, and still remember them today, effortlessly, whereas I remember hardly anything learned yesterday or last week!

The same apparently applies to memorizing poetry and parts of plays. About the only poems I remember in any language are those I learned long ago. I can still recite "Jabberwocky," simply because I read it over and over back when I was in eleventh grade. I can even remember the pretentious verses I wrote at that time, emulating from afar the Lewis Carroll masterpiece:

'Twas out beyond the crale Thores,
A smicky lad did blang and thunch.
His mother pleaned: "My son, don't mease,
Else the dread Organg thee grunch."
"Nix, thou crone," he thobolishly snurled;
Henced he then to shringling wood,
When out from mushy murch there burled
The Organg, and he grangled him to plood.

More important, I remember a number of Sunday Gospels, because the Christian Brothers had the fine idea of having us memorize them week after week. I can still recall by heart several of these, mainly because we learned them when I was back in grammar school. It was splendid to have us learn pericopes of Holy Scripture that would be valuable throughout our lives. I am impressed, too, by the fact that we can remember passages even in foreign languages that were learned early enough. Periodically I will astonish friends by rattling off a French poem or other that

I learned, or some stately selection of Bossuet, though I might not have understood it when I learned it.

A few years ago, here at Loyola, I was asked to be in Sir James Barrie's comedy *What Every Woman Knows*. The director, Dr. Don Brady, asked me to play Mr. Venables, an elderly British statesman. Apparently I astonished the multitudes, because we had eight performances, though I never knew what I was going to say next. My part was not the lead, of course, but it became a bizarre curiosity. I worked very, very hard—dozens of hours trying to memorize a few lines—but on every one of the eight nights the words came out more than a little different. Fortunately, the people playing opposite me were younger and could memorize their own lines. They managed to supply for my confusion too. Apparently nobody knew what had happened, except for the poor students, who were too polite to talk about it, and Don Brady, who seemed to get a large charge out of the fact that I couldn't memorize a few lines, even though I was reputed to have a phenomenal memory.

When Ignacy Paderewski, the Polish statesman and pianist, was on one of several farewell tours to America, around 1930 or so, he planned a concert in the then new Municipal Auditorium in New Orleans. In those days, New Orleans seemed quite some distance from Lafayette, there being no way of driving directly from one to the other. Several times a day, however, there was good train service, and my parents provided me with a round-trip ticket so I could get to see my favorite musical hero. My godmother, Aunt Alyce, and her husband Uncle Oscar (Ernst), whom we always called "Uncle Dutch," met me at the Southern Pacific railway station and drove me to the Auditorium, providing me with a ticket and taxi fare to get home. They lived in the Garden District, on Jackson Avenue, which was some distance from the theater.

Paderewski was as thrilling as I expected, and when he finished the planned program, he offered some fifteen encores, ending with his still popular Minuet in G. That choice so staggered the audience that eventually the stage hands had to start moving the piano off stage, in a not too subtle hint that we were not to expect any more.

Too excited to endure the quiet of a taxi ride home, I decided to walk, despite the distance. In those days one never thought of danger; hence I walked the several miles to my aunt's home on Jackson. When I went to bed I was still so thrilled I could hardly sleep. In the morning, the excitement had turned to a rather high fever, which kept me in New Orleans and away from school for several days—something that rarely happened during my school years. Probably it was the combined thrill caused by my encounter with the world's most eminent pianist and the great statesman who helped Poland get started again after World War I—altogether too much for a youngster.

Since I am not following strict chronology in these casual memoirs, this may be a forgivable moment to add a parenthesis about Paderewski. The next time he entered my life was thirty years later, in 1960 or so, when I was stationed at *America* magazine. The president of the Polish community's cultural club in New York came to see me with the flattering invitation: "We'd like to have you give the homily at a Mass that we're having at St. Patrick's Cathedral in honor of the hundredth anniversary of Paderewski's birth." At first I thought he must be a practical joker, since I couldn't imagine how anyone there would have known what a passionate admirer I was of Paderewski. The group was apparently a little hard put to find a priest-musician willing to invest the time needed to prepare such a homily.

Arriving at St. Patrick's Cathedral vested for the occasion, I paid my respects to Cardinal Spellman, probably the only other non-Pole present. I started the homily with the only Polish phrase I knew at the time: "Praised be Jesus Christ!" to which the congregation roared back, as always on such occasions: "Forever and ever, Amen!" I had picked this up from Thomas Malczewski, a devout Polish refugee from Nazis and Communists in World War II, who lived with us in Grand Coteau. Many years later I happened to be at Grand Coteau when Mr. Malczewski died; this time I started the homily with the same invocation, but in English, for obvious reasons.

Another pleasant memory relating to this period refers to a Mr. Hymel of LaPlace, Louisiana. He died a few years ago, but I first met him around 1970, when I was about to return from my stint at *America* magazine in New York. Something had appeared in the local newspapers about the fact that I was returning to New Orleans. I received a letter from Mr. Hymel asking if I was the son of a Professor C. J. McNaspy, who had taught at Southwestern and who had coached athletics there. I eagerly wrote right back and assured him that I was and would be delighted to meet him some day when I got back.

Mr. Hymel wrote again: "If your dear mother is living, I'd like to have her address so that I can visit her." I wondered whether he realized what a great distance he had bitten off in making such an offer, since he was rather elderly then, possibly about ninety. Mama was at least ninety and had only a year or so to live. It was a great event for her when Mr. Hymel drove up to the Bethany nursing home in some sort of decrepit car, all the way from LaPlace to Lafayette, and brought pictures of my dad that went back to their youth. When, together with Father Don Martin, who knew the family from LaPlace, I visited Mr. Hymel, he opened his cedar chest and very proudly showed us all the pictures he had of Southwestern's teams, which Dad had coached. These were visibly Mr. Hymel's treasures.

Chapter Two

*With God's grace, hoping to become
a companion of Jesus.*

World Without Event

Even a person as uninhibited as I am, or at least appear to be, has a hard time coping with what must seem an easy query: "Why did you become a Jesuit?" My friends (and/or heroes), John LaFarge and James "Hooty" Hart McCown, who, too, came to write their memoirs, found it difficult enough, even with their considerable literary talents, to answer the question honestly and interestingly. Whenever one speaks about someone's "vocation" or calling, one enters the world of mysteries, both natural and supernatural. With such a caveat in mind, I suppose I may rush brashly in, fully aware that I am not an angel and hoping that I'm not a fool.

Not that I consider myself in any way the "greatest of sinners" either, since my faults and limitations are at worst banal and trivial enough, and in no way would rival those of another of my heroes, Augustine of Hippo. Nor do I have the right to imagine myself a worthy "son of Saint Ignatius," that other great convert, or an easily recognizable "companion of Jesus," the real name for a Jesuit (much as some still prefer the earliest known meaning of the word *jesuitical* contained in a list of sins in some medieval prayer books, long before Saint Ignatius was born— "hypocritical," "pharisaical," and so forth).

Almost anyone interested in the vocation question observes that a close study of various *Who's Who's* in America or elsewhere will suggest that distinguished rabbis or other non–Roman Catholic clergymen are disproportionately descendants of other rabbis or clergymen. The same obviously cannot be expected of famous Roman Catholic priests.

At the same time, one often discovers relatives of distinguished clergymen in collateral lines, as if to suggest that vocations and genes are somehow related. In my own case, at least four clergymen of some distinction, while they are not Jesuits, may, if they wish, acknowledge me as a nephew. All four have the surname of Blanchet and are of French-Canadian descent, as I have already mentioned: my great-uncle Clement and his brother Jean Baptiste, both Anglican priests and missioners to Japan, and their uncles, Francis Norbert and his brother Augustin Magloire, both Roman Catholic bishops and missioners to the states of Washington and Oregon. All four were courageous pioneer missionaries.

Without attempting a detailed biography of the four Blanchet missioners, let me briefly tell how I came to learn something about my Uncle Clement (a cofounder of the Anglican Church in Japan) and Uncle Francis Norbert, Pacific Northwest missioner and first archbishop of Portland, Oregon. The latter and his brother Augustin Magloire are pithily described in volume 2 of the *New Catholic Encyclopedia* as sons of Pierre and Rosalie Blanchet, whose families had given "distinguished leaders to both church and state in Canada." Archbishop Blanchet first met Pierre Jean De Smet, the famed Jesuit missioner, in 1842, and drew up plans with him for the development of the Oregon country and successfully worked in Rome and other parts of Europe, returning to America in February 1847, accompanied by twenty-one other missionaries.

When I first visited the Pacific Northwest, I was understandably delighted to discover a number of institutions named after one or other of the Blanchet brothers, especially when contacting the distinguished Jesuit historian Wilfred Schoenberg. He seemed equally enthusiastic at discovering a Jesuit nephew of the Blanchets and immediately showed me the breviary (printed in Antwerp in the late eighteenth century) that belonged to Archbishop Francis Norbert.

My discovery of my Anglican namesake, Clement Blanchet, took place on June 18, 1979, when Don Klugston, the registrar of Sophia University's International College (where I was teaching at the time), escorted me to St. Margaret's College to meet Uncle Clement's successor Bishop Goto. Both the bishop and the entire staff of St. Margaret's showed great enthusiasm at the presence of Clement Blanchet's grand-nephew. They treated me almost as if I were a nephew of Saint Francis Xavier, and thus reminded me of the letter that Uncle Clement had sent me congratulating me on entering the Jesuit Order, which had sent its most famous missioner, Francis Xavier, to Japan. An astonishing ecumenical gesture indeed! Whether these relationships had anything to do with my vocation to the Society of Jesus I cannot presume to decide, since they may simply be coincidental.

Yet I believe that some influences to my vocation may be more obvious, if less dramatic. Professor Stokes, my close friend and mentor, had always spoken highly of Jesuits and their work in astronomy. Though I never was able to attend a Jesuit school, my parents (as I realize in retrospect) did give me opportunities to meet Jesuits they thought would inspire me—friends they knew through athletic contacts with Loyola University or Spring Hill College. These remarkable priests struck me as persons who had lost none of their humanity by becoming Jesuits. In fact, they reminded me a great deal of some of the Christian Brothers I knew at school and whom I admired enough to make me want to join their order as a teaching Brother. But there remained the nagging hope to become a priest, too, like some of the remarkable diocesan priests whom I already mentioned as among my "heroes." So I presented my dilemma to a Christian Brother whom I especially respected. He suggested that I look into the possibility of combining the two vocations of priest and teacher in a religious order. "Why not look into the Jesuits?" my teacher suggested.

An opportunity presented itself without my anticipating it: the school's tradition of having graduates make a retreat with the Jesuits at their retreat house in Grand Coteau, only some fifteen miles from my home in Lafayette. As anyone who knows Jesuits well will realize, the Ignatian retreat—a three-day version of the Spiritual Exercises—was and, I hope, is still often given before graduation from Catholic high schools. The director of the small retreat house, which later developed into a major Jesuit ministry in the South, was a remarkable young Jesuit, variously known as a chaplain in the U.S. Navy and as a remarkable spiritual director for young men and boys, a priest with the unlikely name of Sam Hill Ray. I had met Father Ray several times before venturing on this retreat and found it easy to relate to him in this first "Ignatian" experience. Father Ray knew how to inspire young people, especially through the example of modern-day heroes.

In this he was much like his friend, the even more renowned Jesuit, Daniel Lord from Chicago, whom I had met during a meeting of sodalists in New Orleans. I thus was offered two exceptional role models that fitted my spiritual needs of the moment and age. Years later, when Father Lord was to lecture at Spring Hill College, several of my more sophisticated students expressed doubt about his value as a spiritual director, and I was able to reassure them from my earlier experience. Still later, when studying theology at St. Mary's College in Kansas, despite the skepticism of my contemporaries, I was delighted to find them completely charmed by Dan Lord, as fully as my younger associates had been. Even today, in hindsight, I continue to be impressed by the number of people, of several levels of sophistication, who continue to be disciples of Dan Lord, even people who have never personally met him.

I continued to admire and like Sam Hill Ray even after I had become a fellow Jesuit of the same New Orleans Province. But my admiration cooled somewhat as I found him to be more conservative than I had hoped, and less fond of some of my new heroes, particularly in matters dealing with race and social order generally—such persons as Father Lou Twomey, whose biography I was to write under the title *At Face Value,* for which the distinguished author Walker Percy was generous enough to contribute a preface, and which another friend, Father David Boileau, had had translated into and published in Spanish.

At this distance in time—more than sixty years ago—it is of course impossible to recall the exact process of discernment that led me to believe that God was calling me to become a Jesuit, that he had offered me a vocation. Still, I felt sufficiently sure of this call to mention it to Father Ray, and he felt sure enough to put me in touch with several other Jesuits, who interviewed me regarding my possible vocation. The interviewer with the least forgettable name was Father Will Power, who, as I was to learn later, was one of the most noteworthy Jesuits of the New Orleans Province.

In any case, before I returned home, I found that I had been accepted as a novice for the Society of Jesus. Something of my happiness must have shown in my face, since the first thing mentioned by my father that night seemed uncannily "right on." It was, "I thought they'd want to keep you at Grand Coteau." In reply I must have stuttered something like "They . . . they almost did. I'd like to go back." Dad smiled knowingly, while my mother and sister burst into tears.

Later, I was to discover that for some years my father had been hoping I would some day become a Jesuit, but he was wise enough never to mention or even suggest it. I suppose he realized that I was perhaps too stubborn and self-willed to follow whatever he might hint. In retrospect, it occurs to me that it was no mere coincidence that he kept introducing me to a number of Jesuits who, he rightly thought, might inspire me to want to enter their order. I had already suggested to the family that I would like to be both a priest and a brother and had even gone to visit Bishop Jules Jeanmard, the first bishop of Lafayette and a close family friend. Bishop Jeanmard had tentatively approved me for admission to the diocesan seminary, but seemed not surprised when I returned to see him and told him of my new aspiration. He smiled and assured me that he would follow my career with personal interest and that he was not surprised that I wanted to be a Jesuit.

Bishop Jeanmard was the sort of person one would wish everyone could meet, the ideal bishop in my book and that of most of my friends, a person who combined transparent holiness with profound spiritual insight. I often felt that he must be the best human image of God. In fact when he passed away, after resigning before the obligatory date, it seemed that the entire diocese sensed that a saint had died. Though a person of considerable family wealth, he asked for what is sometimes called a "pauper's funeral." The priests of his diocese, however, realizing that he was so exceptional, saw to it that he was given a proper burial, feeling that someday the church might want to institute proceedings for his canonization. No one who knew him doubted that such a dream was a possibility.

Another personal anecdote regarding Bishop Jeanmard comes to mind. Some ten years after I had entered the Jesuits, the bishop let me in on a secret: his decision to establish the splendid retreat house called Our Lady of the Oaks at Grand Coteau. After sharing the secret, the bishop smiled and said, "C. J., I feel that I can now say my 'Nunc Dimittis'—I've completed my life's work." Happily, God had other plans for Bishop Jeanmard in this life.

Before going on to describe our novitiate, I should at least mention some of my best friends from the time before I entered the Jesuits, friends toward whom I felt and still feel very close. Outstanding among them are Sister Mary O'Callaghan of the Religious of the Sacred Heart, who graduated from high school the same day as I. She later completed a doctorate in history at the University of California in Berkeley, as a protégée of the esteemed Latin American scholar Herbert Eugene Bolton, all this before entering her religious community (where she has served in many important capacities, including missioner to Africa). Another of my friends from that time is Kate Stokes Borne, adopted daughter of Professor Stokes, whom I have mentioned several times, and mother of a number of exemplary and brilliant students—herself a person of unique goodness and high scholarship. Among my classmates at Cathedral High, an exceptional friend was the late Dr. Henry Voorhies, an eminent physician in Lafayette, who wittily prophesied our contrasting careers when he said, "Good-bye, C. J. We go our respective ways, I to kill people and you to bury them!" (A curious coincidence that we often recalled was that Henry served as Lafayette coroner for many years.) Other buddies in my class and/or neighborhood were Ulysse Broussard, Albert DeBaillon, Bill Broussard, and Leon Guidry (who was for many years postmaster in Lafayette).

Father Pierre Landry was always a special friend, both before and after we became Jesuits, as well as his four sisters, both lay and Ursuline. Over the years, perhaps the closest of my relatives in both age and affection is Mrs. John Gidiere, known as Geneviève to her many friends and relatives. To me and to my sister, Mary Agnes, "Gen" has always been another sister.

Ten postulants were accepted for the first entrance date of 1931, which was to be July 20. Why that precise date? Some time later we discovered that it had been chosen so that we would be formally accepted as novices ten days later, on July 31, the anniversary of Saint Ignatius's death and his official feast day. This would mean that two years later, on his feast day, those of us who were accepted for first vows would pronounce them precisely on the great Ignatian day. What we had not realized was that it was a mistaken notion that "postulancy" was not part of the novitiate but something distinct. Thus our novitiate was actually some days longer than canonically necessary! Was this a happy fault, a *felix culpa,* or just a plain mistake? In any case, the confusing error lasted just a few years, and later Jesuits in the New Orleans Province as in others returned to the two-year novitiate, as called for in the Jesuit Constitutions.

Of the ten persons who entered on July 20, 1931, only three survived to celebrate our recent sixtieth anniversary: Ed Sheridan, Harold Weber, and I. Harold has spent almost all his priestly life as a missioner in Sri Lanka (formerly known as Ceylon), where he is highly respected even by strict Theravada Buddhists. Some ten years ago, while I was working in Paraguay, the United Nations ambassador to that country invited me to a lecture to be given by a distinguished Ceylonese scientist. I immediately asked if he knew Harold Weber (not mentioning that he was a Jesuit priest). The scholar exclaimed enthusiastically: "Father Weber? Of course I know him. Everyone in my country venerates Father Weber!" Delighted as I was to hear this, I was in no way surprised, knowing that an important athletic stadium in Ceylon was named for the same Father Weber.

Ed Sheridan, though suffering in his last years from what would be in most men an incapacitating case of arthritis, was no less admired in America than Harold Weber is in Sri Lanka. His career, which spans more than forty years, was principally that of retreat master and spiritual counselor. At the time of his death early in 1994, Ed was the last surviving Jesuit from a highly esteemed family in Macon, Georgia, which has given an exceptional number of nuns and priests to the church, including two classmates of ours, Frank and Arnold Benedetto. A cousin of theirs, Henry Kennington, married my sister, Mary Agnes, and no one could have made a more splendid brother-in-law.

In the Society at that time, Latin was still considered essential for liturgical life, and those who seemed to excel in it were given a disproportionate amount of praise and a feeling of security. I remember that when the time came for novices to be accepted or rejected, the main criterion seemed to be skill in Latin. I shall never forget the embarrassment I felt when some of us were accepted apparently for no better reason than our skill in reading and writing Latin while several others, who seemed to me better Jesuits (one of them the late Ed Sheridan), were turned down or at least made to postpone their vow day.

Not that such criteria were ever made explicit—indeed they would be clearly denied as being decisive, since holiness was always at least theoretically the principal criterion for becoming a Jesuit. Yet, because skill in language is always easier to measure than anything as invisible as interior piety, it became easier to believe in the transcendent importance of Latin. This, I should stress, is not said with personal pique, since I was one of those who suffered least from what struck me even then as a misplaced norm of excellence. My personal distress seemed very important, nevertheless, whenever any classmate was "sent home" apparently because his talent in Latin seemed deficient.

Another point of distress lay in the somewhat narrow standards of spiritual direction. While our director of novices, Father Thomas Carey, was a most gracious and generous person and surely did his best to help us individually according to our needs, the fact that he was almost entirely deaf made communication difficult. The limited selection of available books on spirituality added to one's suffering. Though I know that *The Imitation of Christ* is reckoned a classic of spirituality and was surely one of Saint Ignatius's favorite books, I found it frequently a cause of depression, with the sort of rhetoric that could easily confuse and mislead anyone still in his teens. Even today I can read it only selectively and with great care not to fall into the deepest depression. No doubt some of the problem with *The Imitation* reflects the epoch in which it was composed, but I suspect that much of my problem with it comes from the immaturity under which I suffered when I first tried to read it, without being forewarned.

At length the great day arrived, July 31, 1933, when several of my classmates and I were admitted to membership in the Society of Jesus and entitled to sign our names with the appended "S.J." This seemed such a clear desideratum that I was a bit impatient with a dear relative when he asked me what the S stood for. "I know the J stands for Jesuit!" he explained. So, I started over painfully, explaining that Saint Ignatius had not suggested the word *Jesuit* at all, and that the S simply meant *socius* or "companion"—in this case, "Companion of Jesus."

Then studies started in earnest. We stayed in Grand Coteau for the next two years and still spent a great deal of time in what seemed the life of novices. Further, the curriculum of studies was limited, though several of our teachers were excellent. As I wrote the phrase "in earnest," I recalled instantly one of my greatest teachers, who also happened to be a great punster named "Ernest." This eminent historian, now of happy memory, author of some fifty volumes, Father Ernest Burrus, was then a young and as yet unpublished seminarian, but no less eager to teach us Latin and Greek. More important, Ernie taught us to appreciate learning and wisdom and a love of languages, several of which he had personally mastered.

After teaching us for a few years, Ernie went on to study theology in Valkenburg, Holland, near the German border. World War II was breaking out, and Ernie became engaged in a number of activities that can only be called heroic. He went on, following ordination to the priesthood, to work with refugees, helping Polish, Jewish, and other refugees escape the clutches of the Nazis, combining the difficult tasks of scholarship with what today we often call the "social apostolate." Years later, after I had completed my years of study, I was honored by Ernie at being invited to return to Grand Coteau as a member of the staff, of which he was then dean. When he was called to Rome to dedicate the rest of his life to Jesuit history at the House of Writers, I felt the personal loss deeply and was overjoyed when the opportunity came later for us to do research together.

Another teacher who touched us deeply, a true scholar, a perfect gentleman, and an ideal Jesuit, was Father Ross Druhan, who taught us history and classics and an appreciation of human values at the highest level. Other salient teachers in those early days of my Jesuit formation were certain peers of mine, some of them already deceased—Scott Youree Watson, whom I revere as one of God's favored souls, and together with whom I discovered the poetry of Gerard Manley Hopkins, and at whose departure from this life I was privileged to be present; Auguste Dessommes Coyle, a gentleman and a scholar, too, that rare combination, at whose first Mass I was privileged to be present; Albert Sidney Foley, a man of great piety and learning and one of the outstanding leaders in the interracial and social justice movement in the South; and Joseph Fichter, an author of consequence, perhaps the most eminent sociologist of our generation of Jesuits, who held the Chair of Roman Catholic Studies at Harvard immediately following the esteemed scholar who had been my tutor at Oxford, Christopher Dawson. These contemporaries of mine were among my most important teachers as well as my close friends even back in the early 1930s.

Though music was not part of the juniorate curriculum, I fortunately was able to make something of a virtue out of necessity and apply everything I had previously learned from Sister Emmanuel, Brother John, and other music teachers. Even back in grade school I had considered being something of a composer. In the juniorate this ambition became useful, since we needed a great deal of music for equal voices for use in liturgy and other church services. Fortunately for me, my fellow students were very tolerant and even seemed to enjoy whatever I wrote—masses, motets, and the like. Even then I became convinced, however, that hardly a single musical phrase of mine was original, though I tried to avoid plagiarism and mere repetition. The hard days of juniorate studies were mitigated somewhat by occasional plays, especially plays written by one or other junior. One that I remember especially bore the unlikely name of *Beau Revoir,* being a sort of pastiche of musical numbers from Reginald de Koven's *Robin Hood* and a *Beau Geste*-like plot of all male episodes.

Somehow our friend Jack Curley, with a flair for theater, managed to make use of the varied talents of our two juniorate classes, having Joe Fichter sing songs that he knew from previous radio experiences with accompaniments provided by his youngest associate, me, from an upright piano on stage. Whatever musical quality *Beau Revoir* lacked was somehow compensated for by the enthusiasm of other juniors and the novices who provided the amount of applause typical of starved audiences. In any case, the experience probably helped us all for the days ahead.

Tragedy, however, struck both of us juniors who were from Lafayette. Pierre Landry's father, one of my dad's closest friends, died suddenly in 1933. Then, on December 15 of that same year, fell the blow that I had dreaded for some time, the death of my own father. Although he had been a powerful and renowned athlete in younger years, under pressures from the depression and overwork, he suffered a heart attack. He barely recovered from this in time to accept the invitation to represent the Knights of Columbus from Lafayette in the national convention in Washington, D.C. Unfortunately, not only did he drive those thousands of miles but also he couldn't resist the temptation to climb the Washington Monument, thereby fulfilling a boyhood dream. Some weeks later, he even participated in an athletic event at Southwestern (now USL), although only as a judge.

All this proved too much for his strained heart. He drove home, parked the car in the garage, and providentially discovered my sister studying inside, just before he collapsed. She immediately summoned my mother from Mrs. Pellerin's, next door. They called our doctors and our pastor, who did everything they could until my father died, strengthened by the sacraments. A neighbor called me at Grand Coteau, where my superior very warmly tried to break the news to me. By the time I reached home, half an hour later, my father's body had been taken to the funeral parlor, while my mother waited for me. I remember clearly her first words to me: "God's been so good, C. J." I've never been so impressed by anyone's acceptance of the heaviest possible personal cross.

That was the strangest night of my life, the most curious blend of pride and sadness. Dr. Stephens, president of Southwestern, and other friends crowded into our house expressing the grief felt by Dad's students and admirers. Several friends collapsed in shock; one even died. Monsignor Teurlings held my arm and said tearfully, "C. J., I've lost my right arm." Our yard man Sanders echoed the sentence: "I've lost both my arms." The college closed that day, and the next morning the entire student body marched to the funeral Mass in the cathedral. I had no idea that anyone could be so appreciated by young people as Dad had been.

Academics aside, we were expected during these years at Grand Coteau to learn to live together as brothers. To help in this, every summer two weeks would be given over to some forms of relaxation, though almost entirely at the college itself. Occasionally there would be a bus ride, say, to Avery Island near New Iberia, Louisiana, where Tabasco sauce is made and where the then world-famed salt mines could be visited by people fortunate enough to have made arrangements in advance. Personally I had visited the Avery Island salt mines a number of times before entering the novitiate, but this only served to make the experience somewhat deeper. It is almost impossible for anyone who has not been down in a salt mine to imagine the excitement.

Another attraction of nature found near Avery Island was the exceptional opportunity to see what is known as "the first state- and nationally-owned migratory-waterfowl sanctuaries in the world," started by Edward Avery McIlhenny. There hundreds of egret nests house birds carefully named and studied. The egrets follow a precise schedule of migration, down to South America and back to Avery Island.

Other than these, very few events broke the monotony of those two years of juniorate—a "world without event," in Hopkins's pithy description of the life of a Jesuit Brother.

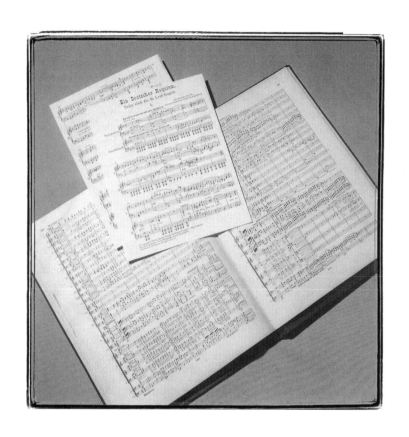

Chapter Three

*Undertaking, with expert guidance,
the serious study of music.*

Doing Humanities Too

St. Louis University, 1935–38

During the 1930s, most young Jesuits from the New Orleans Province went to St. Louis University for the next stage of what we referred to as "formation." The change meant several fairly major adjustments, since St. Louis, though almost a Southern city, differed in tone from the "deep South."

The Missouri Province had been founded by Jesuits from other parts of Europe and seemed to have a more Germanic or Dutch flavor than the French, Italian, or Spanish flavor associated with New Orleans and other parts of the vast geographical area served by Southern Jesuits—including such diverse cities as Mobile, Miami, Tampa, Dallas, El Paso, and Albuquerque. Since the New Orleans Province did not yet have the academic facilities to provide advanced degrees in philosophy and theology and St. Louis University seemed the most available institution meeting these needs, most of my generation of Jesuits "did" philosophy, as we said, at St. Louis University and then theology either there or through its cognate faculty at St. Mary's College, Kansas.

Whether in St. Louis or elsewhere, the change of venue offered both advantages and problems to young Southerners. Granted that we were fortunate enough to have in our group numbers of young Jesuits from Northern provinces, and thus felt perhaps less "provincial" in the unhappy sense of the term, the transition was not automatically easy, requiring adjustments in minor matters, such as differences in Jesuit jargon and other customs. We were frequently reminded that the differences between provinces were simply administrative matters of no real importance to the rank and file, but not all of us adjusted gracefully.

Since my father had been born in Kansas and his father in Baltimore, it may have required smaller sacrifices for me to adjust to midwestern accents than for some of my more strictly Southern Jesuit brothers. Even so, the experience increased rather than diminished my feeling of being a Southerner, and even a Cajun—much as I already detested racism, thanks largely to my parents' example. In any case, St. Louis required a "growing experience."

I must admit that the principal course of studies we were to stress as young Jesuits in this phase of our training—philosophy—proved the one I found least satisfying. Most of the courses seemed deplorably pedestrian, save for those of the distinguished lay historian of philosophy, Vernon J. Bourque. Dr. Bourque seemed, to all of us, a genuine philosopher rather than a mouther of formulas. *The Modern Schoolman,* St. Louis University's journal of philosophy, was at the time the personal inspiration of Dr. Bourque, though the seminarian editors were Robert Henle and Leonard Waters. Somehow these young thinkers, in addition to George Klubertanz, were kind enough to admit me to their group. (I don't believe I ever suspected that I could simply have been their "token Southerner," even if the term had existed.) A moment of genuine satisfaction came, however, when Dr. Bourque not only accepted one of my term papers, awarding it an A, but also suggested that I submit it to *The Modern Schoolman* editor. Whether it was simply kindness on the editor's part, or some unsuspected excellence in my article, I shall never know, but my "St. Augustine on Sensation" was accepted and published and even earned a few complimentary letters. Since I seldom keep copies of articles I have published, and don't even have copies of most of the books I've written, it is no wonder that I can't even remember the year of my *Modern Schoolman* article. It takes little modesty, however, to admit that it did not change the history of Augustinian thought.

Even so, it did lead me to go through, at least cursorily, the *Migne Patrology* volumes of Saint Augustine—tens of thousands of pages in Latin—and gave me some idea of the vastness of that great Doctor's output. Later, during my years at St. Louis, I wrote another paper on some aspect of Saint Augustine's thought, which I cannot now recall. The same happened during my years of theology at St. Mary's College.

It was probably in part because of what I felt was the mediocrity of the St. Louis philosophy faculty at the time (however eminent it was to become a generation later) that my special interests centered then on more "humanistic" studies—classics, music, and art history. St. Louis then, though not nearly so attractive a city as today, possessed a splendid art museum (to which I made repeated visits), a very imposing cathedral (in Romano-Byzantine style, with many of the finest mosaics in this country), one of the best symphony orchestras in America, the incomparable Shaw's Gardens, and certainly one of the very first skyscrapers in the world, Sullivan's masterly Wainwright Building (the perfect exemplification of Sullivan's favorite dictum, "form follows function").

It was not hard for an enthusiastic youngster to find scholars willing to share these treasures. Today, of course, St. Louis offers even more; for example, the Benedictine Priory, with its many echoes of other catenary arches that are the glory of the city, especially crowned by the world's tallest monument—Eero Saarinen's incomparable arch, the "Gateway to the West."

So far as music was concerned, the opportunities that opened up in St. Louis were vast and varied: not only did St. Louis enjoy a superlative symphony orchestra, as I've said, with occasional free tickets available to seminarians, but also a magnificent library of musical scores and a number of fine pipe organs, easily accessible to young organists, notably the instrument at St. Francis Xavier Church on the St. Louis University campus, where the professional organist Devereux seemed eager to help beginners like me. The only limit was free time restricted by obedience.

But the greatest help in my musical development at the time came from Father Gruender, a person well-trained in Germany and endowed with impeccable taste, save for a certain narrowness that excluded Bach and most baroque music on the curious grounds that, in Gruender's words, "Bach is not music, he is musical mathematics!"

Still, Father Gruender taught me to read symphonic scores, starting with Schubert's great C Major Symphony. He placed the score in my hands and started playing what was the finest recording I had ever heard (this was 1935), with no hints as to what the mysterious German terms meant—such words as

posaunen and the like. He almost explicitly made it clear that I
was an idiot for not knowing all this, but his pedagogical manner forced me to learn, and for that I am eternally grateful.

I attended Gruender's music appreciation courses as well
and learned his more simplified manner of visual structure, with
letters like ABA or words like *exposition, development,* and
recapitulation (all now more or less standard and which I
employed in my own teaching). I learned to use various colors
for key relationships, especially full visual projections of scores,
together with pointers and the like. I was always thankful to
Father Gruender for starting me out seriously and for providing
techniques that could be amplified and developed, both by me
and by my more alert students in the United States as well as in
Latin America.

Another competent musician who aided me a great deal was
Father Raphael McCarthy, like Gruender also a psychologist of
standing (and also something of a rival of his, to such an extent
that my ambiguous position as an informal protégé of both complicated my life as much as it enriched it!). In the field of
Gregorian chant and other great liturgical music, St. Louis
offered other opportunities. I was able to come to know and
study under the great Benedictine musician, Dom Ermin Vitry,
whose approach to Gregorian was both related to and different
from that of Solesmes Abbey. This diverse approach saved me
from a tendency toward dogmatism (always present in young
musicians).

Another exciting musical discovery of my life in St. Louis
came thanks to the music library of the city, which opened
opportunities to discover such great choral sacred works as
Brahms's *German Requiem,* Verdi's *Requiem,* and several works
of the English Catholic composer Sir Edward Elgar, notably his
Dream of Gerontius, then enjoying a revival in the English-
speaking world. I had been moved by Richard Strauss's exceptional eulogy of this work, found a copy of the score in the
library, and proceeded to study it in detail, there then being no
recordings available.

It gradually occurred to me that one could, with the diverse
talents available at St. Louis University, simplify the choral work
(one hoped, without destroying it) into all-male voices and spoken choruses. Among the talented singers who made our per-

formances possible were Joe Fichter, John Walsh (of the Missouri Province), Karl Reinert (the future president of Creighton University), and Charles Hunter of Belize, who would later work as spiritual father and novice master in several provinces. Among the speakers were Lou Cervantes (of St. Louis) and Harold Weber (of New Orleans and later of Sri Lanka).

This prolix description of a single event may be justified for serendipitous reasons, especially because of the growth of my friendship with a young professor at St. Louis who seemed to admire the production and support it—H. Marshall McLuhan. While I was never a member of the English department at St. Louis University, either as student or faculty member, my activity as director of the chorus of scholastics helped me get to know several teachers there. Principal among them at the time was Father McCabe. One day, shortly after he had employed McLuhan, a Canadian recently graduated from Cambridge University in England, Father met me in the hall and mentioned that Marshall McLuhan was interested in getting to know someone interested in music. We met in Father's office and quickly discovered interests in common.

My ignorance of modern English poetry at the time was no less than monumental, since our English teachers at Grand Coteau treated the subject as though it had ended in the early nineteenth century. So, the idea of at last learning something about modern English poetry was thrilling, to say the least. In return, I was happy to introduce Marshall to some of the delights of music and to help deepen his knowledge of Virgil and Dante, both of whom were then and continue to be special enthusiasms of mine. Marshall was astonished to discover that I knew nothing whatsoever about Gerard Manley Hopkins, the great Jesuit poet of the late nineteenth century. We started with several of the "Terrible Sonnets," which proved a revelation to me.

Later that same day, Youree Watson and I went for a stroll. Each said to the other: "I've just discovered the most wonderful poet!" The discovery turned out to be identical. We agreed that a week later we should identify our favorite poems among the small but intense volume of G. M. H. To our great surprise, our pairs of favorite poems corresponded exactly, though nothing had been done to influence our decisions. We agreed, thereupon, to choose favorite lines in our favorite poems before the next week, and, again to our surprise, the lines corresponded exactly, or at least with few exceptions. This discovery was rather reassuring to both of us, since we did not fancy ourselves to be experts in the work of a poet we were only beginning to discover. I reported our experience to Marshall McLuhan. He, of course, was delighted too.

Fortunately both Youree and I were able to share our delight in G. M. H. with our own students during the forthcoming experience of "Regency," the term then used to describe a period of teaching between the study of philosophy and the study of theology. Later, too, when Youree was teaching our young Jesuits philosophy at Spring Hill College and I was teaching in the juniorate at Grand Coteau, we were able to introduce our students to the great modern poet. Though my dear friend Gus Coyle, who taught most of the English poetry at Grand Coteau, openly admitted that Hopkins was not his "cup of tea," he showed no objection to my fondness for the poet and even invited me to be guest lecturer when he felt Hopkins could be introduced without violating the historical sequence. I've certainly never met a more generous person in my life than Gus Coyle.

My principal focus of study at St. Louis was somewhat naturally on classics. Before leaving Grand Coteau, I had been able to read all the required works of Latin and Greek literature for a possible future doctorate. This included, of course, all of Homer, the Greek dramas, the extant Greek lyrical poets, and at least the major works of the great prose writers. Roughly the same was true of Latin literature, which proved easier, given the lesser quality and quantity of Latin classics.

One major exception lay in Medieval Latin, where I had the great fortune of having Otto Kuhnmuench as mentor. This was a sort of golden age of Medieval Latin studies, and Father Kuhnmuench was recognized even at Oxford as a top person in the field. It was a delight to "discover" with him the quality of the patristic age Latin poets—such extraordinary men as Prudentius, Ambrose, Fortunatus, and the like—as well as the later medieval poets from Notker Balbulus to the Renaissance Latinists. Happily, Father Kuhnmuench was eager and willing to make use of my music studies, especially in Gregorian chant, and urged me to study the literature of the liturgical "sequences," from the beginning in Notker to the climax in Adam of St. Victor,

and the few remaining sequences adorning the Roman liturgy—
Dies Irae, Stabat Mater, Veni Sancte Spiritus, and the *Lauda
Sion Salvatorem.*

Why this special interest in the sequences? Because, as an
art form, they were among the few works of poetry where
the music came first, this music-poetry order explaining the
unexpected structure found in most of the sequences. Even
today, when few sequences remain in liturgical use, the Easter
sequence (*Victimae Paschali Laudes*) illustrates some of the
variety experienced in most early sequences. For example, the
rhymes and other techniques associated with Latin poetry (of
the Middle Ages) are in general not as strict in the Easter
sequence as in most Latin hymnody, being dependent on the pre-
existing music.

Father Kuhnmuench's prescience eventually became evident to me, as I discovered that much of the material used for
my Latin master's thesis could also be used in work for the
Licentiate in Sacred Music, and even in doctoral work. St. Louis
University was an ideal place to study Medieval Latin, since its
library possessed the entire collection of Latin hymnody gathered by Dreves and Blume, fellow Jesuits who had done pioneer
work in the field and whose major article in the old *Catholic
Encyclopedia* remains a classic.

Other major professors in the field of classics at the time in
St. Louis were Dr. Charles Korfmacher, who proved a sympathetic master in the area of Greek lyric poetry, which I learned
to love as hardly any other; Father James Kleist, a major Christian
Scripture scholar; and Dr. Chauncey Finch, freshly graduated
from the University of Michigan in classics and one of the few
people in St. Louis able to teach Sanskrit. It will surprise no one
to learn that when his course in elementary Sanskrit was
announced in the catalog for the 1937–38 academic year, dozens
of ambitious students signed up for it and lasted exactly one
class, as they discovered how much was presupposed in gram-
matical formation.

Among the few survivors were the later famed scholars
Robert North, James Naughton, John Justin Jolin, and two or
three others already advanced in classical studies. The textbook
used in our course was Edward Delavan Perry's *A Sanskrit
Primer,* then in its fourth edition, and one of the few textbooks

that I still preserve and enjoy "playing with." As I was clearly the poorest of the surviving members of the class, no one was surprised that I dropped out during second semester. Nonetheless, I shall always treasure Dr. Finch's superlative introduction to Indo-European grammar and his appreciation of Sanskrit itself. Not long ago, while visiting St. Louis, I had the presence of mind to phone several of his grandchildren and thank them vicariously for what Dr. Finch had given me years ago.

Shortly before taking my final exams in philosophy and in classics, I recall a very pleasant drive over into Illinois with Marshall McLuhan. We visited several Native American mounds and discussed all manner of personal issues. "Do you plan to get married?" I asked. "I don't think so," replied Marshall. "I plan to be wedded to my work." A few months later when I was at Spring Hill College, I recall receiving a letter from Marshall announcing, "I've just met a marvelous person named Corinne. She is large and has masses of hair and is from Dallas." I saw the handwriting, and my thoughts were confirmed some weeks later when another letter announced, "Just married Corinne. We're very happy!" From then on I looked forward to meeting the marvelous Corinne.

Another special friend whom I was sorry to leave was a Jesuit of my year, Willie Doyle. A person of enormous sensitivity and artistic talent, Willie was the perfect companion for our occasional visits to the museum or other beautiful vistas. His brother Johnnie, also a Jesuit, was a good friend too, but a person of somewhat different tastes. Later he would become my nephews' favorite teacher at St. Louis University High, and the three of us would be ordained priests together on June 21, 1944. Not many years after, Johnnie became a victim of cancer. Willie documented lovingly every day of Johnnie's decline in the most moving set of sketches that I've ever seen.

Chapter Four

*In front of the Spring Hill College
Library, its Ionic columns a backdrop
for the production of* Oedipus
Tyrannus.

Sophocles, Brahms, and Magnolias

Spring Hill College, 1938–41

Leaving St. Louis, we Southerners headed by train for New Orleans, center of our province. The provincial, Father Tom Shields, had news for us about our "status," as we called appointments. Mine was to teach both lay students and Jesuit scholastics at Spring Hill College, in Mobile, Alabama. This seemed terrifying, since I was aware of my youth and limitations. Somehow, the thought of teaching people of my own age or younger was not too frightening, but trying to teach people who were older seemed different. The provincial, however, reassured me and gave me the assignment as a challenge.

Even so, a rather long, tedious summer school had to come first, at Jesuit High in New Orleans—in mid-summer with, of course, no air-conditioning and with cassocks worn to all classes. Further, in the afternoon we were to have courses in physical education, never one of my favorite interests. As the smallest person in the class, I was treated with some sensitivity, being placed on top of pyramids, while my friends suffered the burden of the day. I recall that Ed Donohue (we called him "Pops") weighed 280 pounds, exactly twice as many as I did then. Fortunately for me, he was considerate.

A very pleasant experience, however, happened during the summer school. We were to do remedial work with students who had had trouble passing regular courses. I asked my aunt, who lived in New Orleans, to drive me past the homes of all of the "flunkies," believing that one would learn something about their problems from their status or wealth. One of the wealthiest lads in New Orleans was one of my "flunkies," but it would be indelicate to name him even at this late date. Another, who has since died, was neither too wealthy nor too poor, but he had trouble with studies. I invited him to do two extra hours per day with me for free. He did, and later his parents credited my extra work with his getting through Jesuit High. His name was Rudy Anderson; his brother Bobby's son Bentley is now a very successful Jesuit.

Spring Hill College has one of the most arcadian and loveliest campuses at least in the United States, if not in the world (as a British professor assured me)—avenues of oaks and magnolias lined with every variety of dogwood and azalea. Even today, after storms and hurricanes and mistaken goodwill, Spring Hill remains a favorite of anyone lucky enough to know it.

In those days the dean of the college was Father Andrew Cannon Smith, who had a doctorate in English from the University of Chicago and was truly as brilliant a scholar as anyone I had met at St. Louis. He was happy to let us know what was expected of us and tried to fulfill our needs. I asked him if I could teach elementary Greek. Apparently my predecessor, far more ancient than I, had felt that the Greek situation was hopeless. So I asked Father Smith if I could see the IQ's (or whatever term was used in those days) of the in-coming freshmen and obtain permission to invite (not cajole) them to do elementary Greek with me. He agreed, and as soon as the freshmen arrived they were subjected to a barrage of friendly persuasion.

About a dozen of them joined the course, which took the practical and likeable approach to the language as soon as I persuaded them that the New Testament was probably the only classic that was easy to read in the original. Fifty years later I still keep in touch with several of them, including Warren Clark, shortly before his death. Warren was married to Mary Higgins, the distinguished writer, whose novels grace almost every Sunday book review of the *New York Times*.

I also requested and received permission to start a glee club. What made this volunteer group acceptable was, I believe, the fact that I centered it on some of the best athletes in school. Never an athlete myself, I still appreciated athletics and let it be known. While Spring Hill was not strong in the major sports, it had given scholarships to at least three of the most talented young tennis players of the country: Lou Faquin, Eddie Moylan, and Tony Walsh. During the three years that I taught at the Hill, our tennis team won every match against other colleges. Eddie

Morgan, the sole survivor of this stellar team, seems never to forget his old teacher.

Yet another project that the dean allowed me to get involved in was *The Spring Hill Quarterly,* a smallish outlet for the talents of young poets and the like. Thanks to the generosity of more gifted friends, I was able also to help our Spring Hillians learn to love good music. Sam Betty (who has recently celebrated his golden anniversary with his wife, Lily) had what was in those days a rare collection of excellent recordings. He made them available to me and my classmate Lou Eisele (recently deceased), who was the greatest experimenter I've ever known and perhaps the most generous. Lou had discovered that three or four loudspeakers working together would produce a very special symphonic sound. So this he did in anticipation of the electronics explosion. Between Sam's fine recordings and Lou's superlative "system," we were able to approximate a truly stereophonic sound, though the term didn't enter the English language until 1957. A room on the bottom floor of the library was assigned us, the same group of friends, but under a new title—"Philomelic." The group met every week and eventually was able to provide academic credit. Fortunately, Spring Hill was small, and the dean was alert to opportunities and challenges. He said "no" to very few proposals of this sort. He also allowed me to start a course in History of Art, which I tried to run in conjunction with the "Philomelic."

Other friends in Mobile, not students at Spring Hill, came together with considerable frequency to enjoy the same recordings that Sam had loaned us. We quickly discovered that all of us were passionately fond of Brahms. Whereupon we started the Brahms Society, or rather we simply acknowledged that the Brahms Society already existed. Each of us was nominated and elected an officer. Spring Hill was renamed Karlgasse (the street where Brahms had lived in Vienna) and once or twice a month, especially during summer when the boarding students were not around, we met at No. 4 Karlgasse, which simply meant the bottom floor of the library, or the porch with its classical Greek columns. One or other of us would write a mock serious musical column for the local newspaper, with all the proper apparatus, columns which would duly appear in time. This elicited considerable curiosity in the city. When at length I was able to

visit Vienna and especially Karlgasse—near the great cathedral—my joy hardly knew any bounds.

During my second year at Spring Hill several of us decided
to perform a Greek play, *Oedipus Tyrannus,* to be precise. We
even went so far as to try to build a Greek-style theater down
near the Hill's beautiful lake. Since most of the future performers were no more athletic than I (architecture needs more than
enthusiasm), our theater remained in the dream world. But we
spent a summer making our own translation of Sophocles' masterpiece. David Loveman, from Tennessee, turned my literal
translation into poetry that could be performed, in fact, that
would be performed by Dave himself. F. Taylor Peck (later a
member of the U.S. diplomatic service) translated the choruses
into appropriate meters and planned the appropriate ballet
steps. Decades later, when I was doing mission work in Paraguay,
I several times met old friends of Taylor's.

Other people who worked on *Oedipus* were our future
novice master Robert Rimes and missionary to Sri Lanka
Frederick Cooley. The role of Oedipus himself was played by
David, while the leader of the chorus was tennis player Tony
Walsh. A fellow scholastic, Dick Wooley, who had directed several fine plays at Spring Hill during his own regency, was kind
enough to take charge of *Oedipus.* I trained the chorus in as
painless a way as possible: we sang through all the choruses
once every class day from the beginning of the academic year.
This way I was able to assure them that with fifteen minutes
invested each day they would remember everything effortlessly.
In fact, many years later I find that I can still sing the entire
choral parts with no difficulty. A student oboist did all accompaniments, since the modern oboe is closer to the sound of the
ancient flute; he worked with Frank Kearley—later to be
Professor Kearley of the Spring Hill faculty.

The costumes were created by a close friend of Frank's,
Eugene Walter, well-known designer of floats in Mobile's Mardi
Gras, and later an associate with Fellini and successful novelist
both in Italy and this country. A great thrill was to be given me
when I heard a voice near the Gesù in Rome call out: "St.
Clement the Benign, welcome to Rome!" I was sure that it was
one of the Brahms Society of yesteryear. At our first reunion in
some thirty-five years, Eugene escorted me up to his fifth floor

apartment across the piazza from the Gesù and allowed me to photograph the marvelous facade from that unfamiliar angle. Whenever giving a lecture on the Gesù, I include the view from Eugene's apartment.

Oedipus was performed on the porch of the Spring Hill library, with its Ionic columns predominant. Nothing could be done about the possibility of rain on the night we had chosen, save to leave open the option of a change of schedule. But what about mosquitoes? Here our chemist factotum Frank Kearley came to the rescue, suggesting that the incense of the Greek altar be pyrethrum, the perfect exterminator of mosquitoes. As a double precaution, we sprayed repellent under each of the six hundred chairs provided for the audience. Even so, the night in early May proved perfect, and I've never seen a more receptive audience of students, graduates, alumni, and members of the Greek community of Mobile.

Many years later, when I was teaching young Jesuits at Grand Coteau, we were no less blessed by the elements on a comparable night for our second performance of *Oedipus Tyrannus.* Though the audience was smaller, it included visiting deans from all Jesuit juniorates of the U.S. as well as the distinguished Indian member of the United Nations staff, Jesuit Father deSouza. The outdoor setting, the haunting Greek-like music, the dedicated young performers, combined with Sophocles' high drama to produce once again a performance that was, at least to me, unforgettable.

I hope to be forgiven for apparently overstressing the proportions of what may seem a single event in my life. Yet, whenever I think of regency, *Oedipus Tyrannus* comes first to mind, since it includes some of the finest people I've ever worked with, at a golden moment of our young lives and it relates most of my cultural interests in the classics: dramatic, literary, and musical. Even more, *Oedipus* demonstrated that one doesn't need a genius to be productive, provided that collaboration is richly present. In a sense this production showed the work of a university in microcosm.

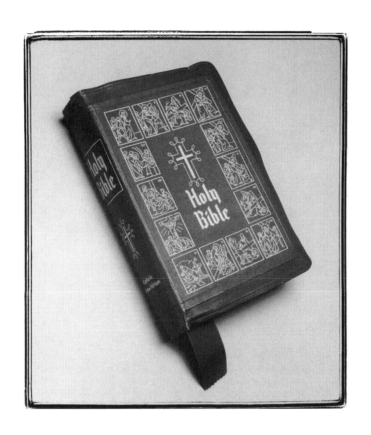

Chapter Five

*God's word, revelation's source, and
the firm ground of theological inquiry.*

An International
Brotherhood on the Plains

St. Mary's College, Kansas, 1941–45

Fascinating as humanistic studies were, both on the receiving and the sharing ends, I remember feeling again and again the intense need of something more. I don't suppose that every Jesuit goes through the same experiences, though I do remember hearing parallel if not identical expressions. One reason why I was so happy to begin the explicit study of theology itself was the sheer need I felt for such knowledge, especially for total immersion in Holy Scripture.

By way of immediate preparation for the study of Holy Scripture, and with some assurance that I could already handle both Christian Scriptures and patristic writings in the original Greek, I spent the summer of 1941 at Spring Hill College, before going to theology at St. Mary's College, Kansas, working on the other sacred language, Hebrew. To my surprise and delight, I found Hebrew, at least in its early stages, far easier than I had expected. The textbook that proved most available started with the Book of Genesis, which, as everyone knows, is both easy to read and most rewarding. I've seldom experienced such poetic surprises as those discovered in its first chapter. To find that the expression for chaos in the original Hebrew was the nearly onomatopoeic phrase *thohu wa vohu* was at least what youngsters today call "awesome." It did not take long for me to become convinced that some of Genesis was highly original and could not be a mere translation.

The journey to St. Louis en route to Kansas renewed old contacts, with the chance to visit Father Kuhnmuench and Doctors Korfmacher and Finch among others. I was able to thank them personally for all they had contributed to my early education.

I had heard enough to realize that St. Marys, Kansas, was not St. Louis any more than it was Mobile or New Orleans. Yet I knew that the college itself, rural as it was, offered a superlative library and some first-class professors, in addition to the renewal of old friendships, since most of my former St. Louis classmates would be back with us again. I also knew that Kansas had been my father's home state and that there would be echoes of tales told by him during my childhood. It turned out that there was more ahead: thanks to one of my Kansas classmates, Austy Miller, I was able to discover that a number of Dad's relatives were still very much alive, among them being Ed Chapman, respected editor of the *Topeka State Journal*.

It was not long before Cousin Ed and his wife Birdie visited me in St. Marys. (Lest you be confused, the town's name, though the same as the college's, is spelled without benefit of the apostrophe.) Their two sons were away in the army, and since my own parents were nowhere near, we provided surrogates to each other, even though our relationship was simply that of second cousins. When the time came for me to be ordained to the priesthood in St. Mary's College's beautiful chapel, my mother was able to make the difficult journey (remember, it was during World War II). She and the Chapmans, though meeting for the first time, felt at home together.

Years later, when I was stationed in Rome, Bill Chapman (Ed's younger son) advised me that he would soon be there. We spent a fascinating time together visiting St. Priscilla Catacomb and the ancient basilica of St. Paul's-Outside-the-Walls. One of the high points of my time in Kansas came when the Chapmans invited me to drive with them to Herington, where my dad's family had lived and where he had been born. We visited other relatives still living in or near Herington and saw the high school where Dad had graduated. To me it was all very much a pilgrimage, a sort of vicarious homecoming.

Later I found it interesting to discover that coincidentally the state of Kansas had a special relationship with the country of Paraguay (where I was then working) and that many excellent Paraguayan students were given scholarships to the University of Kansas in Lawrence. The students included science majors as well as literature and music specialists. Years later during my time as a missioner in Paraguay, the outstanding young Paraguayan instrumentalist, an oboist named Jorge Postel, was awarded the most eminent prize after some years of advanced study in Europe together with the finest award in his instrument at the University of Kansas. I was particularly touched that the Paraguayan award committee decided to name it "el Premio McNaspy" after my dad, an alumnus of the university.

At St. Mary's it did not take long for me to get to know the Ellard brothers, Fathers Gerard and Augustine, both among the giants of American theologians. Gerry was an outstanding liturgist and Gussie a master of the spiritual life and mysticism. To know them was a blessing, and even more to be received by them. Very much as Father Kuhnmuench had done, Gerry recognized me as a fellow scholar, given my advantage in music. When *Caecilia* magazine invited me to write a series of articles on "Great Men of Sacred Music," lives of famous church musicians, I was fortunate to have Gerry as my official reader.

One of the special delights of our years at St. Mary's came in the inauguration of *Review for Religious,* a modest but fruitful monthly magazine geared to the special interests of seminarians and religious women. The founders were Gerald Kelly, our professor of moral theology; Adam Ellis, the professor of canon law; as well as Gussie and Gerry Ellard, mentioned above. Despite great gestures of confidence from their colleagues, the founders believed that subscribers would never number as high as one hundred, and even wagered a free shoe shine if ever that number was reached. Everyone was agreeably surprised when the first issue attracted several times the wagered hundred.

In fact, the entire experience of *Review for Religious* was a constant success story, with thousands and thousands of subscriptions today. By definition the *Review* was hardly a scholarly journal, but instead an effort to provide rather easy spiritual reading, which encouraged a number of us amateurs to compose and submit articles for publication. Gerry Kelly was particularly sympathetic and quick to encourage young and inexperienced writers like me. The slightest encomium from a person so highly admired was enough to stir one to creativity, such as the time Gerry said unblushingly: "You're a good writer, Mac." No accolade from anyone else could have been so inspiring. I forget the article's theme, but it may have been something like "What Does Mary Mean?" Or it could have been something on Our Lady of Guadalupe or on the Shroud of Turin.

While many of the standard courses at St. Mary's proved as uninteresting as one might expect, there were superlative courses in church history (by Gerry Ellard) that more than compensated, as did Gruenthaner's magisterial sessions in Holy Scripture held at night for a chosen few who hoped to major in scripture. Here our star was Bob North, particularly when he ventured to express his sentiments about the course. One evening he fairly attacked Father Gruenthaner: "Dear Father, you give us such excellent courses in private, but our courses during the day are dreadful. How do you explain that?" Father Gruenthaner winced and blushed, proceeding to explain that he had hoped to keep a high standard in all classes but that so many mediocre students complained to superiors that he felt he should give up and be mediocre with them too. A sad commentary indeed. But our private courses continued to be excellent, and by the end of theology I found that I had read in the original Hebrew the entire Hebrew Scriptures, as well as a translation of the Christian Scriptures into Hebrew.

Toward the end of our theology course, the New Orleans Province superior asked me which of three distinct specialties I felt best qualified to pursue. He indicated that I had been invited by the people in charge of scripture at St. Mary's to go on and get the doctorate in biblical studies, although he felt that since so few scholars were available in our province, while the Missouri Province had many, it would be better for me to decline the invitation. So I did. He then mentioned that the philosophate faculty at Spring Hill had invited me to major in the history of philosophy, since I had taught the course at Spring Hill and the people there had seemed well pleased. He asked me to think it over and take counsel.

Providentially, my two closest associates in the area, Youree Watson and Arnold Benedetto, were at St. Mary's. So we went through a discernment process together. The remaining option was a choice between majoring in history of philosophy or preparing to teach in the juniorate at Grand Coteau. History of philosophy was tempting, especially because both Youree and Arnold were going on to major in philosophy, and this would ensure that the three of us would spend most of our lives in the same community.

Even so, as we reflected and tried to discern prayerfully, it gradually seemed to the three of us that, much as we loved the possibility of working together in the field of philosophy, my spontaneous leaning was less toward the abstract than toward the poetic and artistic. This tendency indicated juniorate studies, and our provincial was thoughtful enough to offer me a year of experience as a juniorate teacher before possibly going on to get a doctorate in an appropriate academic discipline, classical or artistic. My dissertation in Latin at St. Louis University had been found satisfactory for a doctorate. All that was needed to complete the doctorate was one, or at most two, semesters of course work. The solution to this dilemma would present itself a bit later.

Meantime, I had been able to publish several more articles in *Review for Religious, Orate Fratres, Caecilia,* and half a dozen other journals before venturing on to the *Catholic Biblical Quarterly.* A minor article was accepted dealing with the topic of immortality in the Hebrew Scriptures, the result of a seminar done with Father Gruenthaner. Later, when Gruenthaner had become editor of the *CBQ,* he urged me to study the still controversial topic of the Shroud of Turin. Though our professor of Christian archaeology, Father Augustine Wand, assured me that his former professor in Rome, Father de Jerphanion, had refuted the arguments in favor of the Turin Shroud, when I read his refutation it struck me as shockingly frivolous. Ironically, de Jerphanion had helped me move from a skeptical to an accepting attitude toward the Shroud. I am quite aware that in recent years some new arguments against the Shroud's authenticity have become popular, and I have studied these arguments as thoroughly as possible. But I must say that, at this time of writing, I find the arguments in favor of the Shroud's authenticity still stronger than those opposed. It seems to me that the facile acceptance of the "carbon counting" theory hardly matches the serious arguments in the Shroud's favor. (See "The Shroud of Turin," *Catholic Biblical Quarterly,* April 1945.)

Theology as an academic discipline is surely very important, though its finality for a seminarian is not purely academic. From the beginning of the Jesuit course of studies, one always keeps in mind (or at least is expected to keep in mind) the priesthood that one feels called to accept when one is officially invited to embrace it by the Jesuit Order's superiors. Nontheological studies possess a high value, though, and should never be trivialized, despite one's zeal for the priesthood; moreover, I in no way wish to suggest that Jesuit brothers are less Jesuit than Jesuit priests. But in a theologate (or to use the more common term today, "faculty of divinity"), the closer the day of ordination approaches, the more one senses the call to this greater fulfillment.

The ordination class to which I belonged included some sixty Jesuits, all roughly the same age (thirtyish), with a majority of North Americans, but four Mexicans and six Filipinos. The day was June 21, 1944, though we still followed the bizarre custom of having the subdeaconate and deaconate on the two preceding days, as a special Jesuit "privilege." Since World War II was on, and our Filipino brothers were completely out of contact with their families, it was a difficult time for everyone.

Other classes at St. Mary's during those years added the poignance of having Jesuits from countries that were at war with one another. The most exceptional of these coincidences was the presence of three German Jesuits who had joined the Japanese mission and who had done work in Japan before coming to the United States. Theoretically they were our enemies, and especially the enemies of our Filipino brothers. Yet, if ever Christian love overcame nationalism, it was at St. Mary's during World War II. Not only did I never see the slightest indelicacy or unkindness, I have been repeatedly assured by our German-Japanese brothers, again living and working in Japan, that the kindness they experienced was incalculable. Those three Jesuits are among the finest friends our country has. Much of this kindness was simply the concrete expression of Saint Ignatius's insistence on Jesuit unity and brotherhood. Yet one can hardly imagine such a successful realization of the Ignatian principle without exceptionally sensitive leadership, specifically that of our superior at St. Mary's, Father Dan Conway, affectionately remembered as "Durango Dan," since he hailed from Durango, Colorado. Anyone who studied at St. Mary's during those exciting days can illustrate from personal reminiscence this sense of international brotherhood.

Father Dan Lord invited me to work in his Summer School of Catholic Action, teaching liturgy and liturgical music. I felt very much obliged to Gerry Ellard for having recommended me and for facilitating my becoming known in these important areas. In fact, this apparently unimportant invitation proved very significant in my life as a young liturgical musician. Among other important people, one very special friend was the Benedictine Ermin Vitry, whom I had come to know during my St. Louis days; another was the dean of the Conservatoire Nationale of Canada, Dr. Eugène Lapierre, whose guidance during my year in Canada was of incalculable importance, as was that of his colleague and mine, Alfred Bernier, S.J.

Certain events stand out so vividly in our memories that we all seem to recall exactly where we were when the events took place. One transcendently important event that occurred during my first session of SSCA was the dropping of the first atomic bomb on Hiroshima on August 6, 1945. I have the sharpest recollection that I was in downtown Milwaukee, where newspaper headlines screamed about the "atom bomb," leaving us in doubt as to what this mysterious expression meant. I later discovered that even the wife of my Chapman cousin knew nothing of the bomb on which her own husband was working.

To end my recollections of the four years at St. Mary's, which roughly spanned the period of World War II, it may serve as an appropriate frame to mention another of those significant memories, one that occurred less than a semester into my theological studies. I am referring, of course, to the world-shattering event that is remembered by everyone simply as "Pearl Harbor." My personal memory situates that happening on the eve of December 8, during our choir practice for the Mass of the Immaculate Conception, when someone burst into the practice room and shouted, "The Japs have just attacked Pearl Harbor!" Where was Pearl Harbor? most of us wondered, though I was lucky enough to remember that our old neighbor, Captain Doran, had been stationed there and his daughter Mary was one of my childhood correspondents. Naturally our Filipino Jesuit colleagues felt the attack even more, since it coincided with the attack on Manila, from which they were cut off "for the duration," as we always put it during the war.

Chapter Six

At work on my standard typewriter,
another life-long companion.

Chant among the Mohawks

Grand Coteau and Mont Laurier, Canada, 1945–47
Grand Coteau in the summer of 1945 was far hotter than the north, but also the beginning of a dream come true. I didn't realize that my assignment was an experiment, so far as our faculty was concerned, since they would be involved in the decision about my immediate future. Being there with Ernie Burrus, my old juniorate teacher, and Gus Coyle, my buddy from scholastic days, Ignatius Fabacher from the wonderful Louisiana families of Fabachers and Bahlingers, and Anthony Achee, the distinguished novice, tertian master, and rector, who later was invited by Father General Pedro Arrupe to replace him as tertian master in Japan and whose grave in Hiroshima is constantly adorned with flowers—all this I find unforgettable.

My principal job during that first year in the juniorate was teaching Latin, Greek, and cultural history, as well as directing choir and drama. It will be clear to anyone who has read the chapter dealing with my regency that the superiors had obviously assigned me subjects that I had shown some competence in and that would give them a chance to judge my capacities for juniorate teaching in the future. They were quick to allow me to extend my tasks to include frequent lectures, ministerial jobs, some radio work, as well as assistance to the Newman Club at Southwestern in Lafayette, the very Newman Club that my dad had founded—indeed the first in any southern college or university. In point of fact, I was allowed to accept the invitation to speak to the entire Southwestern community, which came from President Joel Fletcher, a close family friend.

Among outstanding students during my first year at Grand Coteau were Thomas Clancy, who later became academic vice president of Loyola, then provincial, and more recently director of missions for the province; Robert Rimes, whom I had taught at Spring Hill during regency, and who later became a very successful novice master and spiritual director; and several missionaries to Sri Lanka—Fred Cooley, Lloyd Lorio, and others. When I returned to Grand Coteau after tertianship, I asked Father Achee whether he had known that I was going to return. He replied, cryptically but unambiguously: "No, but I knew what I wanted." This period is often regarded as a sort of golden age of the New Orleans Province at Grand Coteau, especially when we consider not only the faculty but also the number and quality of the young persons we were privileged to teach.

At the end of my first academic year at Grand Coteau, another invitation to teach in Dan Lord's Summer School of Catholic Action (SSCA) arrived and was happily accepted. This particular summer was spent in New York, with the school residing at Fordham University. Once again I taught liturgical music, with emphasis on Gregorian chant.

It had been decided that I should not make tertianship (a sort of second novitiate at the end of the Jesuit course) at Grand Coteau, since I was to spend many years of my life there; a change of venue would be healthy both for my students and for me. Providentially, I believe, I was sent to do this special year in French Canada, at Mont Laurier in Quebec province, where I could deepen my feeling for the French language and for my Canadian-Acadian roots at the same time.

I had discovered that the Mohawk Indians enjoyed the rare privilege of doing all liturgical choral chants in their vernacular, unlike other Roman-rite peoples who were required to use Latin. For years, thanks especially to the great Jesuit liturgist Gerry Ellard, I had become convinced that our liturgical singing would never become truly functional until it could be performed in English. I had also realized that it would be a long time before Rome allowed this radical but necessary change. It occurred to me that while in Canada I should try to study the Mohawk solution to this problem and was fortunately given the occasion to do so in Caughnawaga (now called Kahnawake), across the river from Montreal in the Jesuit Mohawk parish.

In retrospect, it seems particularly providential that I came to know even better Dr. Eugène Lapierre, dean of the Conservatoire Nationale of Canada, partly because we taught in the SSCA together for a second summer and partly because this involved a number of lengthy train rides together. On one occasion Dr. Lapierre happened to be studying a symphonic score. I glanced at it, recognized it, and began to hum it with assurance. Dr. Lapierre seemed astonished and asked what degrees in music or musicology I had. "None," was my simple reply. He quizzed me at length on my knowledge of Gregorian chant, classical polyphony (Palestrina and the like), and baroque and classical European music. Later, when Ermin Vitry, O.S.B., gave me a detailed examination on one of the most elaborate Renaissance motets that I've ever studied, he reported to Dr. Lapierre that he was satisfied that my knowledge of music and musicology was of doctoral quality.

These two scholars, together with Alfred Bernier (the leading specialist in Mohawk liturgical music), determined that if I could do a complete study of the *Liber Usualis* in its Mohawk translation and it passed the doctoral board's examination at the conservatory in Montreal, I could be officially awarded the doctorate in music and musicology. Using spare time in tertianship and opportunities to work with the Mohawks in Kahnawake, I was able to meet the conservatory's requirements for both the licentiate and the doctorate. The latter degree was awarded *summa cum laude* at the Conservatoire Nationale of the University of Montreal on June 10, 1948, surely one of the most memorable events of my life.

The decision to accept this degree—officially "in course" and not *honoris causa*—required considerable thought and reflection. As mentioned earlier, I was only two semesters away from a doctorate in classics at St. Louis University (my dissertation having already been accepted), but at just this time in my life came the unexpected invitation to study for a year at Oxford University, with no special course requirements. Since I already held a doctorate in one of the subjects I expected to teach during the rest of my life and had done virtually all the work required for another doctorate in classics, it seemed far more useful for my future work (teaching young Jesuit seminarians) to spend a year in the ideal academic climate of Oxford, with freedom to attend whatever courses my tutor recommended, than to remain in the United States and satisfy specific academic requirements for the second doctorate.

Campion Hall of Oxford University, whose master at the time was the venerable Father Martin D'Arcy, accepted me as an Oxford scholar, but Father Thomas Corbishley, Father D'Arcy's successor, would be my official tutor (Corbishley held one of the most precious of Oxford degrees, the "double first in greats"). Thus, in mid-September, 1947, together with two dear colleagues, Jimmy Yamauchi and Gerry Fineran, I sailed on the *Mauretania* from New York for Southampton. Yamauchi's blonde Glasgow-Irish aunt met us at the port and drove us to London, where we were billeted at the renowned Jesuit headquarters on Mount Street.

How does one describe the sentiments of young Americans at the first glimpse of the Houses of Parliament, Westminster Abbey, and St. Paul's, even in its comparatively dilapidated state following the Battle of Britain? Monuments abandoned as clichés suddenly soared into life, particularly after the epic of British heroism (even to one whose blood is a blend of Irish and Acadian!). Yamauchi and Fineran implored me to go on with them across the channel to Louvain, where they were to study theology for four years. They somehow felt that even my imperfect French would be better than no French at all. And so it proved. I was delighted, too, at the prospect of seeing Paris for the first time and especially Chartres (still my favorite cathedral). All the more did this seem urgent, since the Cold War had already begun and seemed likely to become hot before one would feel secure in peace.

On October 1, my train pulled into Paris, and I assisted at High Mass in Notre Dame, followed by a quick first visit to La Sainte Chapelle. Needless to say, I remembered how Miss Joor had described it years before as "entering an amethyst." That afternoon I visited two cousins, Ben and Clare Thibodeaux.

Ben, a native of Breaux Bridge, Louisiana, with a Ph.D. in economics from Harvard, was at the time in charge of the Marshall Plan's food project. Prior to military service during World War II, he had worked for the U.S. Department of Agriculture for ten years in South America, the Middle East, and North Africa. At the war's end, he entered the U.S. Foreign Service, was stationed in Paris, then loaned to the State Department's Marshall Plan headquarters for two-and-a-half years, where he was working at the time of my visit. Thereafter, Ben served in various capacities in

American embassies around the world—Vienna, Ottawa, and Tokyo. Since his retirement in 1960, he and Clare have been living on an estate near Grand Coteau, Louisiana.

With Ben hard at work, Clare found time to drive me to Versailles—again an unforgettable "first." Since I was staying at 42, rue de Grenelle, just a few steps from the Thibodeaux's, we were able to start the next day's trip to Chartres fairly early, going by car so that the gradual discovery of the two towers could be enjoyed as in no other way. I prayed that this first pilgrimage to my favorite shrine would not be the last. (Without attempting a count, I believe my prayer has been abundantly answered, perhaps twenty-five times.) Clare and I "did" the Louvre, too, before I returned to 42, rue de Grenelle, in time to start strolling down the Champs-Elysées with a New York Jesuit, in search of a simple dinner to fit our slender wallets.

As a firm believer that "in the kingdom of the blind the one-eyed are kings"—*"dans le royaume des aveugles les borgnes sont rois"*—I brashly undertook to read menus and prices until we found one that seemed appropriate to our needs. We ordered one thing, which I was sure was meat—*"Saucisse de Strass-bourg."* Despite being served with much panoply and panache, it proved to be one "hot dog" apiece. My linguistic reputation, at least with this New York Jesuit, sank to unplumbed depths. Still, it gave us something to laugh about during the rest of our lives.

Chapter Seven

Beginning with England and Central Europe, my first direct experience of Christendom's art and architecture.

Led by a Kindly Light

Campion Hall, Oxford, 1947–48

On October 3, 1947, I discovered the sort of dislocation one can experience going from one European country to a neighboring one: this time it was the contrasting experience of the Paris Metro and the London Underground and the linguistic challenge of a single railway compartment with representatives of six nationalities (something else I had known only in movies). The following day I spent visiting Westminster Cathedral and the Oratory and on the fifth moved on to Oxford. There at Campion Hall, I met a New England Jesuit with whom I was to share many wonderful experiences, Father Tom Grace.

The next day, celebrating Newman's anniversary, Tom and I visited Littlemore, with its several treasured monuments—Newman's pulpit, his garden, the treasured copy of "Lead Kindly Light." On October 11, we went to register with the police and food-ticket office. My experiences with the English police were uniformly happy, as though *police* and *polite* were cognate words. On more than one occasion I was able to get a free ride just by showing need. And what about "food tickets"? Two years after the war, food was still in short supply, yet the fairness of distribution made no one feel the shortage.

One day, however, what may have been a minor miracle took place. I went to Father Corbishley's office bearing a parcel. Brother Parker was there, visibly shaken, rubbing his hands. "Father," I broke in, "we've just received a gift from Puerto Rico. I suspect that it's food." To everyone's delight it proved to be perhaps fifty pounds of sugar. "Thank God," murmured Brother Parker, as Father Corbishley explained his plight: "A miscalculation led us to the conviction that we had absolutely no sugar for the next month. This will carry us through the shortage!"

Brother Parker enjoyed the twin reputation of being both a saint and absent-minded. This episode was obviously a confirmation of the reputation, since the parcel came from a person I had just met once in the United States, a Mr. Ramon Agudo, who thought we might be in need of sugar! The date of this happy arrival is snugly written in my diary: "Wednesday, March 10, 1948"—a day never to be forgotten.

In a sense almost every day at Oxford could be called "never to be forgotten," as I discover scanning over my pocket diary for 1947–48. I decided, for reasons of spatial economy, to jot down only those events that seemed truly exceptional and find now that fewer than one in ten days on the average is unfilled, and even they could have been filled with exceptional class lectures. In fairness, all of E. R. Dodd's lectures on *Agamemnon* would be considered extraordinary in almost any other university, as would E. D. M. Fraenkel's on Horace or Catullus or other classical poets. C. M. Bowra, who brandished the title of "Warden of Wadham," seemed to know more about heroic poetry than many libraries contain. H. M. Last radiated a sense of ancient history the likes of which I had never previously experienced, while J. R. R. Tolkien, who has become a household name today, was just beginning to thrill all of us with his wonderfully fresh creations. His friend C. S. Lewis—already a star for his talks on the BBC, his *Screwtape Letters,* and the great *Perelandra* trilogy—was so popular as a lecturer that his classes had to be held in Examination Schools, those buildings where students take their entrance exams. No mere classroom could accommodate the throngs of his admirers. In this, as in so much else, the C. S. Lewis of the great film *Shadowlands* is true to fact.

A special feature of Oxford lay in the constant availability of outstanding scholars, whether or not they were your personal tutors. Several very popular professors guided such groups as the Socratic Club or the Aquinas Club, or the more specialized Opera Society, to mention just a few. One of the happiest of Oxford experiences took place every Thursday evening in the second term—our Byrd group. Oxford's most distinguished musicologist, Jack Westrup, invited seven of his students to read aloud the entire *Gradualia* of William Byrd, the giant Tudor composer, sometimes called the Shakespeare of music. Byrd, as every musician knows, was the eminent Roman Catholic composer at a period when to be known as a Catholic subjected one to the danger of martyrdom.

True, Queen Elizabeth I loved music and admired William Byrd enough not to have him hanged, drawn, and quartered. At the same time there remained serious risks for anyone in such a high position. As a consequence, much, perhaps most, of Byrd's religious music could seldom be performed. His three masses, for example, were never publicly performed, though today they are recognized as among the finest in all musical literature. The *Gradualia,* all in Latin, were no less obviously Catholic, and probably were never performed in the intervening centuries until Professor Westrup succeeded in having them published. It was our privilege to be perhaps the first persons ever to sing these hundreds of compositions since the Elizabethan age, and even the non-Catholics among us felt the awesome privilege that was ours.

Years later, at Grand Coteau, a group of juniors who read music well did something analogous: we read through, as musically as we could, all of the Palestrina masses—more than a hundred of them. The same group of readers also went through Casimiri's editions of classical polyphony in search of masses and motets that would prove both high in quality and within the range of amateur singers. This was, obviously, a by-product of my Oxford experience.

The other arts were well served too. At the time I was at Oxford virtually all of the colleges could boast at least several major works of architecture, ranging over a considerable number of years—from the fourteenth to the twentieth centuries, from William of Wyckam to the present, somehow mysteriously harmonizing together. When Sir Kenneth Clark addressed us in lectures that were to become his masterly *Civilisation,* we could find in the Ashmolean Museum at Oxford living proofs of what he claimed, nor were we far from most of the masterpieces of European schools, whether British, French, Italian, Spanish, or German. Furthermore, the academic year was designed to allow for many months of salutary travel. During the six weeks of Christmas vacation, I was able to visit at leisure all of England's great cathedrals from Durham to Winchester. There was time, too, especially during Easter vacation, to journey on pilgrimage—both religious and secular—to Italy, from Milan to Monreale, including the mosaics of Ravenna, the Giottos of Padua, the whole panoply of Venice and Florence. It seemed that all of European art and architecture was at arm's length. Long before Easter, Tom Grace and several of his lay friends invited me to join them on a pilgrimage to Rome. The group encompassed Jim Hester (Rhodes scholar, later to become head of NYU and the United Nations University in Tokyo, and whom I was to meet many years later in Tokyo); Alfred Latham-Koenig, a Mauritian scholar later to become one of the founders of Oxfam; and Antonio Fernandes, a Sinhalese scholar and friend of friends in Ceylon. We were scheduled to meet in Rome two very special friends of mine whom I have already mentioned, both doing graduate studies at the Gregorian University, Youree Watson and Arnold Benedetto, my colleagues in theology at St. Mary's in Kansas and ordination classmates of June 21, 1944. Each of them knew Rome better than any of us, and they divided their time so that one would spend mornings with us and the other afternoons.

As a special treat they had arranged for us to enjoy a papal audience with Pius XII, the pontiff who had survived World War II and was then recognized as a hero. A curious episode, little noticed by others, took place when the master of ceremonies explained the procedure we were expected to follow when the pope came in. Suddenly one of our group—a nonpracticing Baptist—grabbed my arm and in all seriousness whispered, "C. J., if I kneel down before the pope, won't that be the sin of idolatry?" I was surprised that he remembered the word idolatry, or that he accepted the concept of sin. But I had to take him seriously, not sure whether he was lapsing into superstition or facing a call of grace. So I muttered, "Well, I'm sure the pope wouldn't want you to commit a sin. I plan to kneel, not adoring him but as an expression of veneration for his office. Do whatever you believe you should do." "I don't know what I'll do," he whispered in response. A moment later, however, when the pope appeared, he was the first one on his knees—his good old rusty Baptist knees.

The Italian elections forthcoming at the time were most crucial because they would determine whether Italy was to be ruled by the Christian Democratic Party or the Communists. Rome became a sounding board for what was to be the future. Every morning during those critical days, especially Holy Week and Easter Week, the rival parties turned every available square meter of space into the most captivating, if not always the most tasteful, propaganda pieces known even to Italian artistic wit. Though serious, it all seemed a gigantic circus, and this was surely an ideal time to be on pilgrimage to the Eternal City.

The throngs that normally fill St. Peter's Piazza extended all the way to the Tiber on that Easter Sunday, as though an outpouring of fealty to the beleaguered pontiff. St. Peter's Basilica is looked upon as the center of Catholic Rome, indeed of the Catholic world, inasmuch as it has been the pope's residence for some centuries (though not technically "the Cathedral," since the Basilica of St. John Lateran had been designated Rome's Cathedral back in the days of Constantine). In retrospect it is hard to imagine the tension of those days, since we know how thoroughly the Communist party was routed. Nothing seemed clear or even clearly probable in those hectic days.

An encounter that I had in St. Peter's Basilica on Good Friday brought me, for a moment at least, close to home. I happened to spot a familiar looking face, at some distance across the transept. He looked so much like other members of the McCown family of Mobile, Alabama, that I overcame my timidity and went right up to him with the query: "Are you a McCown from Mobile, Alabama?" He looked terrified, apparently suspecting I was a member of the FBI or worse! I reassured him more or less with these words: "You must be a relative of Hooty and Helen and Larry and the whole family of McCowns. I know them all but can't account for you." He was, in fact, Bobby McCown.

There were concerts that Easter afternoon, one by the Budapest String Quartet (doing Beethoven) in what was technically a *teatro,* the other performed by the symphony with the Busch brothers doing the Brahms Double Concerto (a rarely performed masterpiece). Which would I go to? My decision was determined quite simply by church regulations as they stood rigorously before Vatican Council II. Had I gone to the Beethoven performance in a *teatro,* I would have been suspended from priestly functions, while the Brahms (being done in the Santa Cecilia Hall, not technically a *teatro*) could be enjoyed without ecclesiastical penalty. And some people still think of the "good old days before Vatican II" as a better time to be alive!

Since I have often tried to describe the marvels of Rome (in books like *A Guide to Christian Europe* and *Rome, A Jesuit City Too*), feeling frustrated at every step, it may prove safer here simply to mention some of the more obvious: the four great basilicas so dear to Saint Ignatius and other founding fathers of our Society, the great churches founded by or for Jesuits (Sant' Ignazio, the Gesù, Sant'Andrea al Quirinale), of course the masterpieces of Bernini and Borromini, and perhaps most of all several of the catacombs, notably Santa Priscilla, which even after thirty or forty visits remains my favorite.

The splendid church of Trinità dei Monti with the memorable shrine of Mater Admirabilis was one of the first I visited and at which I celebrated Mass, my principal reason being the fact that it was the shrine perhaps dearest to the Religious of the Sacred Heart, the community Sister Mary O'Callaghan belonged to and with whom my mother and godmother had studied. The shrine of Our Lady of Perpetual Help was another family favorite, since it belongs to the Redemptorists, in whose parish in New Orleans they lived. I was to become especially close to the Redemptorists during my years in Paraguay.

Nor did I forgot my favorite teachers, the De la Salle Brothers. I quickly went out to their generalate, where I inquired whether there was any American brother in residence. In a matter of moments there arrived Brother Edwin (Hernandez), not one of my former teachers but an old friend from New Iberia, Louisiana, a relative of our Pellerin neighbors and of General Charles Doran. At this surprise, both of us whooped with delight. Brother Edwin informed me that two days later, on April 4, the Brothers were to have a new Blessed named— Brother Benilde—and invited me to participate in St. Peter's at this rare and wondrous beatification ceremony.

With the genuine fear that World War III might break out any day, we decided to make the most of the days remaining before our train would leave for London, with a sort of blitz visit down to Naples, Pompeii, Salerno, Sorrento, and the Amalfi Drive. The hotel we stayed at contained a chapel bedizened with statues of Jesuit saints, which made us feel at home and which led me to ask the concierge where the statues had come from. He told me that the hotel had been a college of the Society before the time of its suppression in 1773.

Then on to Capri, the Blue Grotto, and back to Naples. One of our group, the Mauritian nicknamed Popin, ventured outside the hotel alone, against our warning, only to return minutes later having been held up and robbed. He was livid, more at the loss of dignity than of lira, and would have flown back to London that night had there been a flight available.

We returned to Rome to bid our adieux to Youree, Arnold, and other friends at the Gregorian, notably a person destined to be among the greatest in Jesuit history, Father Joseph Dezza, now Cardinal Dezza. It would be almost forty years later before I was to see Father Dezza again; by then he was quite blind, but remembered my name and voice, and especially my friendship with Fathers Watson and Benedetto.

Back at Oxford we recalled "Oh, to be in England now that April's there!" One would not gainsay Newman's observation: "Of all human things, Oxford is nearest my heart." But, then, there's also Newman's letter to his sister Harriet, written even before he became a Catholic: "And now what can I say of Rome, but that it is the first of cities, and that all I ever saw are but as dust (even dear Oxford inclusive) compared with its majesty and glory?" How does one compare infinities?

The ultimate privilege of spending a year at Oxford was yet to come: a phone message waiting for me from the least likely person—my favorite cultural historian. When Christopher Dawson called Father Corbishley to offer to any one Jesuit student his help as a tutor, Corbishley very generously mentioned me. I almost trembled as I took the bus out to the Dawson cottage on Boar's Hill in the Berkshires, on one of those incredible April days.

I had met Dawson several times before, the first being six months earlier on October 27, when I ventured to introduce myself to him after a lecture, adding the fact that I was from Louisiana. As if he were awaiting such an encounter, Dawson immediately asked, "Since you're from Louisiana, Father, would you explain to me why the diocesan see was moved from Natchitoches to Alexandria?" I was startled, not least because he was the first non-Louisianian I ever met who knew how to pronounce Natchitoches! Whenever anyone suggests that no one can write as many great books as Dawson did and still be a professional historian, I quote this anecdote. He was certainly the most erudite historian I ever met, Carlton Hayes included in that exalted list.

Dawson was at the time involved in composing his Gifford Lectures, the prestigious series of lectures on religion and culture given in Scotland. It was a true privilege to feel that I might make a small contribution to this giant work, but I'm not sure that I ever did. In terms of my own education, it meant a weekly encounter with one of the great minds of the West. Each meeting was simple and unpretentious. Mr. Dawson (I never could bring myself to call him Christopher, much less Chris) would line up the venue of our conversation to fit the broad topic. One day we walked past a large mound. He explained that a town had stood there once, but that after the Black Death the town could not be inhabited. I even forget its name, but the thought of plague remained vivid in my memory and helped me grasp the consequences of the plagues endured by Native Americans, either accidental, or caused by other tribes or by whites.

Many years later, when Mr. Dawson occupied the Stillman Chair of Roman Catholic Studies at Harvard, we were able to invite him to visit Louisiana and the battleground at Chalmette, near the Mississippi River, where, as he explained to me in detail, the future president Andrew Jackson annihilated Lord Pakenham's elegant British army. One of the Dawsons fought and died with Lord Pakenham, whose direct descendant I remembered meeting at Campion Hall, Oxford.

Several of Britain's greatest musicians and musicologists were easy to meet and get to know. Edmund Rubbra, for example, was kind enough to visit us at Campion Hall and spend an evening discussing music. Two days later, quite by accident, I ran into him on "the High" strolling with Vaughan Williams. He presented me to the doyen of English composers, and both invited me to the dress rehearsal of the BBC's first presentation, the following day, of Vaughan Williams's magnificent Sixth Symphony and Rubbra's Festival Overture. Since I studied composition under Rubbra, I began to feel like something of a "grandson" of Williams.

Edward Dent came from "the other place" (Oxonian jargon for Cambridge) for a lecture on opera. Spotting my clerical collar, Dent couldn't resist asking me why all clergymen in operas are villains. I could muster no adequate repartee. Egon Wellesz, distinguished Austrian composer and leading authority on Byzantine chant, was having dinner with us one evening and discussing all manner of musical and liturgical issues when suddenly he was called to the phone. He returned, delighted, to tell us that the Austrian ambassador had just officially invited him to conduct one of his symphonies in Vienna. Not acceptable to Hitler, Dr. Wellesz was overjoyed to be recognized by Vienna's more enlightened new government.

During the late 1940s, Campion Hall was basking in the vicarious glory of Father Martin D'Arcy, then provincial of the English Province, but a frequent visitor warmly welcomed by his protégé Tom Corbishley. "The Hall," as it was known, had become something of a center of British Catholicism, since so many of the galaxy of converts of that time had been either directed or "received" by Father D'Arcy. The greatest of these, Monsignor Ronald Knox, was an especially frequent visitor and would pop in quite informally by the back door from "the Bishop's Palace," as the chaplaincy was familiarly known.

Ronnie (as his peers called him) was at that time on prolonged sabbatical, at work on his *opus magnum et arduum*— the completely new translation of the entire Bible, being done into "timeless English" (presumably English that included nothing in vocabulary or usage that would depend on a single period). It was interesting to hear some of the giants of English literature discuss this with Ronnie himself at tea. In any case, Ronnie's minor works—the books of sermons, the *Spiritual Aeneid*, and dozens of other little masterpieces—establish him as a "timeless classic" of our language.

Evelyn Waugh was another frequent visitor, always on his "good behavior" at Campion Hall, presumably out of veneration for Father D'Arcy, who had received him into the church. I suggest that it must have been out of veneration for Father D'Arcy, since Waugh elsewhere seemed to enjoy nothing more than twitting or even insulting Catholic priests and religious.

One night he mentioned at the table that he was to give a talk at the chaplaincy about his American experience, the visit when he gathered material for that acerbic masterpiece *The Loved One.* I said that I was looking forward to hearing him. "Please don't come, Father. I'm going to say some terrible things about your country!"

Of course, I did go to hear him. It was every bit as acerbic as I expected, and fun to watch the young Britishers enjoying him so much at the expense of us "Yankees." That lasted until his final sentence, which ran more or less like this: "And just so none of my fellow Englishmen should feel the least bit complacent about anything I've said, let me just assure them that the only reason we don't do worse is that WE JUST HAVEN'T GOT ENOUGH MONEY!" A howl from the Yankee contingent greeted this outburst, as the young Brits sank into gloom. A rhapsodic moment for us.

Limits of space hardly permit even a mention of the many people I came to admire and love at Oxford. To mention just a few Jesuits, let me start with Jorge Blajot, a most gifted poet and violinist from a Catalonian family, whose brother Victor served as provincial and held other positions in Bolivia during my time in Paraguay. I got to know Jorge, together with George Croft, at Heythrop, the Jesuit College near Oxford, at Christmastime—to be precise on Saint Stephen's Day—in 1947.

When I arrived at Heythrop to celebrate Christmas with other people of my generation, among the first I met were Jorge and George, both excellent violinists. They were looking for someone who could play the piano well enough to read the piano reduction of the orchestral part of Bach's concerto for two violins. Once again relying on the proverb about the one-eyed being kings in the realm of the blind, I volunteered. It was an unforgettably delightful experience: a Catalonian, an Englishman, and an American sharing the joys of discovering Bach together. Had I been a missionary to Africa like my Jesuit friend Tony O'Flynn, I would have spent time with George Croft once again.

As it was, Jorge Blajot and I became close friends, as he conferred favor after favor on me, always seeming to be on the receiving end. Jorge helped me in Rome, when he headed Vatican Radio, and of course in Spain, particularly Madrid, where he seemed to know everybody and was obviously always eager to share. My eyes watered the other day when I heard he had died.

Having to leave my favorite university and the access it offered to such friends was the only sad aspect of my Oxford experience. Canterbury, with Mass at St. Thomas Church near the cathedral, meant farewell to England via Dover and on to Calais. My hope was to spend the summer of 1948 in immediate preparation for my future work in the juniorate. The train quickly brought me to Amiens, though the city, still in ruins from World War II, was hard to identify. No address that I had in my book was identifiable, but happily the great cathedral was very much erect. The windows, however, had been removed in anticipation of possible destruction. On a later trip I was to see them in their full glory, almost matching those of Chartres.

Deciding to cross over to Rheims via Laon, I was able to stop for an hour or so. Back on the train I began a conversation with a well-dressed lady, who seemed anxious to talk about France. "I'm very eager to see the cathedral in Rheims," I assured her. "Yes," she replied. "I understand it's very beautiful." I was shocked. Here we were only twenty-five miles from one of the most beautiful buildings in the world, and this elegant French lady could only assure me that she had heard it was very beautiful.

The next day, as I was approaching Paris on another train, I heard the same reply about the Holy Chapel, though it was only a five-minute walk from Notre Dame cathedral. Meantime, while in Rheims I had visited the home of Saint John Baptist de la Salle, founder of the Brothers of the Christian Schools, my teachers. Clare and Ben Thibodeaux were waiting for me to celebrate the Fourth of July with Jefferson Caffery, a fellow native of Lafayette, friend of my family, ambassador to France at this time and in general what is known as "An Ambassador's Ambassador" in governmental circles. Later, when I met Mr. and Mrs. Caffery in Rome, living in the Grand Hotel, they were in retirement, a very creative and active retirement in the service of the church. They were also noteworthy as benefactors of our New Orleans Province.

In succession, I was to visit St. Denis, the foundation of Abbot Suger and first Gothic structure, and Beauvais, one of the last and most elaborate Gothic cathedrals, splendid even in its incomplete state. Then down to Bourges and Orleans, other Gothic treasures. But my main reason for wanting to spend the summer in France had little to do with Gothic. Rather it was to spend time at the feet of Father Pierre Charmot, the Christian humanist par excellence. He headed the Jesuit juniorate for southern France in Moulins, not far from Le Puy, and stood for everything I hoped one day to emulate in humanistic education. By way of a small gesture of reciprocation, I offered to teach something in English. To my delight, the library contained enough copies of *A Christmas Carol,* Dickens's short but great book, ideal for a group of young sensitive French Jesuits.

The scholastics escorted me to an ancient chateau at Allier, where one could enjoy a swim. That evening I gave them a lecture—in my best French—on Mozart's G Minor Symphony. The following morning I sallied forth toward Paray-le-Monial, a wonderful Romanesque monastery where Saint Margaret Mary Alacoque and Saint Claude de la Colombière (not yet at that time canonized) practiced profound devotion to the Sacred Heart. Then back to the juniorate for my English class. Almost every day resembled this experience, in intellectual variety and spiritual excitement.

Down at Vals and Le Puy, I just managed to catch André Bouler the evening before he was to leave for Paris and regency with Fernand Léger. As is well known, Léger accepted very few students, this being a privilege that had to be clearly merited. Bouler, a witty Breton, started as most artists do by imitating his masters, and I was thus able to see his growth from a follower to a creator. Today he is generally revered as the outstanding Jesuit painter of France. Over the years, whenever I manage to be in Paris, I look up Bouler and he reciprocates in America.

Down to the Midi, Nîmes and its great arena, the Maison Carrée, and ever so much else. In Montpelier I stopped at a Jesuit house, without warning, where the youngest man was seventy-three years old. They could not have been more hospitable. The superior asked me how I liked my eggs fixed. With a forgivable half-truth, I protested that I didn't want any eggs. He insisted, "All Americans like eggs!" thereupon deciding that mine should be fried. Since no one else at table had eggs, the superior felt obliged to explain, "You Americans did so much for us during the war when we were hungry. It isn't often that we can reciprocate. This is a pleasure for us."

On the way to Lourdes the next day, I passed Carcasonne, Narbonne, and Béziers. Medieval history ran before me, as we approached the nineteenth century and Lourdes. The pilgrims that evening did their singing in English with a very Scottish accent: "And Scotland thy dowry" chanted the leader. It was the ninetieth anniversary of the final apparition at Lourdes and the Pontifical Mass was especially moving. The "Salve Regina" and "Credo No. 3" in fifth-mode Gregorian chant seemed a Catholic International Anthem. Lourdes is one of the Marian shrines that "wear well," along with Guadalupe in Mexico.

Bearing toward the North, past Angoulême, Poitiers, Tours, and the stately Châteaux de la Loire on to Le Mans and Laval, where I visited the other French juniorate. The leading light there was a younger man, Antoine Lauras, who knew a great deal of English and constantly wrote on English and American matters in the Jesuit journal *Les Etudes*. He had also published a major work on classics together with Père Laurand—"Laurand-Lauras" as it became known. When Antoine discovered that I was destined to teach in the juniorate at Grand Coteau and that we had a tertianship at Grand Coteau, too, he began to plan accordingly; Grand Coteau seemed the ideal place for him to study English with me and for me to study and work with him.

After a few weeks at Laval, I was able to get away to Solesmes Abbey, the great center of the Gregorian chant revival. Father Bergeron, whom I had known at St. Benoît-du-Lac, Canada, was there perfecting his chant, as was a Japanese scholar and a Hungarian diocesan priest named Hajtas, whom I later got to know better when I discovered him in New Orleans. I had no idea that I should someday come to know Solesmes even better, but at least the initiation was ideal.

Following a stop in Rouen, I went on to Mont-Saint-Michel, surely one of the wonders of the world and worthy of its association by Henry Adams with Chartres Cathedral. All of these sublime places were given only a brief introduction, since there was, in my mind at least, growing hope that the possibility of seeing them again was not unthinkable. While Lisieux and its shrine to "Little Theresa" seemed superficial and unworthy of the great saint, Saint-Maclou, Saint-Ouen, and so many other shrines were more worthy of their namesakes. Among these was Saint-Wandrille, where ailing Dom David presented vigorously his case against the Mocquereau-Solesmes interpretation of Gregorian chant.

Finally, I had no choice but to tear myself away from Europe, dashing off to England and a hurried viewing of Quarr Abbey, Jersey, before again embarking on the *Mauretania*. The transatlantic journey home was pleasantly uneventful.

Chapter Eight

On the juniorate faculty at Grand Coteau.

Halcyon Days

Grand Coteau, 1948–58

The only element of mystery to anyone who loves to go sleuthing in Jesuit catalogs might be the fact that I did not pronounce my last vows on August 15, 1948, with my classmate Ed Sheridan (now recently deceased), but about five weeks later. Nothing sinister lurks behind this postponement, however. Normally, last vows in the Society of Jesus are pronounced on an important Marian feast. Superiors were not sure that I could be back in a house of our province in time to make my retreat of preparation and still be ready to pronounce vows on the 15th. Accordingly, they assigned September 8, Mary's Birthday, as the date and the Jesuit Church of the Sacred Heart in Grand Coteau as the place, in order to make it easy for my mother and some friends from nearby Lafayette to be present.

When juniorate classes for the fall semester began, my responsibilities were the same as before I went to tertianship and to Europe for studies. Only one precaution was urged on me: not to plan as many plays as we had done in my previous year at Grand Coteau. Then we had performed, if I recall correctly, seven, which in retrospect seems obviously excessive. Now it would be three a year—one on the feast of Saint Stanislaus, patron of novices; one at Christmastime; and a third, presumably a major work, shortly before the end of the academic year.

This gave us an opportunity for a varied pattern of productions—one musical per year (a Gilbert and Sullivan or some equivalent), a modern play (one of Christopher Fry's, for example) and something more classical—a Shakespearean or Greek drama. The productions were designed for giving everyone a chance to participate in some way. Making no claims of infallibility, and with a maximum of consultation, I attempted to distribute roles according to capacity, in general giving the more important roles to second-year juniors, including the role of director, and thus to provide only a minimum of supervision. In the area of musicals, obviously those with some talent for singing won the more desirable roles, while seminarians with talent for staging and set production were often somewhat overburdened, much as I tried to save them from their own generosity.

The "Latin Clinic" became something of a life-saving program. In the 1950s Latin was still essential not only to the liturgy but also to all ecclesiastical studies. This meant that many a young seminarian, Jesuit or otherwise, saw skill in Latin not only as something cultural, as was Greek, but the decisive skill for studies in philosophy and theology. It occurred to me that we should not go on treating Latin as it had been treated in the past century, attempting to make it a matter of so many lines of Virgil, Horace, or Cicero, important as that doubtless was. Experience had taught many of us that this traditional approach was more a matter of luxury than of life or death.

Accordingly, I spent some time at Georgetown University trying to understand the splendid success of their techniques in modern languages. The director did not agree that something similar could be accomplished in Latin. Nonetheless, Fathers Burrus and Coyle were in agreement with my theory and entirely cooperative. We rearranged the first month of the academic year to allow for total absorption in Latin, regardless of the individual student's needs.

Those students who seemed to have problems with Latin were given an intensive training in the language as it was used in philosophical and theological classes, with opportunities to develop practical skills in speaking, reading, and writing. For example, instead of Cicero we read Pinocchio or some easier passages from Saint Thomas, all in Latin. We published a daily bulletin of news, all in easy Latin, and with vocabulary provided. We worked out a simplified but reasonable vocabulary for games; for example, *volifollis* for volleyball, *circuitus grandis* for a "grand slam" in baseball. Of course, such an attempt was not meant to supplant Cicero, but rather to treat Latin as a living language, as Cicero himself doubtless had done.

This was all very good for those students who were beginners in Latin, but what of those who had graduated from a Jesuit
or other classical school with a fine background in Latin? We
provided special attention for them, too, treating them almost as
graduate students, with intensive study of Latin plays or more
difficult authors. Further, each superior student was assigned a
beginner whom he was to help and treat with the attention he
needed. Apart from this, we gave the more advanced Latinists
the opportunity to put on plays in simplified Latin, making the
translations themselves.

One instance was *Everyman* in simplified Latin as *Quisque,*
geared to the beginners; another was what we referred to as
"Plautus and Sullivan," a simplified rewriting of Plautus's *Duo
Captivi* with Sullivan's witty music. This particular work was
created and presented in honor of Ernie Burrus, when he was
called to Rome to work at the Jesuit House of Writers—a great
loss for us but a gain for Rome. On this occasion we invited
Bishop Jeanmard and other special friends of Ernie's, who would
appreciate the Latin effort on our part.

How many vocations were saved through our Latin Clinic
only God knows, but even if we allow for some exaggeration on
the part of those who claim to have had the experience, the
number must still be very high. In any case, with the demise of
Latin as an essential element of the liturgy, followed by a great
decline in its use in the teaching of philosophy and theology, it
was not long before seminaries in general began to drop Latin as
an academic requisite. Meantime, there was an ironic element,
unintended to be sure, in an article that I wrote for the March
31, 1962, issue of *America* magazine, which envisioned a more
widespread acceptance of the idea of a Latin Clinic. Unfortunately, in the aftermath of the Council's Decree on Liturgy, the
idea came too late to be generalized.

Another dream that I cherished reached late fruition—
Spanish as the second language of the New Orleans Province. It
had long been evident to many of us that Spanish rather than
French held prior position, that, in fact, several parishes con-
ducted by southern Jesuits used far more Spanish than French
and that the future pointed more to the need for Spanish than for
French. We began to discover more and more Spanish-speaking

candidates for the Society, and many of them found living in the
Anglo or Anglo-French section of the province very difficult and
saw no immediate signs of a reevaluation.

Thus, when Father Carmelo Tranchese left San Antonio to
come to Grand Coteau in 1955, it seemed like the appropriate
time for me to "put my money where my mouth was," and to
spend less energy praising Hispanic culture and more trying to
acquire some of it, especially a speaking knowledge of Spanish
itself. Father Tranchese was delighted to offer to teach me—
every morning for half an hour immediately after breakfast,
adjusting the place to the weather—and the seminarians, especially those of Hispanic origin, were no less delighted to see one
of their teachers in the role of learner, both from Father
Tranchese and from them. And he was most generous with his
time. When Christmas Day came, I presumed that we would take
a break. "No, no!" insisted Padrecito, as I always called him, "We
must not miss a day."

Father Tranchese was a Neapolitan, destined to work in the
Vatican observatory, who nevertheless wanted to dedicate a year
of his young life to the apostolate of Hispanics in the American
Southland. His year stretched out to many years, since he never
returned to Italy, even for a visit. During the Great Depression,
when San Antonio was particularly suffering, Father Tranchese
went to Washington, D.C., and persuaded Eleanor Roosevelt to
come there to see what his parish was really like. When she
returned to Washington, she was able to persuade her husband
to initiate great changes, and the transformation elicited widespread admiration.

A major article on Father Tranchese's work for the Hispanics
appeared in the *Saturday Evening Post*. Carmelo Tranchese had
very nearly failed to be admitted to the Society, so poor was his
Latin, at least when he applied. A few years later, however, he
had become something of a classicist and enjoyed composing
Latin odes. As his biographer suggests, he was probably one of
very, very few people who ever sent a Latin poem of his own
composition to President Franklin Roosevelt.

On July 13, 1956, early in the morning, our infirmarian called
me: "Padrecito is dying, C. J. Come to his room." When I arrived,
he seemed in a coma. He had already been anointed, but I wanted
to stay on with him. After a while he opened his eyes, recognized

me and spoke in Spanish as we always did when we were together:"Don Clemente, *cómo está?*" "Bien, Padrecito, pero cómo está usted?" *"Mas o menos,* Don Clemente," he replied, understating his condition. I began saying the Our Father in Spanish. He joined with me but died before we could complete it.

Word went out to San Antonio, where he had served so many years; and the next day when several busloads of Hispanic Americans arrived from there to grace his funeral, they joined hundreds of blacks whom he had also served in Grand Coteau. Padrecito was one of my all-time heroes; we shared our love of Dante and of whatever Spanish literature I knew. On his desk when he died were several books of Latin classics, especially the work of the Roman poet and satirist Juvenal, to whom I was introducing him. He loved Juvenal's satirical wit.

Whenever people in Spanish-speaking countries asked me where I was from, I always asked them to guess. The only person who came close to a correct answer was a Spanish lady who said: "You're an Italian who has spent many years in Mexico." This was the greatest possible compliment, since it showed that something of Carmelo Tranchese had rubbed off on me.

The summer after Father Tranchese had taken me on as an apprentice, I had actually spent studying Spanish at the main Jesuit scholasticate in Mexico City, being helped by the young Mexicans and in turn trying to help them master English. Their parents were kind enough to enable me to visit most of the truly famous spots in Mexican cultural history, from the Olmec to the latest Mayan art and architecture. I was also given the opportunity to become familiar with many of the great colonial treasures. When I returned to Grand Coteau, I found it possible to compose a truthful and strong letter of thanks to my Mexican Jesuit hosts in the "most elegant" Spanish I could muster. From that time to the present, hardly a day has gone by without my reading, speaking, or writing Spanish. I've learned that some of my Mexican friends refer to me humorously as "el buen gringo" as though there could be only one "good gringo."

Shortly after I had returned to Grand Coteau in 1948, a cordial letter arrived from Father Bill Leonard, the outstanding liturgist of Boston College. He invited me to teach liturgical music at the summer session that he was directing. I knew Bill only through his reputation as a most amiable and scholarly priest, a former chaplain during World War II in the Pacific area, and a highly literate person, editor of the *Boston Stylus*. It was hard to believe that he knew of me, but I shamelessly accepted the invitation.

When I reached Boston in the summer of 1949, it surpassed my dreams—a beautiful city, richer in diversity than one might expect, with French and Italian heard on the streets near Faneuil Hall and other monuments of our Revolutionary War. As an art center it enjoyed a great reputation, but who can be prepared for the glories, however eccentric, of Mrs. Jack Gardner's Fenway Hall, near the great art museum? During my several summers in Boston, the custodians of both treasuries became familiar friends, since I was enjoying their museums at least once a week. The Boston Symphony and its performances on the Esplanade were other incredibly stunning delights hard to match anywhere else in America. Furthermore, in those days all such treasures were free or almost free, and thus altogether available even to impecunious scholars.

Bill Leonard was the heart and soul of the liturgical movement in Boston, and once I came to know him I could see why. He was a person of enormous sensitivity and unselfishness, more eager to give than to receive, especially fond of sharing friends. Thanks to him I came to know such liturgical giants as Mary Perkins Ryan, Ted Marier, Shawn Sheehan, Martin Hellriegel, and H. A. Reinhold, and to feel accepted by them as a friend. Little wonder that a few years ago, when Bill began gathering his liturgical museum at Boston College, "Liturgy and Life," all were eager to cooperate. And when he launched his volume *Liturgy for the People: Essays in Honor of Gerald Ellard, S.J.,* scholars, like John LaFarge, Josef Jungmann, Daniel Berrigan, David Stanley, and Kathryn Sullivan, were delighted to contribute.

My principal job that first summer was to prepare the music for daily Masses, trying to provide variety and interest. In those days the idea of a daily homily was fairly original, as was the habit of singing the ordinary of the Mass even at a "low Mass." As far as I was concerned, it was mainly a learning experience for me, and I particularly enjoyed sharing reflections on seminary teaching with Tom Stack, of the Hartford archdiocese.

The second summer was somewhat more relaxed, especially since I felt more at home at Boston College, already knowing such scholars as Francis Sweeney, Charlie Donovan, Fred Moriarty (Scripture scholar), and Jim Skehan (seismologist). The opportunity, too, to discover several of Christopher Fry's poetic plays and Menotti's *Amahl and the Night Visitors,* one of the most charming of American operas, could not be overestimated.

This opportunity led me to risk performing *Amahl* at Grand Coteau. In point of fact, as I realized the amount and quality of talent in the forthcoming juniorate group, it soon became clear that we could put it on as our Christmas play. It proved so delightful, indeed, that we performed it several times, even for parents of our novices and juniors, and those of us who worked in it look back upon *Amahl* as a high point of those years at Grand Coteau. The next year, in fact, our scholastics at Spring Hill did their own production, which again proved quite successful.

My third summer in Boston in some ways proved best of all, with more and more opportunities for my own cultural growth. Toward the end of the summer, I visited Father Bill Carroll, the soul of the juniorate in Shadowbrook, Massachusetts, just before the tragic fire there. Bill was outstanding among the Jesuits I've known for his prodigious knowledge of the Society's literary and artistic history. A joke that I accidentally pulled on him was something we both enjoyed for the rest of our life.

Someone had given me a ticket for an early performance of Menotti's tragic opera *The Consul,* and this cut short my visit to Shadowbrook. Bill tried to persuade me to stay anyway, not realizing my fondness for Menotti's work. I insisted, "No, I've got to see *The Consul* tomorrow," whereupon Bill asked, "What Consul?" Half unintentionally I immediately replied, "The Consul of the U.S.A., to get back home after all this time in New England." Fortunately for me Bill was a good sport and could take a joke, especially one like this, obviously meant to be funny rather than malicious. Fortunately for me, too, I was able to spend even more time with Bill, after he was stationed at Holy Cross. His witty and profound lives of great eccentric Jesuits (in fact, he could pass for one of them) constitute one of the great as yet unpublished volumes.

Some years earlier I had asked my old mentor Ernie Burrus what he would most like to see if the opportunity ever presented itself to return to Europe. Without a moment's hesitation, he asserted, "Chartres, of course!" I concurred, doubting that the opportunity would ever come up again. Yet it did, several times. I forget in exactly what year the first chance to return occurred, but sometime around the middle 1950s I suddenly received a phone call from Dr. Clifford Bennett, director of the Gregorian Institute. He had organized a splendid program of advanced Gregorian chant to be held at Solesmes Abbey, known the world over as the "motherhouse" of Gregorian chant. Father Joseph Gajard, O.S.B., supreme master of the Solesmes school of chant, gave the course, but Dr. Bennett wanted me to be the simultaneous translator from French to English and English to French. The task was easy, since I felt almost equally at home in the two languages. Further, it seemed a real honor to be chosen for this assignment. I could think of no better way to be inseparably linked with someone like Father Gajard than by becoming his interpreter.

Not very long after the Gregorian Institute experience, an even more surprising invitation came from the great U.S. abbey, St. John's in Collegeville, Minnesota. To my great astonishment the summer session in Gregorian chant at St. John's was having some trouble deciding on a professor of advanced Gregorian chant and chant aesthetics, two distinct courses. It was never completely clear to me why the Benedictines chose a Jesuit to give such courses rather than someone from their own abbey or some other Benedictine abbey. After all, Gregorian chant is the specialty of the Benedictines, I felt.

On the other hand, the American Benedictine most renowned in this country had these very kind words to say when introducing my book on liturgy, *Our Changing Liturgy:* "I first met him when he, a Jesuit, was lecturing on Gregorian chant in a Benedictine abbey (which would, however, be a lesser reason for surprise today than it was a mere decade ago)." These are the words of Godfrey Diekmann, O.S.B., former editor of *Worship* magazine and doyen of American liturgists. A generation or two must now have passed since the "as-clumsy-as-a-Jesuit-in-Holy-Week" *boutade* was in vogue. I believe it was more often in jest rather than a serious criticism, since at least in theory Jesuits always had some members they could be proud of as liturgists.

One thinks of Gerry Ellard and Bill Leonard in this country, both worthy disciples of the giant liturgist Father Josef

Jungmann and many other Europeans. One recalls also Father Gelineau, his psalmody and other excellent studies in liturgical music. The surprise of surprises came to me on discovering that the predecessor of the Solesmes monks in liturgical chant was also a Jesuit, Louis Lambillotte (1796-1855). While Saint Ignatius of Loyola reluctantly felt that for apostolic reasons he had to deprive himself and other Jesuits of the regular use of the Divine Office in Gregorian chant, he himself loved music, especially sacred music, and found great devotion in its presence, even sending for his dear friend the musician-artist Jesuit André des Freux to lift his spirits with the clavichord and other music.

In 1957-58, Greg Curtin, the assistant director of novices at Grand Coteau, was a man thought of as a legend from the time of his own novitiate, back in 1944-46. In fact when I left Grand Coteau in 1946 for studies in Canada and visited Greg in New Orleans on the way, I felt sure it would be for the last time on this earth. He looked every bit like a pin cushion, so punctured was he with intravenous tubes, as though facing imminent death. It was a very agreeable surprise, then, on my return a year later, to find him quite alive. As the years went on, it was decided to accelerate Greg's course of studies, so that he might live at least until ordination to the priesthood. He was in fact ordained in 1953, after facing the likelihood of death several times.

Greg's repeated stretches of borrowed time made us appreciate him more and more. He had been a very popular athlete back in his first years as a Jesuit, and every time he was sent to the hospital we had prayed with more than conventional zest. Now, when he came to Grand Coteau in 1957, after several years of priestly apostolate to take up a very important job, most of us felt that he was completely cured.

The year 1957 offered great promise for the future of television. *Playhouse 90,* an exceptional program of live drama, became the sort of thing one could eagerly look forward to. I remember feeling and expressing my hopes that at last TV was going to do something significant, analogous to what Haydn had done through the enforced opportunity he felt to create new music—becoming the "father of the symphony, the sonata, the quartet, and the classical concerto."

Greg and I watched almost every program in the promising new series, never bored, often thrilled at the new phenomenon.

Why the program eventually left the air I never knew, but it did last for a splendid year, and Greg and I used the call letters of nearby ABC affiliates that carried the program—WBRZ in Baton Rouge and KLFY in Lafayette—as a whimsical code and reminder of the evening's program. Although Grand Coteau is much closer to Lafayette than to Baton Rouge, we were able to pick up both stations. I called Greg "WBRZ," and he responded with "KLFY" (Lafayette was of course my home town). Since few English words can be pronounced without at least one vowel, try putting the short *i* as in *wit* between the first two consonants of WBRZ and KLFY, just in case you would like to break our code.

———

During those halcyon days at Grand Coteau, in addition to weekly supply ministries in various small towns of Acadiana, where homilies might be expected to be given in French or English (at a moment's notice), I was given the opportunity to do a good deal of radio and some TV ministry. Perhaps more important were the chances to work on weekends in the Newman Club center at the University of Southwestern Louisiana (a center that my dad had been instrumental in launching), with several of the great pioneer priests: Monsignor Irving DeBlanc, Monsignor Alexander Sigur, and Father Jude Speyrer (all then from the diocese of Lafayette, and Jude Speyrer now the first bishop of the diocese of Lake Charles).

It will still be no surprise that I felt a natural empathy for Newman Club work, given my dad's background and my own experience at Oxford. Working with these chaplains and our own Fathers Burrus and Coyle, we managed to invite a host of interesting, important people for special lectures. Much of this activity was made financially possible through the collaboration of Loyola University in New Orleans, LSU's Newman Club in Baton Rouge, and Spring Hill College in Mobile. Thus we were able to invite down to our area Father Martin D'Arcy, Christopher Dawson, and half a dozen other lecturers of international stature.

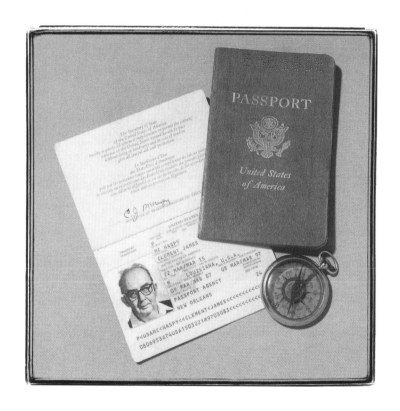

Chapter Nine

*Passport to Christian antiquities, then
to the religious shrines, and artistic
treasures of the world.*

Not Yet Fully One

The Crescent of Christianity

At this stage in a life blessed with so many opportunities to travel throughout the world, it is not always easy to distinguish particular European or Holy Land trips, for example. It has seemed appropriate here and elsewhere in these memoirs, therefore, to depart at times from my efforts at chronology and to let the logic of geography and comparable experiences govern my presentation.

The type of repartee one dreams of but seldom has a chance to practice happily came to me one day in this form. "Can't we talk longer?" I was asked on the phone. I had to reply, "I'm rushing for the plane. I'm off for Egypt!" "Wow!" was the unmistakable answer. Whoever it was, some thirty years ago, I have no idea, but I did have the rare presence of mind to jot down the conversation in my diary. I was playing chaplain-guide for a pilgrimage to the Holy Lands, with stress on the plural. Our flight did go to Cairo, though the plane landed in Frankfurt, where we hoped to meet two friends of my sister who lives in St. Louis; they had somehow not been on the right plane. When morning came we found them finally, after passing Elba and reaching Cairo. The plane they were on was traveling to Karachi, Bangkok, and Tokyo.

This was my very first time in Africa. Following Sicily and Crete, how green the delta of the Nile seemed. In the morning we had Mass at the Franciscan church of St. Joseph, followed by a trip to the museum—the Museum of King Tut, again a "first" for me. Fortunately I have had many later opportunities. Then a trip to the palace of Muhamad Ali (the monarch not the prizefighter), which was followed by visits to the great mosques in the "old city," with a stupendous panorama, and a short sailing journey on the Nile, in all its evocative splendor. Across the Nile in Giza, one suddenly leaves the greenery of the delta to enter total desert, in sight of the pyramids. Also near the three greatest pyramids one sees perhaps the world's largest sculpture, the Sphinx, and near both the ultimate tourist opportunity—a camel ride, well photographed, of course!

That evening a flight was available down—or rather "up," since south is upstream as in the Rhine and the St. Lawrence Valleys—to Luxor, gateway to the great temples and pharaonic tombs. Noteworthy was the total absence of light over the desert. In the morning we went by rowboat over the Nile to the Valley of the Kings. The temple of Queen Hatshepsut (the queen's statue was defaced by her envious brother) is one of the greatest architectural wonders even of Egypt, since the Colossi of Memnon are more properly considered statuary than architecture.

We took a buggy ride to Karnak and there met a guide who was manifestly Christian, eager to have us discover this as he showed the sign of the cross in Coptic letters (the term *Coptic*, a simplification of the Greek word for Egypt, is reserved for those descendants of the ancient Egyptians who remained Christian despite severe Muslim taxes). It turned out that our guide's name was Hannon. In the sand near us was the world's largest obelisk (some five hundred tons, and hence immovable). Few obelisks stand in Egypt, only one in Istanbul, one in Paris, one in London, a smallish one in New York—all the remainder, some fifteen or so, are found in Rome, having been sequestered by monument-greedy caesars. The great temple at Luxor is in good condition, much of it being a mosque with a surprisingly well-preserved Christian apse and Constantinian inscriptions. A statue of Ramses II, probably the pharaoh who persecuted Moses and his people, stands awesome and monumental.

Back in Cairo we met Pieter van der Aacker, a young Dutch Jesuit, who took a few of us to visit the Coptic ghetto, including the allegedly oldest church in Egypt, where the Holy Family is said to have rested during the flight into Egypt. Today it is a synagogue. From Cairo another Dutch Jesuit, a close friend of Father Ayrout, "Egypt's John LaFarge," drove me in a jeep over the desert to the nearest surviving monastery. He was in possession of a letter from Father Ayrout to the Coptic abbot, which assured entrance and hospitality to us.

The monk who was our host proved to be a graduate of the college of agriculture at Cairo University. He could not have been more charming. In flawless English, he spoke most warmly of the revitalization of the church under Pope John XXIII. Escorting us to a very large icon he rendered a most plausible interpretation: "To me this image suggests this, this other image that, and so forth." There remained one final image, which proved to be blank. "What does this mean?" I asked. "To me," he replied, "it suggests the sadness engendered by the fact that we are not yet totally united: Rome, Constantinople, Alexandria, the various other Christian churches. This cannot be the will of Christ. But the blank is not entirely empty; it suggests that more is to be. Christ's will cannot be frustrated. I see signs of hope in your Vatican Council II and especially your wonderful Pope John XXIII." After a prayer, our host sent his greetings to Father Ayrout and bade us a warm adieu.

While a venerable city, Cairo is by no means old by Egyptian standards. Curiously, too, it is one of the few Egyptian cities with a Latin origin, its Latin name *Fustat* coming from *fossatum* or *fossa* (trench, ditch, fortification), by way of Greek *fossaton* (camp). In his splendid article "Biblical Geography," Raymond Brown explains that "only after the Muslim invasion did Cairo rise here, over a Roman fort named Babylon and near the place that legend made the terminus of the flight of the Holy Family into Egypt (Mt 2:14)." An interesting detail about the Coptic tradition is the dating system: instead of A.D. (*Annus Domini*), the Copts date important events by the Year of Martyrs (*Annus Martyrum*)—A.M. 284, referring to the persecution of Diocletian in the first year of his reign.

When we got back to our hotel in Cairo, a surprise was in store for us. One of the group who had not made the trip to Luxor told us, with great excitement, "Guess who's in the hotel with us—Malcolm X!" I thought she was dreaming and almost told her so. Then I thought no more of it until, a few hours later, I entered the elevator and discovered, facing me and smiling in a friendly way, none other than the great Black Muslim himself, popularly known as Malcolm X. I swallowed my fear, smiled and said something like "Good morning" to which he replied something equivalent.

I should not have been so surprised, since we had read in the papers that Malcolm X made the hajj, or pilgrimage, to Mecca very devoutly. We had even heard rumors to the effect that he had changed his philosophy from that of revenge to one of brotherhood. When we returned to the States, we heard even more and read his remarkable profession of brotherhood, printed in the *New York Times.* We also knew that some of the more radically conservative Black Muslims were infuriated at him.

On the evening of February 21, 1965, not long after our return to America, my friends Charlie and Cathy Vukovich were driving me over the George Washington Bridge back to the *America* residence on 108th Street. Our conversation was so animated that we missed the usual exit onto the West Side Highway and quickly found ourselves in Harlem. The strange silence that covered Harlem that night made us wonder, but we didn't think to turn on the radio. When we reached the *America* residence, we found the entire staff silently glued to the television set, trying to make heads or tails of the bits and pieces of the horrible news of the assassination. If, as seems likely, Malcolm X was assassinated because of his conversion from vengeance to forgiveness, I think of him as a martyr of charity.

My subsequent visits to Egypt quickly taught me that the legends about Father Henri Ayrout were entirely true. A most memorable person. In fact, he seemed the best loved man in Egypt. Thanks to him we were to meet not only monks of the desert but also patriarchs and bishops. Years before the word *ecumenical* became stylish, he had introduced the reality of ecumenism to a land where Copts hardly spoke to Orthodox or Catholics, or Muslims to Christians.

When he died suddenly, on April 10, 1969, during a visit to the *America* residence, our shock was shared by the many Muslims and Christians who knew and venerated the man. All the Cairo newspapers found space to print his obituary on page one. Henri had become a Jesuit in 1926 and was ordained a priest in 1938, becoming the first Jesuit in the Melkite (Byzantine) rite. This helps to explain something of the bizarre circumstances of his death—at Mass, which he celebrated in his own rite, during one of the long periods of prostration. When we realized that the ceremony seemed too long, we approached him and called him by name, but there was no answer. In many ways Ayrout resembled Father LaFarge, notably in his openness to others and his great concern for the underprivileged. In Egypt he had founded 122 schools and centers for the poorest of the poor.

He died on the fourteenth anniversary of the death of his great friend Teilhard de Chardin, with whom he had worked. Since we associated him with Father LaFarge in many ways, it was appropriate that his wake in New York, before the body was brought back to Cairo for a state funeral, was held in the lounge of the John LaFarge Institute, under the joyous portrait of Father LaFarge, coincidentally stressing the similarity of the two men who dedicated their lives for the underprivileged and for all humanity.

Apropos of Father LaFarge and Africa, I suddenly recall that when the distinguished French poet Léopold Senghor, president of the African republic of Senegal, visited us at the LaFarge Institute, as our staff's only Francophone member I was asked to interpret for him. He stressed that the two people who most attracted him to visit New York were the late John LaFarge and Pierre Teilhard de Chardin, then recently deceased in New York and buried among the New York Jesuits in the cemetery of Poughkeepsie. We thereupon drove out in the presidential car to visit Teilhard's grave. It was President Senghor who coined or at least gave dignity to the word *négritude*.

For centuries Egyptian culture had been largely Hellenized, and it is even hard to think of Cleopatra as a Greek name. Alexandria, indeed, was the second Hellenistic city, neither entirely Egyptian nor entirely Hellenistic. In Egypt, Hellenistic art was progressively replaced by an indigenous art impregnated with the Orient, as several historians of art point out. In fact, Coptic art finally eliminated figures, almost entirely replacing them by the rich ornamentation borrowed from Syria. In other words, Coptic art ended as a national Egyptian art, modified by contact with Syria, and as distinct as Syrian art was from Byzantine.

My close Jesuit friend, the late Pierre du Bourguet, head of the Louvre's Egyptian and Early Christian sections, spoke enthusiastically of "pharaonic and Moslem art, the two colossi between which Coptic art developed in the same soil." Much influence came from Alexandria, Palmyra, and the Sassanid, Byzantine, and Muslim cultures. This influence led, according to du Bourguet, not to "deformation but to transformation according to the profound soul of Egypt, and would have reached a supreme rank if not stopped by Moslem conquest." It rather provides a link between the classic and Byzantine arts in icon and illumination. Further it influences Ethiopian art in its light relief, geometric and vegetal forms, decorative, fanciful arabesques, all unique in Christian art. Everything is worked: there is no empty space. (It may be that my short article on Coptic art in *Liturgical Arts* magazine, February 1966, can still be read with some interest.)

Byzantium (A.D. 330 May 11 to May 29, 1453) is "the city sovereign above all others," as Villehardouin put it, or in the words of my old professor at Oxford Dr. Powicke, "the greatest, most active, and most enduring political organization that the world has yet seen." Yet one must not forget the revolutions that came close to destroying Byzantium, or the recorded fact that of 107 sovereigns, only thirty-four died in bed, eight in war or accident, and all the rest by poison or assassination.

Scholars speak of the "Byzantine Compromise" between the classical and the nonclassical. Several words mysteriously appear in Byzantine literature—the *phanariots,* the *latinophrons,* and especially the *gasmules.* This last term is found in few dictionaries or encyclopedias and may bear explanation here: a gasmule is (somewhat like a mule) a cross between two types— a Greek and a Frank (or simply European), presumably combining the best (or worst) features of each.

Yet, when one thinks of Byzantium one inevitably thinks first of Hagia Sophia, obviously the masterpiece of Byzantine, if not of universal, architecture. Despite myths and wishful thinking, this extraordinary structure is not translated from another place or dedicated to some nonexistent Saint Sophie, but rather to Holy Wisdom, the Divine Logos, the Second Person of the Holy Trinity. No wonder, as you view it in partial dilapidation, that you are tempted to echo Procopius's description of it as "suspended from the heavens by a golden chain," or Justinian's praise: "Glory be to God who hath deemed me worthy to compete in so great a work! I have outdone thee, O Solomon!" Everything is astonishing, not least the fact that Hagia Sophia was built in five years, between 532 and 537, a third of the time required for that other masterpiece of antiquity, the Parthenon, dedicated to Athena the goddess of wisdom.

Hagia Sophia is, in strictly structural terms, far more wondrous. One is reminded that between the two masterpieces the whole Roman experience had been epitomized in Hadrian's Pantheon, and that the most modern techniques of physics, statics, mathematics, and geometrical projections had been assimilated by two Greek engineers, Isidore of Miletus and Anthemius of Tralles. But despite the complexity, it is clarity itself, in the words of Auguste Choisy—"unity, tranquillity, satisfaction of the spirit—one sees nothing which does not explain itself—this is the clarity of Greek art."

Yet the partial tragedy of Hagia Sophia remains in the disappearance of the original mosaics in their full splendor, thanks to the ravages of the iconoclasts and the Muslims. Still there are many later mosaics of high quality and the large thirteenth-century mosaic of the *deësis* (the representation of Christ enthroned, flanked by the Virgin Mary and John the Baptist), whose subtle, delicate colors and humanistic outlook seem to presage the developments in the West a century and a half later. I personally thrill to the incredible frescoes of the *Anastasis* (Resurrection) in the Kariye Jami (originally called Our Savior in the Field, since it was outside the original walls of Constantinople) for its realism and almost Renaissance excitement.

My very first visit in Constantinople (the first of six or seven) caught me almost unprepared, for the lack at that time of anything resembling ecumenism. To be sure, that wondrous person, Patriarch Athenagoras, could not have been more helpful in creating openings to Sinai and other treasured spots. On the other hand, it was difficult to reach the Patriarch since obviously, at least in those days, the Turks bore no love for him or anything else Christian. Our Turkish guide either could not or did not want to help us locate the Patriarch.

An Orthodox guide, on the other hand, could not have been more forthright. He showed us the medallion he wore but indicated that he did not dare wear it when he went swimming. "Otherwise," he smiled, "I might not be allowed to swim back up!" The freedom with which he said this put me so much at ease that I ventured to mutter something snide about the Muslims and their destruction of Constantinople during the Fourth Crusade.

He patiently but firmly reminded me, "It wasn't the Muslims; it was you Catholics!" This comment also reminded me that the phrase attributed to Lucas Notaras could well be more than legendary: "Rather the turban than the tiara!"

It was neither the first nor the only time I felt embarrassed at the un-Christian behavior of some of my forebears. One evening, after looking down from our hotel to where I had been told the Jesuit church lay, I phoned Father Pasty, and asked if I could come down. "Bien sûr," he assured me. But on the way over I spotted some hoodlums apparently up to no good. After a few minutes with Father Pasty, I started back, being assured that I could celebrate Mass the next morning. On the way I noticed what seemed the same group of possible hoodlums and back on the hotel porch heard the sound of shattered glass. Sure enough, as I discovered the next morning, the "young Turks" had been doing their best, as Father Pasty put it, to chase him out of Istanbul.

But not all in Istanbul was saddening. The stunning quality of Topkapi, the glory of the Blue Mosque, the Mosque of Suleiman the Magnificent, the marvel of Hosios Lukas, remained to reassure one. Most of all, perhaps, there was the greatness of Sinan, a Christian architect (who died in 1587 and who was at least the Christopher Wren of Istanbul), leaving even more treasures in the dozens of mosques he created than Wren did in the churches he was designing at just about the same time.

A later visit to Istanbul was enhanced and enlivened by two former students of mine, both persons of artistic and literary culture and colleagues who helped enormously in the creation of this memoir: Jack May of Louisiana State University and Clyde LeBlanc of Weston School of Theology.

Petra is a famous stone city—the word *petra* means "stone"—today in southern Jordan. It was once occupied for about one thousand years, starting from 500 b.c., by the Nabataeans, a nomadic Arab tribe. The city was captured by Antigonus in 312 B.C., and used as a storage place for plunder. Little by little Petra began to build a unique blend of Greek, Egyptian, and Assyrian traditions, later taking on Roman and "baroque" Hellenistic elements. The Nabataeans carved quarried blocks for royal mausoleums and temples, which are most impressive, a two-thousand-seat theater and a complicated system of channels and cisterns for water supply. The city eventually declined, but it was rediscovered in 1812 by Johann Burckhardt, who described it in enticing detail.

Shortly before I managed to visit Petra, the eminent Scripture scholar Jean Steinman and a group of pilgrims (on April 6, 1963) entered the long narrow gorge, only to be caught in a flash flood from which none of them escaped. An almost unprecedented calamity this was, which made me scrutinize closely all weather reports as well as the piercing blue skies. As I reached the opening of the gorge and viewed with a sense of awe the vast temple-like "treasury" (really a tomb), I began to feel terror on seeing four Arabs on their steeds, shouting as though ready for battle. Happily my terror was short-lived, as I noticed a movie camera recording the entire event. Years later, while watching Sean Connery in *Indiana Jones and the Last Crusade,* I recalled the ambiguous experience filmed on the same spot. My young guide Sunor tried to persuade me to give him my rather elegant kaffiah rather than the dollar we had agreed on. I compromised—to my advantage—by offering him two dollars but no kaffiah!

The Dead Sea, enlivened by history, is always an awesome sight. On each of my visits to the Holy Land I managed to visit Qumran, the monastery of the Essenes, roughly contemporary with Jesus, and possibly the "desert" to which John the Baptist went as he prepared for his vocation as precursor of Jesus. Impressive as is the Qumran area and the monastery itself, one senses the terror of the desiccating heat of the desert just about everywhere.

Fortunately I was able, at least once, to visit Masada, one of the most thrilling and tragic spots on earth. Apparently impregnable, this vast rock fortress had been fortified by the Maccabees and used by the Romans as a stronghold, but it fell into Zealot hands in A.D. 66. The Jewish historian Josephus dramatically recounts the story of Zealot resistance until the year 74 and how they died to a man—in what is sometimes called "the last gasp of the First Jewish Revolt"—not allowing even their own wives and children to fall to the Romans. "Masada Will Not Fall Again" is, of course, modern Israel's battle cry.

The Dead Sea Scrolls were for the most part discovered in 1947, and for some time afterward in the wadi that Arabs call

Qumran, and contain biblical fragments spreading over three full centuries, from 250 B.C. to A.D. 68. Included are a complete scroll of Isaiah, from the first century before Christ, and a great deal of Jeremiah and other biblical writings. Today many of these treasures are in Jerusalem, in the Shrine of the Book, and are easy to read for anyone familiar with biblical Hebrew. They are surely among the world's most precious treasures, both for Christians and for Jews.

"Going up to Jerusalem" was simply a phrase to me until we started literally from the Dead Sea, a quarter of a mile below sea level to a half a mile above. The horrid heat at sea level, or even below, made one short of temper. I never thought I'd be disagreeable toward my dear friend Father Elmo Romagosa, nor that he'd reciprocate. But alas! How dreadful the miserable sensation of suffocating heat. I thought of poor Bishop Pike, who some months earlier had died of suffocation and thirst, a most horrible death. But then, as one climbs up, up, up to Jerusalem, suddenly one is in spring.

In those days, the Mandelbaum Gate meant a real threat, but I wanted to cross the Gate before the assigned hour, not through arrogance but simply to meet my good friends from the United Nations Mission, the Kirchman twins. They were eager to have me meet the community of Christian Jewish priests, most of them Roman Catholic, one an Anglican, almost all converts: Père Joseph Stiassny (of Ratisbonne), Père Jean Roger (Assumptionist), Père Michel Dutheil, the great Dominican scholars Bruno Hussard, Marcel Dubois, François (whose surname I forget), and the Carmelite Daniel (once known as Oswald Ruffeissen). We celebrated Mass in Hebrew and then enjoyed dinner together.

A special word must be said about Brother Daniel, a former leader of the Polish Jewish resistance against the Nazis during World War II. To the Nazis, Oswald Ruffeissen was "public enemy number one," and they were just on the point of capturing him. As a Jew he had, in the words of Justice Silborg of the Israel High Court, "risked his own life times beyond number during the dark days of the Holocaust in Europe, to rescue his brother Jews from the very jaws of the Nazi beasts" (*The Bible Today,* December 1970, 182–85). In his own words, he was desperate and could think only of the Carmelite convent, where nuns lived who might be willing to risk their own lives for his sake. So it happened. The sisters immediately gave him a nun's garb, had him shave and assume feminine attitudes. When the Nazis came in, they found only nuns, though they searched and searched the convent. At long last they gave up, and Oswald was able to make his way across the border. Meantime, the heroism and true Christlike quality of the nuns made him take steps toward Christ.

After a few years he asked for and received baptism, changing his name to Daniel. Meantime the war had ended, and Israel had been established for Jews by the Law of Return. Daniel (like the other converts to Christianity) did not look upon his baptism as a renunciation of his Judaism—rather as a fulfillment. Accordingly, he petitioned Israeli citizenship by the Law of Return. This action caused a national crisis. No one who knew how many Jews he had saved wanted him turned down. Yet how could an "apostate" enter Israel as a Jew by the Law of Return?

A special Supreme Court session looked for a middle course and came up with the idea that a "Jew is one who was born of a Jewish mother and who had not been converted to any other religion, or who not being Jewish, is converted to Judaism." Daniel was disappointed at not being accepted as a Jewish Christian but did accept the invitation to become an immigrant Israeli as better than nothing. Some days later, while visiting Mount Carmel, I discovered that Daniel had just left for a mission station. We sped up and reached him before too long and had the joy of presenting him to our own group. An unforgettable meeting.

The experience of discovering Beirut, years before the destructive civil wars, was quite incredible. I had heard much about its beauty and serenity. As a Jesuit I was charmed by the prospect of visiting Université de Saint-Joseph. My Oxford companion, Father Dick McCarthy, came to visit me at our hotel and invited me to see his university and to meet the great Father Peter Hans Kolvenbach, one day to be elected successor to Father Arrupe as general of the Society of Jesus. I did not of course expect that at the time, nor did I guess that I would outlive Dick McCarthy, then the picture of health and at work on his eleventh book on Arabic philosophy—in Arabic.

We moved on toward Damascus, past snowcapped Mount Hermon, and the consummate work of Roman baroque known as Baalbek, in the Bekaa Valley, crowned by the Temple of Jupiter built by Nero and Caracalla. Damascus itself is the largest city in Syria, very ancient, independent from the reign of Solomon until the Battle of Issus in 333 B.C. Damascus was important under the Byzantines, but fell to the Arabs in A.D. 635. The Umayyads made it their capital, but this brilliant period ended in 750, when the Abbasids removed the seat of the caliphate to Baghdad. The Great Mosque and the Street Called Straight are both unforgettable.

Dura Europos includes one of the earliest Christian churches (dated about 225), a Mithraic temple, the oldest known synagogue (lavishly decorated with scenes from the Hebrew Scripture, despite Jewish prohibitions against the use of images). The little Christian building features themes of salvation, much like the catacomb of Saint Priscilla in Rome. I looked forward to rediscovering these Christian symbols in the great Yale collection on my return to the United States. Then on to Amman (original name for Philadelphia) and down, down, down into the intense heat below sea level to Jericho, reckoned the oldest continuously inhabited city in the world.

The view of Mount Nebo, traditional spot of Moses' death among the Mounts of Moab, reminded me of a typical Israeli joke, rich in irony. The story goes that when Moses reached the spot from which he could see the Promised Land, he collapsed, a victim not of excessive joy but of disappointment! Not, to be sure, that the Holy Land is devoid of beauty, but because this beauty has to be "earned" in order to be recognized. Unfortunately I failed to make a note of who it was that first told me the joke, but it could have been Alan Paton—not the famous South African writer, author of *Cry the Beloved Country*—but an Israeli guide who has had to explain hundreds of times that he is not the famous writer.

I came to know this Alan Paton during a long bus ride, my first in Israel, toward the end of a moving but taxing day, when confidences are rather easily exchanged. "Are you disappointed in Israel?" I asked him. "Not in the dream, what Israel stands for and hopes to become," he replied, but forthwith added, "I am disappointed in many of the Sabras, the native-born Israelis of the first generation. They already seem so spoiled with the good life. I wonder whether they would stand up in case a real crisis arose. I'm afraid not." This was decades ago, before Israel's toughest wars. Many conversations with Christian Arabs could hardly have been more opposed to Paton's assessment. The bitterness of the Arabs, quite understandable, strikes me as hard to remedy.

One afternoon several decades ago, I was flying from Jerusalem to Amman. A young steward sat next to me after we were airborne, and I launched into a conversation: "Looking at all this beautiful country," I suggested, "I find it hard to believe that peace will never come. I suppose your generation will solve the Arab-Israeli problem." "Oh, no," he insisted rather bitterly, "not until I get my house back. Every time I see it from the air, I hate the Israelis more than ever. Peace will never come until we are treated justly," he added decisively. No wonder that after my first visit to the Holy Land, when people asked how soon there would be real peace there, I replied, "As soon as both sides display the wisdom of Solomon and the goodness of Saint Francis. I see no sign of either, at least for now!"

Not surprisingly, I suppose, some memories of my first trip to the Holy Land still crowd out more recent experiences there: The first view of Jerusalem, cool and golden—"coelestis urbs Jerusalem"—and the visit to the traditional spot of Lazarus's grave, where several of us chanted the "Ego sum resurrectio et vita" ("I am the Resurrection and the Life") and our friend Marian, recently widowed, wept as Jesus had wept in the same spot. The Mass of the Agony in the Church of Nations at Gethsemani followed, and my happy, ever so surprising meeting with my old Oxford friend and superior, Father Tom Corbishley—our respective greeting was "What are you doing here?" which called for no reply. Then the drive with Alice Kirchman down to the Dead Sea by full moon, followed by a boat ride amid unforgettable beauty. Another drive toward Emmaus, again with Alice and her sister, and echoes of "Stay with us, Lord, for the day is far spent!" The opportunity to plant a tree in memory of Father John LaFarge, sponsored by Rabbi Tannenbaum and the American Jewish Committee. For "he is one of the Lamed Vav— the thirty-six good people whom God keeps on earth to save the earth from destruction," the rabbi explained.

As we reached the site of the ancient Basilica of the Incarnation in Nazareth, all of us felt particularly moved, since whether or not the traditional spot was historically exact, we knew that we were as near the spot of the First Joyous Mystery as could be ascertained. We asked for the sacristan in order to arrange for Mass. Father Romagosa secured the permission and the promise of adequate bread and wine for the Eucharist. He suggested to me that I get started on the readings of the Mass and the homily, assured that by the time I reached the offertory we would have the bread and wine. I followed his suggestion but suddenly faced a problem after I finished the readings and went ahead on what was to be a brief homily. It was not destined to be so! So I went on and on, almost the time of a full rosary—the Annunciation, Visitation, and so forth—while Father Romagosa renewed his search for the sacristan.

Both of us confessed later that we had recalled the outrageous story about the sacristan who had started saying the Rosary, waiting for the priest to come for Benediction, and feeling free to improvise additional mysteries. When the priest arrived, he was astonished to hear the sacristan announce the sixteenth mystery of the Rosary: "Pontius Pilate Stabs Judas Iscariot!" Happily my imagination was not so creative.

On a later pilgrimage to Nazareth, I was able to see the splendid bas-relief doors of the new basilicas, recently done by a friend of mine from Connecticut, Fred Shrady. It was a happy coincidence that I met him just before leaving for the Holy Land, and he was able to inform me about his contribution to the wonderful new doors, which he had not yet personally seen.

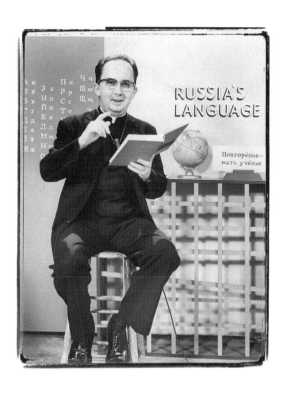

Chapter Ten

*Teaching an elementary Russian-
language course that aired weekly
on New Orleans public television.*

From Fertile Crescent
to Crescent City

Loyola University, New Orleans, 1958–60

One day in 1957, Father Jude Speyrer, then chaplain of Southwestern's Newman Club, came to see me at Grand Coteau and proposed the possibility of a European tour for special students, adjusting expenses to the realities of student budgets. We worked for hours on the project; meantime, he had made tentative arrangements for travel at minimum expense. Rather quickly we were able to get the minimum number of students required and then opened the tour to other friends, personal friends like my widowed cousin Geneviève Billeaud (now Gidiere), General Doran's wife Martha (who had been my baby-sitter many years earlier), Jerry Hughes, a former Jesuit novice then teaching at Spring Hill and destined to re-enter the Jesuits and (recently) be ordained, several adults from the area not far from Grand Coteau, such as Mrs. Irene Petitjean and a Mrs. Meche, whose first name I can't recall.

Mrs. Meche was a person of enormous wisdom and Christian humility, who was not afraid to ask questions and secure help. Before signing up for the tour she came to see me to ask whether with her slight education she might be wasting money going with college students. I assured her that all of us would be happy to help and urged her to sit near me on the bus and never to hesitate to ask questions. She thereupon told me she had been to a "Charm School" in Opelousas, though I wondered why such a person would need to acquire more charm. She explained that, after mastering the technique of entering a car without too much leg exposure, she had turned to the instructor and inquired: "Dat's fine, chèr, but tell me how you get off a tractor."

On the whole, the students appreciated Mrs. Meche's wit and wisdom, though some of the more "sophisticated" adults treated her a bit condescendingly. She may not have previously known about the Mona Lisa, though she quickly learned; but truly important cultural and religious treasures were not at all beyond her grasp. For example, she spent the whole day at Lourdes on her knees behind the high altar, unintentionally giving us all a lesson in true devotion. Moreover, she enjoyed the entire experience so thoroughly that she returned to Europe with a friend the following year to go more deeply into the meaning of such high realities as St. Peter's Basilica, Chartres Cathedral, and the like. When I recently heard that Mrs. Meche had died, I felt a real loss.

This thrilling spiritual-cultural tour of several countries of western Europe directed by Father Jude Speyrer and me in the summer of 1958 came to a happy ending on the same ship *Mauretania* that we had used on the way over to Europe. About the third day, however, a startling radiogram was brought to my table at lunch. It contained the one word "CONGRATULA-TIONS!" My close friend Jerry Hughes read the bewilderment sketched on my face and came over to ask if it was some bad news, something perhaps I would have to break to one of our group. "No, Jerry, I can't make heads or tails of this one word." He read the full text of the radiogram, address included. It opened, "Rev. C. J. McNaspy, S.J., Dean, College of Music, Loyola University, New Orleans" and was signed simply "Amos Vincent." Father Vincent had joined our group in London and returned early, reading the dire news of my appointment in one of the New Orleans newspapers, assuming I knew about it already. No such luck. In fact, before leaving New Orleans, I had been assured by Gus Coyle, then dean of the juniorate at Grand Coteau, that I would be back at Grand Coteau for the next school year.

The reason I found the news "dire" would have surprised most people who did not know me well. They, I suppose, would look upon the appointment as a "promotion," though to me it seemed calamitous. I knew I had no administrative ability whatever and had even begged the officials at Loyola University not to propose my name for dean of the College of Music. They agreed, but no one had anticipated what is often called "an act of God." This sad development, totally unforeseeable, had to do with the death of the previous dean.

But why didn't my superiors at least let me know in time for me to present a case against my appointment? Though such a procedure is not required, granted our tradition of Jesuit obedience, it is still reckoned normal, for obvious reasons. Later I discovered that the superior of the New Orleans Jesuits had indeed written me in Europe, but that the letter had never caught up with me. Hence my shock. Jerry was kind enough to sense my distress and to stay up with me for many hours helping me to accept this cross (granted it may sound absurd to refer to this as a "cross"; nevertheless it was, or seemed to me, the worst news I had heard in ages).

When our ship reached New York, I didn't have the stamina to endure what ordinarily would have been a pleasant day or two in the metropolis; instead, I returned immediately to New Orleans and went to Loyola to discover some explanation for the "disaster." There it all made sense, except that it was obvious to me that I could never be a good, or even an adequate dean. Several of my best friends there, who probably knew that my self-evaluation was correct, did manage to suggest something hopeful: "At least you can't complain about your secretary, who is the finest in the entire University."

I had met Mrs. Yolanda Tallman before, never dreaming that she would one day be my secretary. As soon as she returned to the office from her short vacation I met her again, thanked her for her heroism, and asked if she would allow me to use as a nickname (in French) "Simon"—for Simon the Cyrenean. Her sense of humor was such that she could appreciate what others might look upon as blasphemy. As a rare person, thoroughly trilingual and blessed with a full knowledge of the College of Music, its faculty, alumni, and traditions, I began to understand what Fathers John Keller and Tony O'Flynn had meant. Fortunately, Mrs. Tallman could and did compensate for many of my inadequacies, leaving me with a reputation that I felt was completely unmerited.

The other members of the faculty, save for one "prima donna," were altogether cooperative and did nothing to make me ask to resign. They seemed to understand my plight and to be in no way offended when I started several arts and sciences programs—History of Art and Russian Language and Literature—and gave an average of two lectures a week to various clubs in the city. They somehow even seemed to be, if I may venture to suggest this, rather proud of their eccentric dean and the publicity reflected on them. The strange fact is that even today a number of New Orleanians find it hard to believe I was there only two years as dean of the College of Music. Perhaps it was the number of TV and radio programs I hosted during that time, making me more of a public figure than the academic post alone would have warranted. The weekly elementary Russian language course that I offered on WYES-TV for a year or so was widely followed, as was the music program performed by our star pianist Istvan Nadas and hosted by me, at Nadas's request. It had become so, in those early days of educational television, that anyone with a weekly or biweekly program was almost as well known in certain circles as the TV stars. This particularly delighted my mother because we started to be recognized almost everywhere we went, especially at every restaurant we visited. One day, however, an Easter Sunday as I recall, no one seemed to notice us. Mama mentioned this, apparently feeling a bit hurt or maybe wanting to tweak me in fun. As we left the restaurant, however, the doorman bowed, wished us a happy Easter, and mentioned how much he enjoyed my TV programs.

The College of Music stood on its own merits at the time that I was dean, with an international reputation already built up in the world of opera, thanks to Norman Treigle, Elizabeth Wood, Dorothy Hulse, Mary Tortorich, Barbara Faulkner, Anthony Caruso, and a galaxy of younger stars—Nadas in the world of piano, having been a star pupil of Bartók and a stunning performer of almost the entire piano repertory; Charles Braswell, the shining light of the then new discipline known as Music Therapy, a protege of Dr. Gaston at the University of Kansas, and later recognized as the outstanding scholar in that field; the late George Jansen, a stellar band director, especially in the field of Brass Ensemble; and last but not least, the first chairs of the respected New Orleans Symphony, who were happy to add to their prestige by teaching in the College of Music.

Another very positive feature about Loyola in the late 1950s was a deepened sense of racial justice in the community, thanks especially to Father Lou Twomey, a real pioneer in the area, and to Jimmy Yamauchi, Alvin Pilie, Joe Fichter, Henry Montecino, and a number of outstanding lay people. One of the most courageous of these was none other than my secretary, Mrs. Tallman, who was occasionally insulted if not threatened by anonymous people with a KKK leaning, particularly when it became known that we saw eye to eye on the matter. It was easier for me, belonging to groups of priests and religious, Jesuits, Josephites, and others in favor of interracial justice, but people like Mrs. Tallman did not enjoy the same group support.

I'm sorry not to be able to recall all the details of this next episode: One day a mature student came to my office in the College of Music and asked to be enrolled as a special organ student. She presented her credentials, which were unimpeachable. The only possible problem that could be brought up was her race. I asked for a day or so to examine the papers. Meantime I consulted Mrs. Tallman, who was completely in favor of accepting the student. "Do you foresee anyone possibly making trouble?" I asked her. She reflected, then suggested that I ask the president of the student body. The only problem he foresaw was one person, who is still living and whom I don't want to identify now. I realized that he was one of the weakest students and would probably be afraid of the dean, on principle. So I sent for him. He came in obviously nervous. I proposed the problem as well as I could, asking his advice on the question of admitting a black into the College of Music. He seemed so relieved that I was not going to expel him from school that he assured me there would be no problem at all. He was right.

It is a tribute to my predecessors and to my successors in Loyola's School of Music that neither my arrival there nor my departure appreciably changed its reputation. In later years, such internationally esteemed scholars and artists as Joe Buttram, Harry McMurray, and Philip and Ellen Frohnmayer would hold their own in any world faculty, as would Joe Hebert and Joe Mahoney in the field of jazz performance. Much of the credit for Loyola's internationally growing repute surely goes to its most recent dean, David Swanzy, and associate dean, Anthony Decuir. More than to anyone else, I owe the launching of these memoirs to David Swanzy.

Shortly after I had begun my brief tenure as dean, a very important event in church history took place. On October 28, 1958, the patriarch of Venice, Angelo Roncalli, was elected Pope John XXIII on the twelfth ballot. At the age of nearly seventy-seven, he was regarded by many as a "caretaker pope," though his election would prove a turning point in the history of the church. My memories of the new pope are fairly slight; however, I do recall how enthusiastic my new friends connected with the College of Music seemed to be, especially with the new pope's wit and charm, following the dour solemnity of Pius XII. But would he be only a "caretaker"?

The decisive answer to our questioning came on January 25, 1959, when he startled the world—at least the non-Vatican-watching world—by calling an Ecumenical Council. Most of the nonspecialists were astonished, believing that such a council would never be called after the definition of papal infallibility by Vatican I, which seemed to make no other council necessary, or perhaps even thinkable. How could such a council not be super-fluous? Or, as some of my more conservative friends put it, "Why break up a winning team?"

I wondered about all these matters, which I intend to say more about later, when suddenly in 1960 (I can't remember the exact date) a quite unexpected phone call came from New York from Thurston Davis, the editor of the Jesuit weekly, *America*. I had met Father Davis a number of times but was totally unaware that he wanted me for his staff or that he had already asked my superior in New Orleans for permission to invite me. At first the idea seemed too ridiculous for words, particularly when he mentioned that he had looked on me as someone who could replace Father LaFarge when the time came. "You have exactly the same interests," Davis assured me. "You are a liturgist, very much inter-ested in the race question, interested in music and the other arts, and you write well." "Not nearly as well as Father LaFarge," I protested. "You will in time," was Davis's ready answer. I was quiet for a while, then asked, "How much time do you give me for an answer?" "Whatever you need," replied Davis.

This seemed to me the most honorific invitation of my life, and it was hard to evaluate objectively. Moreover, it wasn't the type of invitation where I could ask for advice: not from my rel-atives or close friends at Loyola, who would have opposed the move; nor from other Jesuits from other communities, who would automatically approve the idea. After some reflection and prayer, I tried to invoke the Ignatian principle of the magis or "the further good." Much as I loved Loyola and the College of

Music, I could not believe that at this moment of my life what I was doing there was more important than what I might be able to achieve as an editor of one of the leading weekly magazines in the United States. But making the discernment was only the beginning. How to break the news to my mother and other relatives, to Mrs. Tallman and other special friends at Loyola, or in the New Orleans music and arts communities? Fortunately, one of my nephews was in New Orleans at the time, and he seemed able to evaluate both opinions and to back up my decision.

Chapter Eleven

On the roof of America *House, 1970.*

America and the Wider World

New York City, 1960–70

The community of Jesuits that I joined in New York was one of the most cosmopolitan I have ever known. It was stationed on 108th Street near Riverside Drive, and thus near Columbia University, the Juilliard, and St. John the Divine Cathedral, and its fuller vista encompassed the country, or perhaps even the world. Not that ten men, even well-qualified men, could suffice for such a goal. No one of us would be able to write on all the areas assigned to him. But the presumption (not a rash one) was that each staff member would know or come to know other persons of similar aspirations—whether on social, theological, philosophical, or artistic subjects—who could happily be invited to collaborate on our mammoth task. Nor was the staff absolutely permanent, but able to be changed as need suggested. During my ten years there, I saw a continuous turnover, with at least one new person a year. The person who obviously appealed to me most was Father John LaFarge, then in his seventy-eighth year following some thirty-two years on the staff of *America* magazine. I could never imagine myself as his successor, such was his stature. His modest autobiography, published in 1954, *The Manner Is Ordinary,* was complemented by *An American Amen* (1958) and *Reflections on Growing Old* (1963), a veritable *De senectute,* which has helped countless thousands of people of a certain age. "Uncle John," as I've mentioned we called him, was totally unselfish, a model priest, social activist, and scholar, eager to share with others his vast experience.

If any American of this century can rightly be called an aristocrat, surely worthy of that title was his father, John, who anticipated impressionism and was one of America's foremost artists and architects and, according to Henry Adams, "the most complex mind in the U.S." His mother, Margaret Mason, was the grand-daughter of Commodore Matthew Perry and great-granddaughter of Benjamin Franklin. Their eldest son, Christopher Grant, was the architect of the choir of St. John the Divine Cathedral and, among other important structures, St. Matthew's Cathedral in Washington. Their second son, John Louis Bancel, was an important religious artist, especially in mosaics, murals, and stained glass; he became president of the Liturgical Arts Society. Oliver LaFarge, Christopher Grant's second son, was a novelist, social scientist, and ethnologist who worked with Franz Blom at Tulane University, both of whom I had brazenly met as a young boy. I was privileged to have been with Uncle John when he died, as I have mentioned in the preface, and assisted Cardinal Cushing in the stately funeral.

Thurston Noble Davis was director of the entire publishing venture of America House, including *Catholic Mind* and other projects, and tended to control every detail of it, at least until what I consider his Vatican II conversion. He was a most gifted man, graced with a Harvard doctorate and surely one of *America*'s outstanding editors. The superior of the community, former provincial superior of English Canada, was Father Noonan, a lovely man, who made me feel quite at home. Father Vinny Kearney, a New York Jesuit, was the "minister" or administrator of the residence, always ready to remedy what needed remedying. Another New Yorker and close friend of Thurston Davis was Father Gene Culhane, managing editor during my ten years at *America* and writer on Latin American topics, while serving as Davis's constant consultant and "alter ego."

In my own areas of special interest, Harold Gardiner seemed the most accomplished editor. He was selected as literary editor of the *New Catholic Encyclopedia,* an obvious choice, given his vast literary background and sane taste. Harold seemed universally loved and had a great deal to do with the Campion Award and with launching the writing careers of young authors. His favorable review of novelist Walker Percy's first masterpiece, *The Moviegoer,* was later credited by Percy himself with its critical success.

In matters of social justice, following the leadership of Father LaFarge, Ben Masse did much to set the tone of *America* during the early 1960s. Not only did Ben support unions and the labor movement in general, but he was at least partially responsible for *America*'s undeserved reputation as a "leftist-leaning" journal of opinion. Robert Graham, of the California Province, was a historian of high competence (especially in church matters) and served the magazine well in the 1960s, before he was called to Rome to work on Vatican documents, where he continues to work fruitfully. During recent visits to Rome, I have always enjoyed renewing contacts with Bob.

At about the same time at *America,* there arrived two very scholarly new associate editors: New Yorker Frank Canavan, political philosopher with a doctorate from Duke University, and Bostonian Walter Abbott, Oxford-trained classicist and Scripture scholar, who was to coauthor the important first edition of *The Documents of Vatican II.* A short time after our arrival, two important younger editors were to join the *America* staff, Don Campion (destined to be Davis's successor as editor-in-chief) and Dan Flaherty, my closest personal friend during the tougher years there, a man of universal competence, who is credited with great service to the *America* enterprise, to Loyola University Press, and to his own Chicago Province, of which he was made superior following his years in New York.

America magazine has long been one of the most respected of Catholic journals of opinion and is thoroughly available in libraries throughout the English-speaking world, thanks to its well-indexed files. Whenever, for example, one wishes to find significant articles on a topic with religious or philosophic implications, the *Index of Periodical Literature* will be of inestimable help in locating important articles in *America,* either under topics or by names of authors. The same can be said of book reviews. Sometimes it happens, in fact often happens to me, that I may want to find what or when I wrote on a given topic; the *Index* is my unfailing source of information.

The most difficult part of producing a weekly journal of opinion is, of course, the ruthless weekly deadline. While general articles can and usually must be prepared ahead of time, editorial materials have to meet regular deadlines. During my years with *America,* we had two regular board meetings: one to identify important events of the week and to select the most urgent ones, together with the editor best equipped to write on the topic; the other, three days later, to prepare the final draft.

Meantime, everyone on the staff was required to proofread every word of an issue before copy went to the printer. Under the eagle-eyed scrutiny of Thurston Davis, with the responsibility of each editor to initial the text, woe betide the unwary editor who took his task lightly! The fact that the inevitable rebuke came from one's contemporary, and was indeed justified, made it no easier to endure. It took me some time to learn exactly what was expected and perhaps even more to become used to feeling like a schoolboy again after years of teaching and serving as a dean. Someone remarked that this scrupulous policy would surely guarantee that *America* would never be tainted by any small errors.

A feeling of comparative success came only after several months, when my carefully researched article "The Culture Explosion" received ample quotation and high accolades from the *New York Times.* A reference to my work that particularly tickled my vanity can be found in *The Critic* for October-November 1963 in the column "Stop Pushing" by Dan Herr and Joe Wall: *"America* is now way OUT, with the sole exception of Father McNaspy who is incredibly IN." All this attention led to a number of interviews from other magazines and an awareness of being somewhat established in the arts world of New York. Invitations came, too, from colleges and seminaries, the two most surprising from Jewish Theological Seminary in New York and from Woodstock College, the esteemed Maryland and New York Province's theology faculty then located in Woodstock, Maryland. I had never expected to address an audience that included Avery Dulles, John Courtney Murray, Gustave Weigel, and other theological giants.

Thurston Davis was never one to rest or allow his staff to rest. Soon he had me giving a weekly radio program at Fordham University's station, and judging that to be successful, he asked me to start the production of a monthly recording of classical music in what was called the "Music for Everyman" series. Several thousand subscribers helped make the series a financial success for at least five years, and again this modest reputation elicited more and more speaking invitations, which resulted even in some invitations to lead groups to the Holy Land on pilgrimages (recalled in chapter 9 of this memoir).

———

In 1961, I was invited to Spain, and Thurston Davis asked me to take advantage of my several weeks there to interview the widest spectrum of Spanish intellectuals, while assuring them that their anonymity would be strictly respected. It almost goes without saying that today (in the 1990s) such reassurances would be neither desirable nor thinkable. But thirty years ago, secrecy was no luxury. My questions were carefully thought out, while the replies were spontaneous and, I believe, useful at that time. *Sign* magazine for January 1962 was brave enough to trust both my choice of people to be interviewed and my honesty in offering a composite reply, titled "The Reign in Spain." The *Catholic Mind* for 1962 gives an accurate reprint of the interview. I should add one startling effect of what would otherwise seem a bland article: the wife of the Spanish ambassador in Washington told my editor that the article caused the heart attack and death of her husband. Such was surely not my intention. It tells us something about this time that such could even be thought to be the effect of an innocuous article like mine.

One of the questions I put to them was, "What will the future bring to Spain?" The composite reply: shrugged shoulders and hands thrown up in a gesture of utter skepticism. This was the only question that met with an unanimous response. From there on came a bedlam of opinions, including the following: If Franco were to die suddenly, many are afraid that total chaos would return. Yet, we can't stand another civil war, said most, anything but that. Very likely the army will take over, though how long they can hold power or what they would do with it is uncertain. Again that shrug and that typically Spanish gesture. Spain is a car going down a highway; the highway will end, but the driver knows neither when nor how, said a very wise theologian. The American forces in Spain may help prevent a disaster was one helpful suggestion. The contacts with other countries will help. There will be a king. But will he be able to hold the country together, with so much apparent indifference or even hostility, especially toward a monarch of Bourbon blood? Spain has not been very fortunate in her kings, for some time at least, I was reminded.

Meanwhile, criticisms of the regime were multiple and various. Criticizing the government is a more popular national sport today than bullfighting, I was informed. The Generalissimo was adorned with many nicknames, some less innocent than others. When he came to Madrid, something he did very rarely, for the splendid Goya exposition commemorating Madrid's fourth centenary as capital, I heard someone shout across the street to a friend: "Paco Paredes" is coming to town! He explained that "Paco" is the diminutive for Francisco and "Paredes" means "Walls." Franco's picture is on all the walls! No one seemed conscious of the police, who were all about. It is hard to imagine such overt criticism occurring in Moscow (remember, this was in 1961).

The most serious criticism seemed to be that Franco has absolutely no trust in anyone, least of all in the people of Spain. Because of this, he has not allowed any political expression or development, and Spain remains politically a child. We have absolutely no training in politics or self-government, I was told again and again. The trade unions or syndicates, like everything else, are controlled from above. While an order of succession, in the event of Franco's death, has been established juridically, few seemed confident that this succession would work out. There has, unquestionably, been a substantial improvement in Spain's gross national income and dollar balance. Much of Madrid—the part seen by tourists—is elegant and makes other capitals pale by comparison. To the deep resentment of hard-working Catalans and Basques, tax money has been pouring into the capital and (it was alleged) benefits only the capital. Further, many conversations with working men right in Madrid showed that they believed Madrid's beauty was a sheer front, a facade (*fachada* was their word for it.)

After personal exploration in slums where no tourist nor even public transport goes, I found conditions that staggered the imagination, with large families living in tiny, one-room huts. Of all university students, fewer than 2 percent are from the working classes. On the other hand, I was happy to discover one bright ray: that the Jesuits, in spite of certain changeable opinions to the contrary, were educating more than twice as many poor boys as middle class or rich. I closed my article with a caution. In such a babel of conflicting sentiments on almost every subject touching Spain, no visits, however many or long, can give one assurance in his own judgments about that unique and beguiling country.

Strange, isn't it, that one who doesn't keep a diary every single day often forgets even the year of a particularly moving event in one's life, but before one of the first of my many visits to Spain I made it a point to ask Rabbi Marc Tannenbaum (recently deceased) if there was anyone there in the Jewish community that he would like me to look up. Marc thought for a bit, then wrote out the name and address of Dr. Max Mazín, who was not a rabbi (at that time Spain had no resident rabbi), but was the informal leader of the Jewish community in Madrid. At my further suggestion Marc added a note to his friend. When I reached Dr. Mazín's address, clerically clad and thereby constituting something of a "first" in that part of Madrid, the receptionist seemed a bit bewildered, but did reply, "Un momento, por favor." After the "momento," there emerged a very distinguished gentleman, who presented himself simply as "Max Mazín, padre, mucho gusto." He read the message Marc had sent, smiled broadly and stated, "Padre, su visita viene de la Divina Providencia." It seems that I was the first Catholic clergyman he had ever met, and coming under the auspices of a distinguished rabbi, I could not have been totally evil! I suspect that the news from Marc had something to do with an event that I happily read about some weeks later—the restoration of that splendid ancient synagogue, called for centuries "Santa María la Blanca," to the descendants of the Jewish community that had created it.

If anyone is interested in pursuing this small personal history, I am pleased to report that the noble synagogue appears in the 1963 edition of my *Guide to Christian Europe*. Too bad, I feel, that I cannot claim any credit for having helped bring about the restoration. Meantime I was happy to discover that Saint Ignatius Loyola is quoted by his close friend, Pedro de Ribadeneira, as saying with tear-filled eyes that he would consider it a special grace to come from Jewish lineage: "Just imagine, Pedro, being possibly a kinsman by blood with Christ Our Lord and Our Lady the Glorious Virgin Mary."

Even the very first time I was able to get to Spain, some ten years earlier, I found it impossible to resist fulfilling the dream of visiting the caves of Altamira. I had barely enough money to go from Madrid to Bilbao but managed to stop in Santillana del Mar in Santander Province, begging a ride from friendly foreigners (Swiss, I believe they were) who wanted to fulfill the same dream. These caves were the first of their kind to be discovered (1868). A scholarly Spaniard was visiting them with his daughter Maria, who spotted a painted bison on the ceiling of the Great Hall—the apex of 150 or more representations of animals, some twenty to forty thousand years old.

I was fortunate enough to have access to the principal caves quite alone, with a flashlight and the shelter of a raincoat to save me from dampness when I lay down. While years of further study have not revealed the full meaning of the symbols, either to me or to scholars like the Abbé Breuil, one senses that this is a holy place, a shrine, where our prehistoric ancestors sought to enter into some sort of communion with a power above themselves.

On another occasion, while guiding students through southern France, we were able to have comparable experiences in Lascaux, another "Sistine Chapel of the Paleolithic." After thousands of years safe from ecological damage through human breathing, both these treasures have began in this century to suffer seriously and irretrievably. Only recently have Spain and France had the good judgment to invest in perfect reproductions, together with air-conditioning that should render these treasures safe from human contamination for as long, one hopes, as humanity inhabits this earth.

The replica of Altamira is right in the heart of Madrid, in the museum of anthropology, and surely must not be missed. Never had I imagined the possibility of communicating so clearly with human beings so many thousands of years removed, yet so much like ourselves. Next to these great caves, even the pryamids of Giza seem upstart.

Another of my favorite places in Spain is Córdoba, in Andalusia, which throughout the Middle Ages was a cultural capital for Islamic and Jewish philosophy and art, the home of Moses Maimonides, Averroës, and Avicebron. At a time when books were rare throughout Europe, it boasted of some four hundred thousand volumes. Back in Roman days, the two Senecas and their relative the poet Lucan were the pride of Cordoba. But, as often happens in "Catholic Europe," the most valued structure there, sustained by some 850 monolithic marble columns, is the

Cathedral, often called "the Mosque" or *la Mesquita,* a veritable forest of marble, going back to Muslim times.

The new part of the cathedral itself is—to my taste—a baroque horror, ordered built by Charles V; but somehow the hundreds of horseshoe arches still allow a space for holiness to remain. In order not to lose my few hours waiting outside, I quietly stayed in place when the order came to leave the cathedral, entering the *mihrab* where it was easy to pray the rosary and whatever other prayers I knew in Arabic or Hebrew. Those extra hours of meditation are among my very special memories.

During this time two close friends of mine were assisting at the Council in Rome, Bishop Maurice Schexnayder of Lafayette, the successor of Bishop Jules Jeanmard, and his auxiliary Bishop Warren Boudreaux (consecrated July 20, 1962). Bishop Schexnayder having been called back to Lafayette, Bishop Boudreaux invited me to stay on until the end of the first session of the Council as his informal *peritus.* A splendid opportunity.

Bishop Schexnayder, whom my dad had helped found the Newman Club at LSU, was always very generous to me. He had heard a lecture of mine on the use of vernacular in liturgy (based on my experience in the Jesuit Mohawk parish across from Montreal, mentioned earlier) and although admitting that he was not in agreement, he congratulated me. When *Worship* magazine published the text of this lecture in March 1961 (30:4; 241–50), Bishop Schexnayder ordered several hundred reprints to be sent, together with his personal card, to all the bishops of North America. He did this despite his known aversion to the vernacular liturgy and my promotion of it in the article. Several bishops wrote personal letters thanking me for writing the article and stating that it had changed their thinking and voting during the Council.

Being a sort of *mini-peritus* at the session on the Sacred Liturgy gave me an opportunity to meet a number of impressive theologians from several traditions. Some of these encounters evoked mirth, such as when I asked in broken Italian what language an Egyptian preferred to converse in. "In English, Father, if you don't mind" was the reply.

My warmest memory of Pope John XXIII dates from the ending of the first session, December 8, 1962. The pope was clearly almost moribund as we sang the concluding "Te Deum." He was smiling, however, especially when he opened and closed his hands at the words: "In you, O Lord, I have hoped, nor should I be confounded forever." He was so feeble that he felt compelled to use the *"sedia gestatoria."* He blessed everyone with whatever vigor he could muster, but on reaching his old friend Cardinal Gerlier of Lyons, his gesture of blessing spontaneously turned into a kiss. Standing behind Cardinal Gerlier, I could not miss this unforgettable moment. It is the way I always remember Pope John XXIII.

In consequence of my articles on vernacular in the liturgy and on problems of liturgical music, I became a close friend of Rembert Weakland, the Benedictine monk of St. Vincent's, Latrobe, who was appointed music editor of the *New Catholic Encyclopedia*. Rembert, in turn, came to New York to invite me to share the music editorship. Nothing could have pleased me more, apart from possible difficulties that Thurston Davis might have. He gave an unequivocal no to Rembert's invitation, no doubt feeling that such a division of labor would distract me from my job at *America* and possibly lead me permanently into encyclopedia work as it had done for Harold Gardiner. He did allow me, however, to contribute several articles to the *New Catholic Encyclopedia,* to the *Encyclopaedia Britannica,* and to other encyclopedias, so long as I secured his permission in each case. But I happily recall that during Vatican II his approach became altogether more flexible, and for this I could never thank him enough. He also grew to trust me more and had me invited to appear frequently on TV and radio.

When Cardinal Montini was elected John XXIII's successor, June 21, 1963, and took the name Paul VI, we "liberals" rejoiced, since many of us had seen him on his visits to America, and the following day we were further reassured when he promised to continue the Council. On September 29, he opened the second session, closing it on December 4 with the promulgation of the decrees on the liturgy and on mass media.

A month later he made an unprecedented air pilgrimage to the Holy Land, meeting with Orthodox Patriarch Athenagoras in Jerusalem (January 4, 1964) and praying with him for universal peace and Christian unity. All of us who witnessed the ceremony on television were thrilled. For me, in a special way, it meant the opportunity to appear again on the *Today Show.*

America was asked to provide someone fluent in French, Italian, and Latin, since no one knew what language the pope would use when he spoke to the world. Thurston invited me to do the job, and I got up early that cold morning to go to the NBC studios. As I sat waiting to be received, I suddenly discovered that I was sitting next to Mickey Mantle. One of my best friends in New Orleans, Jesuit Brother Jimmy Maitland, was about the most fanatical Yankee fan of my acquaintance. So, I whipped out a card and asked Mickey to autograph it for Jimmy. "Sure," the star replied, laughing magnanimously as he scribbled, "Best wishes, Brother Jimmy!" Later Jimmy enshrined the card as a sort of icon. I remember thinking that my dad would probably be proud of me for at least knowing how important an athlete Mickey Mantle was.

At length my time came, and I entered the studio facing my host, Hugh Downs. He introduced me and announced that I would translate the pope's remarks. When the pope appeared, I discovered that I was completely useless, since the entire conversation was in English. Still, thanks to Hugh Downs's graciousness, I stayed on camera, bringing delight to my mother and godmother, glued to their TV screen in New Orleans. Not for long, however, because their friends kept calling enthusiastically to say, "C. J. is on the *Today Show* right now."

The meeting of Paul VI with the Patriarch Athenagoras happened to touch my life in yet another way. An old friend of mine, a fellow Jesuit and former student, Joe McGill, told me many years later:

I was in Tanzania, running a retreat house in Nyegezi, for all practical purposes "in the bush," with few if any retreatants. As I reconstruct it, it must have been the Christmas season following the wonderful encounter of pope and patriarch. There were no newspapers, in fact so little news that one day before Christmas when I want into Dar es Salaam, a nun tried to stop me, telling me that there had been a coup and that the president was in hiding and the situation was too turbulent to risk a visit. Finally, when I did go in, on what I thought was Christmas day, to have dinner with two fellow Jesuits, I found them putting up their crèche, and much to my surprise discovered that I was a day early—it was Christmas Eve! On the way back

to the retreat house, somewhat dejected over my confused
state, I picked up the BBC World News Service on my car radio,
and for their religious segment they announced that they had a
report from one of their "special correspondents, Father C. J.
McNaspy," and it was an archive piece on the momentous meeting that had taken place almost a year earlier. Hearing your
voice was all I needed to regain contact with reality.

Needless to say, Joe and I have had many a laugh over the affili-
ation with the BBC that I never knew I had.

The following year, when Paul VI came to New York to visit
the United Nations, I was invited by several radio stations to do
a simultaneous translation from his French text. On the feast of
Saint Francis, instrument of peace, Paul VI delivered before the
assembled delegates what his biographer Peter Hebblethwaite
calls "the speech of his life, a thirty-minute address for which
thirty years of Vatican diplomacy had prepared him—cordial,
discreet, human, and radical, in the sense of going to the roots of
the institution."

The magnitude of this event cannot be overstressed, nor the
response of the people concerned about the United Nations
itself. As a student of the United Nations in those early years, I
was excited almost beyond belief to do the simultaneous translation of the pope's address. True, I was given a provisional translation to help, but Paul VI spoke so clearly in French that I did
not have to depend on the text in hand. The climax, as almost
everyone remembers, came as he proclaimed, then echoed, the
unforgettable phrase "Jamais plus la guerre!" ("Never again,
war!") I believe my eyes watered more than they ever had at any
human phrase.

Yet the day was not over. That same night, October 4, 1965,
the pope celebrated a High Mass in Yankee Stadium, and the television networks invited me to help their announcers in report-
ing the event. We were shuttled over to the stadium to prepare
for the broadcast. That was actually the only time in my life that
I ever entered Yankee Stadium, which must also have delighted
my dad, watching from heaven. My colleagues in the media quite
modestly recognized that as a priest I had the advantage when
it came to explaining the structure of the Mass. No one coun-

termanded my explanation; rather they seemed grateful that someone from the "club" was eager to help.

The most thrilling moment came early in the Mass. I had been wondering whether the pope would venture to use the vernacular, in this case English, rather than "play it safe" and stick to Latin. Nothing was announced in advance, but never have the words used to begin the Mass seemed so welcoming as the pope intoned, not with the remote, arcane "In nomine Patris," but with the truly familiar "In the name of the Father."

I was still atingle as I started out of Yankee Stadium, for the long freezing trek to mid-town Manhattan. Slowly my fingers began to thaw, so that toward midnight I got to my typewriter and, as quietly as possible, began thumping out an article on that unforgettable day in the life of Pope Paul VI and of so many of us ordinary Christians, to appear in the New Orleans Catholic paper, the *Clarion Herald,* edited by my friend Father Elmo Romagosa.

My early years at *America* (1960–63), enhanced by the strong presence of Father LaFarge, gave me the opportunity to know leaders in a range of special interests: such giants as Kenneth Clark, George Hunton, Roy Wilkins, and other interracialists; liturgists like Maurice Lavanoux and the Rambusch family, cofounders of Saint Ansgar's League, who made me LaFarge's successor as chaplain of the Liturgical Arts Society; and, with only slight exaggeration, several of our country's top ecumenical and interfaith leaders—like Martin Marty, Jack Egan, George Higgins, Alexander Schmemann, Marc Tannenbaum, the editors of *Commonweal, Christian Century, Commentary,* and so many others. Obviously, in such circles, friendship with Father LaFarge was the key to opening many important doors.

Anyone of a certain age recalls exactly where he or she was on November 22, 1963, at the moment of John Kennedy's assassination. Most of us members of the *America* community were enjoying a postprandial conversation when our youngest colleague, Don Pugliese, popped into the recreation room with the incredible news. "You must be kidding!" I muttered nervously. "How could anyone kid about such a terrible thing?" Don rejoined. Thereupon we all clustered around the TV set as the dreadful news gradually unfolded. Even Father LaFarge, no devotee of television, seemed glued to the set for the rest of that day and the following, with hardly a sound save for occasional sighs of dismay.

Thurston Davis pulled me aside and very quietly asked me to go to the NBC studios: "They want us to give a statement, and I don't feel quite up to it." Embarrassed, but somewhat flattered by Thurston's confidence, I agreed to do the job as well as I could. Thurston's parting words were, "Give those right-wingers hell!" Fortunately I reflected during the subway ride that we hadn't any proof of who the perpetrator of the heinous deed was, right- or left-winger. We simply didn't know, though Dallas's reputation as a conservative city seemed to point to the right. I limited my remarks to the horror of the crime and the climate of hatred, with nothing about the political orientation of the assassin.

Two days later, November 24, that gloomy Sunday afternoon already mentioned in these memoirs, we at *America* had to endure a second shock, closer to home, as the death of Father LaFarge followed so closely upon that of his Harvard colleague.

As the likelihood increased that the assassin had been Lee Harvey Oswald, we began to wonder about his background. A phone call from my good friend Father "Steve" Foley at Spring Hill College advised me and asked me to advise my confreres that Oswald had, only a few days before the assassination, visited his cousin Gene Murret, a Jesuit seminarian at Spring Hill and close friend of mine; furthermore, Oswald had given a low-keyed talk about his Russian trip and impressions.

Steve had called with some urgency, fearing that enemies of the Jesuits might cook up a conspiracy myth, as some had done following Lincoln's assassination. He felt that we at *America,* in a sense spokesmen for Jesuits in the United States, should be in possession of the full story before any falsehood began circulating. He followed the phone call with a fuller account of everything regarding Oswald and his visit to Gene. To be sure, nothing sinister had occurred during the visit. The following year, on September 27, I rushed to the nearest bookstore to secure a copy of the *Report of the Warren Commission* on the day it appeared, to check on the treatment of the Spring Hill College visit by Oswald. Happily, it had been faithfully reported by the Commission, and this made me feel more secure about the Commission's handling of larger issues.

The other most distressing assassination that took place during my tenure at *America* was that of Dr. Martin Luther King, Jr. While I had never known him personally, any more than I had John Fitzgerald Kennedy, I felt as crushed by his murder as I had felt by J. F. K.'s. Again, I remember distinctly where I was on that night of April 4, 1968. I had gone by cab to my doctor's office because a bus strike had paralyzed the city. Dr. Maloney's receptionist came into the office breaking the news: "They've just shot Martin Luther King!" After some minutes of reflection with the amiable doctor, I set out on foot to mid-Manhattan to the apartment of my closest black friend in New York, Jim Broady. Jim was delighted to see me and reassured me with the words: "I knew you'd come." I had gotten to know Jim when guiding my first Holy Land pilgrimage, some years earlier. We had shared experiences, both joyous and tragic, and he had even named me executor of his will before undergoing very dangerous surgery.

Somehow, that tragic night, I felt no fear while walking several miles through the streets of Manhattan. To be sure, few people were on the street, but those few seemed more human than usual in the vastness of the city's canyons. I stopped and addressed every black that I met, expressing condolences. No one failed to respond cordially. This seemed like the night of the first blackout in New York when everyone's characteristic iciness toward strangers seemed to melt in the presence of the shared uncertainty. I've heard that the English enjoyed some such experience during the Battle of Britain.

Suddenly and unexpectedly, at 3:45 on the afternoon of October 11, 1963, my phone rang. The voice was that of Thurston Davis, and I sensed what seemed unusual excitement as he invited me to come to his office. Something was clearly "up," and I replied that I'd be right down. Thurston was as excited as I ever remember seeing him. He explained that he had just heard that the next day (we both realized that it was Columbus Day) his old classmate Father Walter Ciszek was to arrive at Idlewild (as Kennedy Airport was then called).

I had long admired Wally Ciszek as a hero of our times. In fact, like other Jesuits then living in the New York area, I had offered Mass for the repose of his soul, so sure were we that he had already died. "I thought Wally was dead," I remonstrated. To be sure, after twenty-three years out of contact with his family and fellow Jesuits, Wally could reasonably be presumed to have gone to the heavenly kingdom. So Thurston went on to explain almost breathlessly that Wally had been released from Siberia and had already reached London in his homeward trek.

Why, I wondered, was Thurston advising me particularly? He answered my unexpressed question before I could ask it: "It seems that Wally has forgotten his English, and since you're the only one here who speaks Russian, maybe you should plan to come with us. Would you like to?" "Of course," I gasped—excitedly.

As it happened, before we could set out for Idlewild, Wally's taciturnity was explained. He had not forgotten his English; he had only been thoroughly obedient in following the instructions of the American ambassador in Russia to speak to almost no one until arriving in New York. Since I was no longer needed, his old associates from the New York and Maryland Jesuit Provinces could more appropriately be invited to join Thurston in meeting him. Though disappointed, I understood the change of plans and was happy to wait at *America* residence to meet Wally. Not only did he speak English enthusiastically when he bounced off the plane, I was told that he used words like "fox-trot" to describe the rock and roll music he heard at the airport.

Later, Dan Flaherty very generously invited me to work with him on the autobiography that he was to help Wally compose. For me it was a privilege to meet and work with one of the heroes of our time, and Dan was kind enough to give the autobiography the title I suggested, *With God in Russia.* How apt the title proved became obvious as one relived with Wally Ciszek the years spent in Russia as he prepared to work among the Poles, he himself being Polish; his captivity by the NKVD, the Soviet secret police, and his years of imprisonment in Moscow, especially in dreaded Lubyanka; his years in the prison camps of Arctic Dudinka and Norilsk; and the thrilling details of his unexpected release. While not a writer of Pasternak's or Solzhenitsyn's stature, Wally Ciszek grips the reader by his total sincerity and unaffected love of God and humanity. One could hardly improve the autobiography's final words: "I blessed myself, then turned to the window as we took off. The plane swung up in a big circle; there were the spires of the Kremlin in the distance. Slowly, carefully, I made the sign of the cross over the land I was leaving."

If any readers of these pages have not read Wally's and Dan's superb account, I urge them, in the words of the reviewer for *Best Sellers,* to devour these objective pages, from which there emerges "a picture of a man of invincible faith and heroic fortitude, who is sustained by a great love for God and his fellow man." Would I ever get the chance to visit Russia myself, I wondered at the time. And if so, what would my experiences be?

In retrospect, I have come to think of Terry Anderson and Wally Ciszek in comparable terms though they would seem to have very little in common, except what matters most. Like Jesus and Stephen (who first forgave his enemies in imitation of Jesus), Terry Anderson, a hostage of the Islamic Jihad for 2,455 days, openly proclaimed, "I'm a Christian and a Catholic; it's required of me to forgive, no matter how hard it may be." Wally Ciszek, years before, following twenty-three years of imprisonment in Moscow and Siberia, disappointed only the John Birchites and other similarly narrow-minded Christians by truly forgiving all the people who hated and tortured him. Their principal difference seems to be that Ciszek, a Jesuit priest, was not a political hostage. As I write these memoirs, I have yet to meet Terry Anderson, though he's still very much alive, whereas Father Ciszek has long since gone to God. I was not surprised to learn, a few years ago, that his "cause" for canonization has already been introduced in Rome.

Getting to know Wally Ciszek proved a personal blessing in unexpected ways, particularly since through him I became much better acquainted with such great thinkers in New York as Schmemann and Meyendorff, giants of Orthodox spirituality. No one enthusiastic about Russian classical novelists like Dostoevski or Tolstoy, not to mention J. D. Salinger and his charming *Franny and Zooey,* can be unaffected by the traditional Orthodox "Jesus Prayer," which meant so much to Wally.

Like many others I found this wonderfully simple and scriptural series of ejaculatory aspirations, rhythmically repeated, very helpful in heightening a mood of inner silence. My favorite form is "Lord Jesus Christ, Son of God, have mercy on me, a sinner"—recited over and over, in Old Slavonic or Russian, while pressing through hectic crowds, or quietly and devoutly venerating an icon of Rublyov.

One day while I was working at the *America* residence, Rabbi Arthur Schneier, a close friend, called to ask whether I'd like to participate in an informal memorial service for some fifty persons hanged by the Baath party in Baghdad for no stated reason save that they were not members of the party. The exact number of these heroes I cannot recall, but when I arrived at the meeting place I discovered some fifty wreathes bearing Iraqi names, with no identification as to whether the person named was Jewish, Muslim, or Christian (since names like Yitzak, or Isaac, could be borne by a member of any one of the three monotheistic religions, just as the Arabic blessing "Allah yibark-hak" may be reverently used by any Christian, Jew, or Muslim). I never knew whom the wreath given me to carry commemorated. But I hope that God accepted my prayer for him or her. We marched in silence to the Iraqi United Nations embassy and left the wreathes at the locked front door. Arthur had advised both the police and the TV networks of our innocent intentions.

While it is always hard, if not impossible, to discern saints who have not been canonized, a number of the Sufi Muslim mystics have written passages that Christopher Dawson describes as of "unsurpassed beauty and religious significance. . . . Thus it is related of Rabi'a, the saintly freed woman of Basra, that at night she would go to the house-top and pray as follows: 'O my Lord, the stars are shining and the eyes of men are closed, and the kings have shut their doors and every lover is alone with his beloved, and here am I alone with Thee. . . . Thou art enough for me.'"

During the recent Gulf War, every time Basra was mentioned I thought of Rabi'a and her likeness to Saint Teresa of Avila. Even more remarkable are the prayers of Al-Hallaj, the great "Martyr of Sufism," who suffered at Baghdad in A.D. 922. He regarded Jesus, in Dawson's words, "as the type of deified humanity—the second Adam in whom the divine vocation of the human race is realized." His disciple, Ibrahim ibn Fatik, relates, "When he was brought to be crucified he prayed: 'O Lord, I beseech Thee to make me thankful for the grace that Thou hast bestowed upon me. And these Thy servants who are gathered to slay me, in zeal for Thy religion and in desire to win Thy favor, pardon them and have mercy upon them. Glory unto Thee in whatsoever Thou doest, and glory unto Thee in whatsoever Thou willest.'" The Sufi may reason like a pantheist, but when he prays it is with the humility and adoration of a creature in the presence of his Creator.

Walter Kern, a priest from the diocese of Buffalo, whom I consider a good friend, publishes a program of prayer motivated by the spirituality of the Heart of Jesus, titled *Priestly Heart Newsletter.* Issue no. 56, April 1982, was titled "Muslim Mystics and the Heart of Jesus." Father Kern points out that

> Muslim mystics in a specific context [are] also related to Christ's Heart. Vigorously rejecting any idea of a Trinity, Muslims who follow Jesus as the model of sanctity want to become fully submissive to Allah, having nothing in their hearts but His will. They want to practice Islam as Jesus practiced it according to the Koran. They firmly believe that, when Jesus will come again at the end of time, he will join the Muslims in prayer and refute the prayer of Christians, thus showing publicly the futility of their creed. Muslim mystics are genuine followers of the Jesus of the Koran. . . . Since Al-Hallaj wanted to be completely like his model, Jesus, he was ready for crucifixion if Allah so wished. By his life and death (crucified in 922), he propagated the imitation of the personality, the heart, of Jesus. Ibn Arabi (died 1240), also a mystic, stated that he saw Al-Hallaj in a dream and determined to follow him closely. Thus, Jesus became his personal friend. He writes that Jesus helped him to overcome the crisis of his conversion, so he often asked Jesus for perseverance in his religious life. Jesus, the seal of universal holiness, imparts soul-quickening spirituality to his friends after having received it himself from Allah. In the course of the centuries, the personality of Jesus was dealt with in many Muslim spiritual books. For example, A. Palacios lists many in his "Logia et Agrapha" of Our Lord Jesus Christ found in Muslim writers, especially the ascetics (found in *Patr. Orientalis* 13, 3 Paris, 1919, 335-431 and 16, 4 Paris, 1926, 531-624).

Pious Muslims tried to imitate Jesus' heart, his personality, in the way they understood it—according to the teaching of the

Koran, the Sunna, and the doctrines of the Sufis. Father Kern then quotes Norman Daniel: "The Christ of the Koran is not the Christ in whom Christians believe, and yet there is only one Christ, whose praise must always be grateful to Christian ears. Medieval devotion to Christ and His Mother was too powerful to grudge an alien devotion that was genuine" (*Islam and the West,* Edinburgh, Edinburgh University Press, 1962, 166–75). Perhaps now is the time to revisit the meeting place the mystics found in the Heart of Jesus. (My own knowledge of Islam is so limited that I have to trust the accuracy of these quotations from recognized authors.)

In 1932, the Jesuits of the New England Province opened Baghdad College at the request of the Chaldean Patriarch Emmanuel and the Christian hierarchy of Iraq. They followed the policy of full compliance with government educational policy and were seen this way by all those, non-Catholics as well as Catholics, who knew their schools—the College and, from 1956 on, Al-Hikma University, recognized as the great educational institution of the country. Jealousy caused accusations against the U.S. Jesuits to be raised, but at the request of my Oxford friend Father Dick McCarthy, president of the university, the prime minister investigated Al-Hikma and made it clear that nothing detrimental to the country was being done by the Jesuits. Unfortunately, on November 25, 1968, after Saddam Hussein came to power, the Jesuit professors and administrators of the university were compelled to terminate their years of service to the cause of higher education in Iraq.

I have personally been able to discuss the matter with non-Catholic Iraqis, who agreed that the quality of Al-Hikma's educational work was far superior to that of any other institution in the country. The loss to Iraq was irretrievable. Father Dick McCarthy wrote the government in these unequivocal words: "We respect you, as we respect all sincere citizens. And we respect ourselves and our profession—and this is the right and duty of every man. We love this country and its people and we appreciate hospitality, which we shall never forget. We ask God Most High to bless our dear Iraq and its dear sons with the best of His favors and blessings in this world and the next, for God is the One who hears and answers."

Several winters in the early 1960s I was invited to give our U.S. army chaplains a short, liturgically-oriented retreat geared to the needs of chaplains and their assistants, whether choral personnel or otherwise. While late January is not my favorite time of year in Europe or North America, I was always happy to find an occasion to be apostolically present in central Europe—Vienna, Prague, Salzburg, Munich, the Rhineland, Berchtesgaden, or wherever—enjoying myself culturally while, I hope, doing helpful apostolic work. In point of fact, my very first trip to Vienna—which can't help being a favorite central European city of anyone who's been there—was on the occasion of a chaplains' retreat not in Vienna, but in Berchtesgaden across the border in Germany (though near Salzburg, and thus not terribly far from Vienna) in a hotel that was used as a rest center for U.S. officers. I don't suppose any winter scene can surpass for sheer beauty the one near the General Walker Hotel, where "rest and recreation" were and perhaps still are generously provided our military service personnel.

It so happened that the final night of the retreat one year coincided with Mozart's birthday, January 27. Three chaplain's aids, real music lovers, invited me to go with them down the mountain from Berchtesgaden and across the frontier into Salzburg for the final concert of the celebration. It was a glorious performance of Mozart's celebrated *Vespers,* lasting till about eleven o'clock. The evening seemed mild and unlikely to deteriorate. My three friends dressed appropriately, laughing at the pessimism shown in my heavy topcoat and Russian cap, plus galoshes. I was prepared for the worst and joined in their laughter. As we started across the border, it began to snow, at first gently. I remember expressing relief that Ralph (from a mountainous U.S. state) was driving, since I had never driven in mountains, much less in mountains deep in snow. Ralph replied, "Well, I hope we make it." He sounded a bit ominous, but I put it down to weariness.

Toward midnight blizzard conditions of a sort developed, and we were still not at the hotel. We had failed to use the snowchains in our naiveté, and felt the car stalling. Ralph tried to cheer us up: "There's a fork in the road a quarter of a mile ahead. You drive, Sally, and make a left turn when you get there. The hotel is just beyond it." "But I can't drive!" moaned Sally. As the second least powerful I was elected, tried to get signals straight, and with their pushing got started. The fork appeared in the thickening snow, and I managed to spot the left turn. I took it and drove as fast as I could safely, hoping to see the hotel soon.

Several minutes went by, but still no hotel. Finally the car stalled completely, so I got out and yelled as loudly as I could: "Ralph, Emile, Sally!" No answer, save the swish of the gathering blizzard. I could just see that the left side of the road opened onto a chasm, perhaps a thousand feet deep. I realized that I had to feel my way carefully, since it was a blackness like none I had ever experienced. (I had forgotten that snow in total darkness is not white!) I also realized that every road, in mountains or not, led somewhere and determined not to stop to rest, lest I fall asleep and die, as I had seen happen in movies.

To survive, I simply had to keep moving until I reached the inevitable village. I must have walked at least an hour before I met a wall of impassable, solid iron. I banged on what must have been a door, but no response. I banged again and again, but still no answer. At about this point I realized that I was in real danger, that this was the only road in Europe that led nowhere that night. I had, in fact, reached Hitler's "Eagle's Nest," on a night when there was no guard, no custodian, no help. To stay alive I would have to walk carefully, for at least five more hours. It was midwinter, one of the longest nights of the year. But especially I must not stop to rest; that would be as fatal as falling over into the chasm.

I must say that that night I prayed more fervently than perhaps ever in my waning life. It really seemed like the last night of my life, barring some sort of miracle. Along toward three o'clock in the morning, the miracle appeared: lights of a car or jeep or truck coming my way. As the vehicle approached I began to wave desperately. There was no need to, since the vehicle obviously was in the process of searching for me. At last the jeep stopped and a very Irish face with a thoroughly Brooklyn accent greeted me: "Hey, Padre, are you O.K.?" I was, then. "Where are the others?" I asked.

On the way back to the hotel, I gradually pieced the night's drama together. Arriving at the fork, Ralph, Emile, and Sally realized they had misled me. They found the car, by then completely in snow, with no footsteps visible. Then they rushed toward the hotel but had to attend to Sally because she was in a panic, feeling that it was her fault. They stopped at a cabin, woke the inhabitants, spoke to them in German, and explained everything. Sally stayed with them for the next hour or so, warming up, while Ralph went on to the hotel, from which he called the Alpine Rescue Squad. No answer. Then he called the nearest U.S. station, frantically trying to get help. When a voice answered, its only message was: "What's his rank?" (meaning my rank in the service). Ralph used his head, remembering that they were treating me like a colonel, and simply said so, plus a few expletives and earnestly-meant threats. This prodded the Irishman from Brooklyn into action, and I was saved. The next morning I discovered that the three youngsters were sick in bed with flu, while I had survived, thanks to my galoshes and other caparisons. *En tout cas,* as they say in the Alps, every year I offer a Mass of thanksgiving on Mozart's birthday.

Whether it was the year before or after my "Eagle's Nest" fright, it was certainly around Mozart's birthday, that Colonel Charles and Bernice Medinnis, both of California (in fact, Bernice had been "Miss California" a few years earlier), participated in a chaplains' retreat with me at Berchtesgaden. This time we drove from Salzburg to Paris, then to Amiens where we visited a wonderful liturgist friend of mine, even though my collapsing memory won't resuscitate his name, and he has since gone to God (where I presume he's laughing now at my plight). We stayed several days in the Amiens area, thoroughly enjoying the Cathedral's beauty as well as that of Laon, Rheims, and Beauvais. My only problem on that occasion was how to get a view of the new windows in Notre Dame (Paris) without missing my plane out of Orly. I've repeatedly thanked God that Chuck was as fine a driver as a colonel, not to mention his choice of Miss California as a stunningly beautiful and no less brilliant wife. Our last get-together was in the summer of 1990, when we managed to visit San Juan Capistrano, swallows or no swallows. To be with the Medinnises is a joy forever.

The present residence of the *America* staff is 106 West 56th Street in New York City. How the move took place bordered on the miraculous. I shall recall it as accurately as possible, with no adornments. One morning back (I believe) in 1963 or 1964,

Thurston Davis awoke with a great idea—at least it seemed great to him. It was to send Father Walter Abbott to Boston to ask Cardinal Cushing for a million dollars. When he mentioned this to Walter, a collapse seemed imminent.

Being a man of strong obedience, though, Walter sallied forth. He knew Cardinal Cushing quite well, but never in terms of asking for that kind of money. The Cardinal was almost as taken aback as Walter was. "Well, Walter," he drawled, "I don't think I can give you a million. Would half a million do?" Walter survived that shock and returned to New York with a check for half a million dollars. Thurston had managed to save some funds toward the project and, with the Cardinal's immense gift, was able to take advantage of the pending sale of a nine-story build-ing in the most advantageous part of New York City, which he was able to buy for something like $800,000 cash. Don Pugliese, a young New York Jesuit with immense talents, was placed in charge of the renovations, and in a matter of months we had a virtually brand-new building, with no debt.

Meantime, I begged Thurston to invite Father André Bouler, then living in Paris (whom I mentioned earlier as having been one of Fernand Léger's few personal pupils), to come to New York to size up the situation. With enormous imagination André spotted the problems of turning what had been at least five or six rooms in the hotel into something worthy of a chapel. The liturgical changes of the Second Vatican Council were very much in the air, and André had to be prophetic as well as practical. Almost every liturgical artist who comes to New York visits André's chapel—the tapestry, the stained-glass windows, the medieval statues, the metal tabernacle (designed by André's asso-ciate Father Tézé), everything miraculously works together. It was the only New York chapel in my time that merited inclusion by Maurice Lavanoux in the splendid magazine *Liturgical Arts.*

Around this time, several members of the Liturgical Arts Society, originally founded by Father LaFarge and associates, called me (as their chaplain following Father LaFarge) and asked whether I would favor the idea of a papal knighthood being con-ferred on Maurice Lavanoux. "Of course, who could be opposed to such a fine idea?" I asked. "Well," replied my associate, "the problem is that normally knighthoods are conferred by the Cardinal Archbishop of the city, and I don't think that Cardinal

Spellman would like such an honor being conferred on Maurice—they seem to have different values." "What do you suggest we do?" I asked. My friend had thought the matter through and had a powerful ally in Rome who, he felt, could expedite matters. "Fine," I replied, "you have my vote." We agreed to keep the matter quiet, and for some time I thought no more of the "conspiracy."

Then one day a phone call from the Cardinal's office advised me that I was invited to the palace for the conferral of a knighthood on Maurice Lavanoux. The hour was set, and when I arrived I found most of my lay friends, all members of the Liturgical Arts Society and of the Quilisma group within the Society, with only Maurice unaware of what was about to transpire. At length Cardinal Spellman entered, radiating his usual bonhomie. He already seemed to know each of us by name. Another Jim Farley, I thought. He opened the papal document and said in mock distress: "Oh, it's in Latin. Can anyone here read Latin?" After teaching Latin for some twenty years, I felt I could volunteer: "I believe I can, Your Eminence." The Cardinal laughingly protested: "I thought you were a vernacularist, Father?" "I'm a vernacularist because I am a Latinist, your Eminence," I laughingly protested in turn. "Fine, Father, go right ahead." Fortunately the text was not in difficult Latin.

———

Cathy and Charlie Vukovich from Maywood, New Jersey, quickly and lastingly became among my best friends in the East. The parents of both were from Dubrovnik, but they did not meet until they reached New Jersey. Both obviously were Croatians. Perhaps I should say "are" Croatians, since though Charlie died while I was in Paraguay, I'm sure that in heaven he's still as loyal a Croatian as ever. I came to know Charlie through good friends at St. Peter's in Jersey City. He created a new technique of glass work, which I encountered for the first time in 1962. Glass it was, to be sure, and stained, but not what we normally mean by stained glass.

Never a mere imitator, Charlie had taken glass from broken colored bottles, with some of their op art vigor, years before the term was coined. He set them into rough concrete to express the "Stations of the Cross" with a piquancy seldom matched, while the "Resurrection" was glass on glass, brilliantly pointing up the mystery and glory of the Resurrection.

Over the years I have seen almost all of Charlie's work, from Staten Island to Omaha and never found it less than thrilling. His "Soldier" in Veterans' Memorial Park (River Edge, New Jersey) was a most unlikely success. Right at the height of the peace movement—which sometimes took on warlike tones—he managed to create a welded steel alloy statue of a soldier, poignant rather than militaristic. But his "Crucifixion on 8th Avenue," in New York's Covenant House, is overpowering.

I could go on and on talking about Charlie and Cathy, my two favorite Croatians. They were forever deeply in love, Cathy working at NBC to enable Charlie to be fully creative. Shortly before Charlie died, Cathy did me the ultimate favor, phoning me in Paraguay so that we could share an immensely important moment in both our lives. What friends they were! Happily, the chapel of Javier College in Asunción is dedicated to Charlie's and Cathy's memory—a chapel made possible partly by gifts, at the time of Charlie's death, from his many friends.

I've only been to Dubrovnik once. The opportunity came almost by accident. I flew from Rome to the Dubrovnik airport and from there went by bus to the seminary. I brought notes of introduction, since my Croatian language is the poorest. But the brother at the door received me most cordially and gave me the bishop's room, commanding the Adriatic. It was the perfect place to watch a storm at night, over the very castle where the ghost scenes of Olivier's *Hamlet* were filmed. At breakfast we discovered that though I could speak to each member of the community in a modern European language, only in Latin could we all bluff our way through—laughter and all!

The Jesuit superior accompanied me to the homes of Charlie's and Cathy's parents, who made me feel like the proverbial member of the family. A Slovenian seminarian escorted me all over the city, to the oldest pharmacy in all Europe, to the splendid stairwell built by Croatia's greatest sculptor, Ivan Mestrovic, a native of Split, the city built inside Diocletian's palace, with a cathedral encompassing Diocletian's tomb. Mestrovic is highly appreciated all over the United States, perhaps in part because of his long stay at the University of Notre Dame. Amazingly enough, the Louisiana Arts and Science Center in Baton Rouge houses, after the University of Notre Dame, the second largest collection of Mestrovic's sculptures in the United States. Notre Dame Seminary here in New Orleans proudly displays an exact replica of his statue of the *Woman at the Well.*

———

A special delight of working at *America* House was the opportunity one had to meet interesting and famous people, some of whom I've already mentioned. Another was Jim Farley, Franklin Roosevelt's professional "nomenclator," whose fabulous memory I experienced personally. The Roman Emperors, you may recall, always had someone at their side to remind them of the names of important people who might otherwise be forgotten.

I had heard a fair amount of the mnemonic prowess of Mr. Farley, some of it from people who had known it at first hand: Father Russell Dornier's father, for example, who was called by name years after he had met Jim Farley. My experience was less dramatic, but nonetheless shocking. While at *America* House I happened to meet Mr. Farley one evening. We hardly spoke, since Jim Farley had far more important people to talk to. Still, about six months later, in a totally different context, not *America* House, I ran into him and before I could offer my name he asked, "How are you, Father McNaspy?" An extraordinary gift.

As I have been writing this account, a student of film here at Loyola University asked me what famous movie stars I had met. "None," I replied tentatively, but I thought a moment longer before realizing that I had inadvertently forgotten about my favorite actor, Alec Guinness. It surprised my student that I could forget anyone so important. "How did you get to know him in the first place?" he asked.

So I explained how while I was working for *America,* I had the chance of seeing Mr. Guinness about once a week when he came to our residence on 108th Street to have lunch and see friends, especially Father LaFarge. Guinness had come to know several English Jesuits when he was received into the church. They were happy to recommend Father LaFarge and our community to him as a pied-à-terre when he was in New York.

Another famous person of stage and screen whom I met, thanks to Father LaFarge, was Helen Hayes, now of happy memory too. Father LaFarge invited me one morning to a rehearsal of some TV program in New York, on which he was to appear with Miss Hayes and very generously presented me, mentioning my various interests. Among other things, she said that she was to give a talk on Phyllis McGinley, the charming, ever-popular poet whose work fascinated me, especially during the 1960s. I mentioned that I had been thinking of her verse style as a sort of "verbal inlay," and noticed that it would be easy to create a rhyme more or less in her style: "the verbal inlay of Phyllis McGinley." With the modesty of a great artist, Miss Hayes expressed delight and even used my phrase during her talk.

A third movie star whom I cannot explain having forgotten even for one moment is Bette Davis, with whom I shared a table at a banquet in New York, given by B'nai B'rith, at which I had been invited to give the invocation.

Once again, the combination of *America* House and some slight linguistic skills led to a memorable encounter, this time with Roger Garaudy, who was at the time the leading French Marxist philosopher. The subtitle of his just published book was *A Marxist Challenge to the Christian Churches.* My role in the encounter was minuscule, if not less, though I personally found it interesting, and I treasure the autographed copy dated "December 1, 1966, *au Père McNaspy en souvenir d'un acceuil fraternel à l'institut LaFarge, très cordialement,* R. Garaudy." Why to me?

It must have been a Saturday morning, when my phone rang to register a curious request: "We need someone who speaks French. Can you come?" "Where are you, and who are you?" I asked. "One of the editors of *Commonweal,* and we're downstairs in *America* House." "Give me a moment to shave, and I'll be right down." Why no one on the *Commonweal* staff spoke French, I have no way of knowing. And how they knew that I did was equally mysterious. The editors were from Herder and Herder, and the coauthor of the volume was Leslie Dewart. In any case, I was flattered and determined to do the very best I could.

As I shook hands with M. Garaudy, recalling that he was officially an atheist but a friend of Jesuit Father Calvez, it occurred to me that he might enjoy a bit of whimsy. So, I held my fingers like horns on either side of my head and observed, "I see we both left our horns at home!" He enjoyed my effort at humor, and we seemed likely to get along.

The job was surprisingly easy, especially since I had determined to be simply accurate and not to slant anything. After some minutes of easy sailing, I hit a snag. M. Garaudy was talking about the changes in attitude between Christians and Marxists, away from anathema toward honest dialogue. "I feel sure that if Marx were alive today, with John XXIII and Vatican II he would smell less of the scent of. . . ." "What was that last word, M. Garaudy?" Almost painfully he practically spelled it out "o-p-i-u-m," which in French doesn't sound like "opium" in English. We all caught the joke simultaneously, and it turned on me. Even if it had been intentional on my part—which it was not—it could not have been better calculated to win sympathy. Seldom before or since have I thanked God for my own mistake.

One of Garaudy's finest sentences was, I believe, the following: "We Communists do not ask anyone to stop being what he is, but on the contrary we ask him to be it more fully and to be it better." At the time it seemed to me that he was speaking more as a free human being than as a Communist. I was not entirely surprised to read somewhere, not long after our encounter, that M. Garaudy had become a Christian and had been expelled from the Communist Party. It is hard to believe that all this happened only a little more than twenty-five years ago.

———

How do you identify yourself with assurance when you can't be seen, either in person or on television? During my period at *America,* I was invited to direct a retreat at Spring Hill College. A phone call, said to be from Ceylon (now Sri Lanka), summoned me, and the person on the other end, never having heard my voice on the telephone, registered some doubt. "Are you really Father McNaspy?" I tried to convince the person on the other end of the line, Father Bill Moran, then provincial superior of Ceylon, that it really was me.

Fortunately, I could recall a nickname—"Frog"—that I shared with Pierre Landry, which Pierre and I had given each other years before, when Bill Moran was a scholastic with us at Grand Coteau. Bill had overheard us using this odd nomenclature and started, uninvited, to use it at least with me. Why "Frog," which we pronounced "Frahg"? Because the person we were mimicking always pronounced the letter *t* like *g,* making the Latin *frater* (brother) sound something like "frahger," with the shortened form "Frahg" instead of "Fraht" roughly the equivalent of calling "Brother" simply "Bro."

It didn't take a stroke of genius to think of calling Bill Moran "Frahg"; we had jokingly done this over the years any number of times. So, quite spontaneously I almost shouted, "Hey, Frahg, come on; this is your old Frahg." At that, Bill realized who I was and that gave him the assurance he needed. He had an important question to ask, which only I could answer (though, of course, I can't remember either question or answer today), and our code worked. It certainly saved him a lot of money since Ceylon's distance from Mobile is not slight.

It must have been around the same time when this next solution to an unimportant problem was provided by another ruse. I had arrived, unexpectedly, in the city of Rome and called my friend Garth Hallett, a New Orleans Jesuit teaching at the Gregorian University. I started out: "Garth, can you guess who this is?" "I don't need to guess," Garth responded with confidence, "I'd know your voice anywhere, Tom Culley." "No, it's not Tom, it's C. J." was my answer. "How can you be C. J. if you're Tom?" Garth responded with characteristic insistence. Having Garth change his mind once it was made up was something I never dreamt possible. Yet I tried.

"Do you remember, Garth, when you gave a talk at Grand Coteau, comparing Dante and Virgil?" Garth hesitated a moment, then admitted, "Yes, you were there, too, Tom." Crestfallen, I had to try again, becoming more and more specific, hoping to convince him, however hopeless it seemed.

Happily I recalled a more complex episode. "Do you remember, Garth, the day that you, Don Didier, and I went on a picnic on the road to Opelousas, a road that was never finished, all red mud, and eventually we sat down under a palmetto bush and read Horace's famous satire *Ibam forte Via Sacra?*" I could imagine the computer clicking as Garth, the noted Wittgensteinian scholar, actually went through the process of moving from one certainty to the opposite certainty. At length, he gasped, and I shall never forget my surprise at his surprise: "By golly, it is you, C. J." (In Garth's defense, I should add that Tom Culley was also in Rome at the time, doing research at the American Academy, and that Tom and I do sound very much alike on the phone.)

Another event that took place toward the end of my stay at *America* was the sudden death in 1969 of my mother's only sister, my godmother Aunt Alyce, leaving us uncertain as to where Mama would feel most at home. Mary Agnes, with her large family, was in St. Louis, where she still lives, and of course I was in New York. After Aunt Alyce's funeral, Mary Agnes and I began looking for a suitable nursing home, where Mama would be reasonably content. No such home could be found in New Orleans where none of us had many friends, or where Mama could be made happy.

I began asking my old friends in Lafayette, especially priests there who could give guidance. Fortunately, one of these priest friends knew the Sisters of the Most Holy Sacrament, who directed the Bethany Home for the Aged. The first response was expected—no room, quite literally.

At this point, one of the sisters spoke to the superioress: "Isn't this the Mrs. C. J. McNaspy whose husband used to teach at Southwestern?" Indeed she was. Several of the nuns were consulted and remembered that, some thirty years earlier, when nuns weren't allowed to attend secular universities in that area, my dad had offered to teach them in their own convent. His qualifications were, of course, unimpeachable in both undergraduate physics and chemistry. I recall clearly driving him to the convent of these nuns on Saturday mornings, together with the basic instruments needed for elementary courses. True, I can't recall how many years Dad did this great work of zeal and kindness. But it must have been a considerable time, since the sisters, many years later, remembered and succeeded in returning the kindness a hundredfold—by accepting Mama into Bethany Home.

Chapter Twelve

At the 1972 Jesuit Institute for the Arts in Mondragone, south of Rome, with friends Larry McGarrell (left) *and Tom Culley* (right).

Bridging the
Sacred and the Secular

Cultivating the Arts in the Society

The phrase "Cultivating the Arts in the Society" is not my personal fabrication, but the official title of *Document No. 30* passed by the Thirty-first General Congregation of the Society of Jesus in 1965. Such a title could have been somewhat surprising, given the long reputation among Jesuits, however unmerited, as being pragmatic if not philistine. *Document No. 30* "hails the importance of the fine arts" since they "provide a special pathway to the human heart." Though brief, *Document No. 30* is quite explicit about what the Society needs to do to carry out its aims; namely, 1) that "all Jesuits today be given opportunities to become acquainted with and to appreciate the arts as part of their general education," and 2) "that measures be taken to permit those who manifest outstanding talents in this field to develop them."

Even before the documents of the Thirty-first General Congregation, a number of articles had helped the subject of Jesuits in the fine arts become appropriately alive. The Christmas 1966 issue of *Canisius,* a magazine of the German Jesuits, had featured the order's "old artistic tradition," pointing to the Brothers Tristano, to Brother Seghers's works found in many important museums throughout the world (and to his friendship with Rubens and Poussin), to Brother Pozzo's great mastery, and to other important Jesuits in the visual arts.

The role of Jesuits in drama was no less stressed and so was the importance of music, especially in the German College of Rome. The distinguished Jesuit musicologist Thomas Culley did his Ph.D. dissertation at Harvard, studying in depth the music of the earliest Jesuit colleges in Rome and was awarded the Prix de Rome in appreciation of his work. Tom and I prepared and published a careful study of "Music and the Early Jesuits (1540–65)," which was published in the 1971 *Archivum Historicum Societatis Jesu* (pp. 213–45), based entirely on original Roman documents. Our younger Jesuit colleague, T. Frank Kennedy, did his Ph.D. in musicology at UCLA, studying principally the work of Domenico Zipoli and other Jesuit musicians of the Paraguay Reductions, and more recently produced one of the earliest operas in the Jesuit tradition *The Apotheosis or Consecration of Saints Ignatius Loyola and Francis Xavier,* originally composed for the saints' canonization in 1622 by Johannes Hieronymus Kapsberger and the Jesuit Orazio Grassi, architect of the church of Sant' Ignazio in Rome. This sketchy epitome of Jesuit involvement in music and other arts does not begin to do justice to their incredible missionary and academic accomplishments.

I hope not to be or to seem self-serving, therefore, when I stress the role in recent years of the Jesuit Institute for the Arts. It was Tom especially who inspired other Jesuits and me personally to help in founding the Institute. Away back in the early 1960s, Tom, Bill Lynch (the Jesuit philosopher who wrote *Christ and Apollo, Christ and Prometheus,* and other seminal works in theology and literature), and I, all living roughly in the New York area, had a number of informal meetings regarding the cultivation of arts in the Society. Out of several such meetings, plus the help of Father Ernest Ferlita, doing his doctorate in drama at Yale while Tom was at Harvard, there developed the idea of a full summer workshop staffed by Jesuits for other Jesuits, to be held at Holy Cross College (Worcester, Massachusetts), which provided not only excellent facilities in several arts but also the chance for academic credit.

At the first summer institute in 1970 at Holy Cross, we were fortunate to have André Bouler (already often mentioned in these pages) and some Americans who had known him in Paris, such as Lee Lubers and Ed Lavin, in addition to Gene Geinzer (who was then in the process of earning the first of several advanced art degrees), Larry McGarrell, David Lawrence, T. Frank Kennedy, the brothers Jimmy and John Armstrong, Denis Leder, and a host of other artists and critics, some no longer on this earth—like Youree Watson and Ed Cuffe. We could never thank sufficiently the great Lithuanian Jesuit musician Bruno Markaitis or director Vinny MacDonnell, or that incredibly versatile Christian Brother Alexis Gonzales, who did so much to secure impressive grants from the Hearst Foundation, thereby making several summer workshops financially feasible. Among other important guests who participated in the final Mass of the 1970 meeting at Holy Cross College were Cathy Vukovich and her late husband, the distinguished sculptor Charles, and Maurice Lavanoux, friend of all religious artists, deceased not long after.

The Institute had its second workshop in 1971 at the University of Santa Clara, with similar personnel and the addition of several Mexican Jesuits of exceptional talent. I had hoped to have the 1972 meeting in Mexico City, for what I believed were obvious reasons, but was voted down in favor of Rome, a great favorite of Tom Culley's. Tom proved right, I have no hesitation in saying, for reasons that were more than obvious. For it turned out that we had access to the splendid Renaissance palace at Mondragone in Frascati, near Rome, where the Institute was heartened by gracious visits from none other than our beloved Father General Pedro Arrupe (himself a singer of no mean accomplishments and a great lover of the arts), the Fathers Assistant Vincent O'Keefe and Harold Small, and other members of the Jesuit Curia.

On one of these occasions, Father General thoughtfully surprised the assembly by reading a paper of his own, which manifestly captivated his audience. It also caught the attention of the *New York Times,* leading to the publication of a special issue in April 1973 that featured the address of Father Arrupe, "Art and the Spirit of the Society of Jesus," and, to my great surprise and delight, an article of mine titled "Art in Jesuit Life."

Most of the "founding brothers" of the Jesuit Institute were, I believe, quite uncertain of its possible future, or indeed of whether it would have any future. By temperament many artists are understandably disinclined toward organization. We were delighted at the outcome of the first three summers, but were not sure whether to plan ahead.

When we returned from Mondragone, however, we felt the desirability of at least one more session, planned for Guadalajara (Mexico), but since Tom Culley at that time felt rather exhausted by the Roman experience, the question arose as to who might be willing to take charge temporarily. A dozen or so of us, roughly representative of all the U.S. provinces, met informally and found Ernie Ferlita the most likely leader among those available. He had been a "founding father," was a close friend and associate of Brother Alexis, and, while not aspiring to power or any possible honor involved in the job, seemed willing and able.

In point of fact, the Institute has continued meeting, at least from time to time, principally on the West Coast or at Creighton University, Omaha, with added inspiration from poet Joe Brown, sculptor Lee Lubbers, and photographer Don Doll, among others. We were happy, too, to discover that André Bouler, Joseph Tézé, and the famed Jesuit painter Brother Venzo have continued the European tradition, both individually and as a group. In any case, we "oldsters" feel that our work, such as it was, is probably done—we pray, satisfactorily.

I hope to be forgiven some self-indulgence, including here the final paragraph of my aforementioned article:

> Jesuit artists, it goes without saying, can and do provide something of a pastoral presence among those highly imaginative persons who are often on the cutting edge of culture, but who all too commonly, since the baroque era, have been disaffected toward the visible church. With all due allowance for many other factors, it seems the Suppression of the Society (1773) and its minimal participation in the creative world since its Restoration (1814) may have had much to do with the general non-presence of Christianity in major movements of the nineteenth and twentieth centuries. For I believe it was (and should be) one of the Society's main functions to serve as a bridge between the explicitly sacred and the explicitly secular. Our Ignatian spirituality and at least our finest traditions suggest that this is where part of the action is—and a large part, too.

Many of the Society of Jesus' greatest artists were brothers, like Brother Andrea Pozzo, mentioned earlier. I stress the "Brother" part because dictionaries and encyclopedias still seem to think that to be a Jesuit is to be a priest, even though a number of the most important artists and scholars of the Society were brothers. One thinks of Brothers Seghers, Castiglione, Primoli, Bianchi, Bressanelli, and Kamel (of "camellia" fame), all occasionally referred to improperly as "Father." Though Brother Pozzo is probably most often thought of for his incredible trompe l'oeil ceiling of Orazio Grassi's marvelous Church of St. Ignatius in Rome, he was no less esteemed for his incredible work in the Gesù, together with Vignola, as well as Giacomo della Porta and Giovanni Tristano. The latter (if anyone) was believed to have a perfect grasp of Ignatius's concept of a church and is often thought of as the father of "Jesuit architecture" (if such a thing exists).

Saint, Site, and Sacred Strategy, subtitled *Ignatius, Rome, and Jesuit Urbanism,* was being worked on by Jesuit Father Thomas M. Lucas during my last lengthy visit to Rome. At the time, Father Arrupe was thought to be dying, but Father Peter Hans Kolvenbach, the newly elected Father General, was very much alive, and the "Ignatian Year" already in preparation. More than fifty people were working with Tom Lucas to restore the rooms of Saint Ignatius and the corridor of Andrea Pozzo that adjoins them. It was a work of discovery, peeling away ornate decorations of later ages, revealing the simplicity of the man who lived and died there. Lucas describes the startling discovery of the corridor that Andrea Pozzo painted as "a kind of hymn about the simple man who lived here, a place to discover God's grace and glory." Should I ever see Rome again, this is where I should like to start my pilgrimage.

The name Athanasius Kircher comes readily to mind in the context of Jesuits and the arts; he was surely one of the truly exceptional polymaths of the Society, touching on or even mastering just about every human discipline. (Kircher was born in Fulda, May 2, 1601, ordained in 1628, and died in Rome on October 30, 1690. His heart is at the shrine of Our Lady in Mentorella, not far from Subiaco.) The Kircher Museum is one of the first and most important of the Roman College, though taken over by the Italian government in 1870. It holds many important books; for example, his *Muisurgia Universalis,* said to be the first important work of musicology, and all sorts of works on linguistics; some of his other achievements include the invention of the magic lantern, first observation of sunspots, and a treatise on plagues and theory of microbes. In Erik Iversen's *The Myth of Egypt and Its Hieroglyphs* (Copenhagen, 1961, 89, 97-98), we read:

> When Egyptology emerged from this confusion as one of the
> first separate disciplines, it was due mainly to the erudition,
> the almost superhuman industry, and the unswerving dedica-
> tion of Athanasius Kircher. . . . He substantiated the phonetic
> value of the sign M, with a brilliant reference to the Coptic
> word for water MU. This is undisputably correct, and the
> method corresponds in a remarkable way to that used by
> Champollion for his decipherment. It is, therefore, Kircher's
> incontestable merit as the first to have determined the pho-
> netic value of an Egyptian hieroglyph . . . . Egyptology may
> very well be proud of having Kircher as its founder.

Wonderful praise, coming from a critic who is neither a Jesuit
nor even a Catholic.

The following remembrances are all so obviously related to
the arts that it seems appropriate to recount them in this chapter on "cultivating the arts." The artistic experiences are both
creative and appreciative, and to the extent that they concern
classical and Christian art, they are centered in Italy, Sicily, and
the Greek Isles.

During my summer session at Solesmes Abbey in the mid-
1950s with Father Joseph Gajard, O.S.B. (described in chapter
8), I had had several occasions to discuss with the learned
expert in Gregorian chant what could and what could not be
adapted into the vernacular. On the whole, Father Gajard
belonged to the very strict school, believing that very little
Gregorian chant could be done properly in any language except
Latin. My own leaning, on what I believed to be liturgical
grounds—namely for the people and their needs rather than for
abstract beauty—was in favor of working hard toward making
the language and the music coalesce happily, rather than one
dominating the other.

On one occasion I ventured to sing (if one may generously
call my vociferations singing) the lovely Gregorian piece *Salve
Mater Misericordiae* for Father Gajard in English: "Holy Mary, O
Mother merciful." It was a translation I had laboriously worked
at and hoped he would judge to have succeeded adequately.
Gajard was surprised at how well it went, and he was kind
enough to say so. I then did my own translation of the *Salve
Regina,* keeping carefully faithful to the Gregorian rhythm. He

was equally pleased. Then something a bit freer, since I was convinced that a literal translation would not work: *Christus vincit* as "Christ Lord of glory" keeping the exact rhythm, according to Solesmes. I did the same with the Advent "O Antiphons," in a translation which many people find satisfactory, since it has been published by McLaughlin-Reilly together with verses from the *Magnificat,* again adapted to English-Gregorian rhythm and is now rather widely used.

With this background I believe the following episode will become less improbable on several grounds. It is also ironic, since it involved going from the original vernacular into Latin, rather than vice versa. One day in 1963 I received another surprising phone call, this time from Harvard, more specifically from Professor Elliot Forbes. I wondered how Mr. Forbes knew my name at all. Then I realized it had to be through my close friend and his distingushed student Tom Culley. Mr. Forbes had gone to Tom for help on a matter of translation, but Tom had unselfishly sent him on to me.

The very idea could hardly have been more astonishing: it was to translate a forgotten text of Beethoven into singable Latin for use by the Harvard chorus on its forthcoming European tour. "Why do you want it in Latin?" I asked Mr. Forbes. "Because the Latin may provide an element of dignity, of sacrality," replied Mr. Forbes. "And why that?" I insisted. "Because the work, though quite good, is virtually unknown in Germany and the chorus is afraid that if it were sung in German, modern students would laugh it to scorn; the words sound so sycophantic and pompous." "Send it on, and I'll mail my best efforts to you within a week," I pledged, perhaps foolishly. When the score came, I was thrilled at the quality, the *Fidelio*-like maturity of the youthful Beethoven, under twenty at the time. But I realized that the words would be an insoluble problem, unless I could make them more singable in Latin.

The terrifying problem was that of Germanic monosyllables as opposed to polysyllabic Latin. How to sing German *riss* as Latin *corripuit?* In retrospect I recall clearly that I had to spend more time on a few monosyllables than on entire paragraphs. Should anyone have time and inclination to examine my little work, it is titled *Cantate auf den Tod Kaiser Joseph des Zweiten* (published by G. Schirmer, Inc.) and beautifully performed by

Thomas Schippers and the Camerata Singers, with the New York Philharmonic. The work is of course performed in Latin rather than German. I believe, perhaps with some bias, that it is one of the young Beethoven's most impressive works, and in this judgment I am in the good company of Brahms! At the time of the performance, I asked Schippers why he had done it in Latin, and he replied because it sounded better that way. I then thanked him for the compliment—obviously unintended!

It was Miss Ruth O'Neill, formerly Leopold Stokowski's personal secretary, through whom I met the great maestro and was brought in to appraise Richard Yardumian's *Mass* commissioned by Fordham University and performed by Stokowski at the New York Philharmonic. It was also Miss O'Neill who had so much to do with my opportunities to discover Italian baroque. She persuaded two of her best friends—Dr. Max Silberman, Viennese by birth, and his adoptive nephew, George Hutzler, lecturer at the Metropolitan Museum of Art and a profound art historian—that I would be of some assistance were they to make it possible for me to visit Rome purely on a baroque and classical journey, together with Sicily, which she knew I had never seen. These two absolutely exceptional opportunities fortunately came while I was stationed at *America* House, when both flexibility of schedule and usefulness of any travel could be assured. By then I had visited Rome perhaps a dozen times, always trying to deepen my knowledge of ancient Rome, as well as early Christian, medieval, and baroque Rome, and a fair amount of this study appeared in my *Guide to Christian Europe* and *Rome, A Jesuit City Too,* in both of which I tried to use only what I had personally experienced.

Since one of my graduate courses in classics had been on Roman and Greek inscriptions, there was very little in the catacombs (even the Jewish catacombs) and in other early Roman works that I had trouble understanding. In fact, on several occasions, notably for the facade of the chapel of Jesuit High School in New Orleans, I was invited to compose Latin inscriptions. (This invitation makes the Beethoven cantata translation into Latin less surprising.) Even so, after some dozen visits to Rome, I had never had the opportunity to visit Magna Graecia (Sicily and Southern Italy), which proved particularly exciting.

Shortly before I left New York, I visited Maurice Lavanoux to share my joy. He was even more excited than I, since he knew better than I what was ahead. I remember almost his very words: "When you get to Palermo, check and see whether the Monastery of Monreale and the Capella Palatina and their mosaics are as wonderful as I remember them from fifty years ago." Indeed they are, as two visits now assure me, and as everyone whom I've urged to visit Palermo will agree, including my Jesuit colleagues with diverse intellectual interests, from Tony O'Flynn to Ransom Marlow.

I must now tell in some detail how Monreale was revealed to me. George Hutzler and Max Silberman offered me the car they had been using, so that I might have a free hand for viewing what would probably become my favorite parts of Sicily. Early one morning, I came down the mountain from Taormina (one of Newman's favorite spots) and started before dawn toward Agrigento, Gela, and other gorgeous Greek cities; we had already visited Siracusa and its catacombs and enormous Greek theater. I had decided to skip meals that day, content with cookies and an occasional stop for a cappuccino, economizing both in time and in cash.

It was no longer impossible to believe what Cicero had said about Siracusa, that it was the most beautiful of all Greek cities. I wondered, however, as I visited the ruins of Selinunte and Segesta, whether Cicero had somehow forgotten about them. In any case, as I drove into sight of Palermo's incomparable harbor, realizing that I was not expected at the train station for some three hours, to rejoin Max and George, I decided to get a sort of preview of Monreale, only three kilometers to the west on the road toward Palermo.

It was nearly five o'clock when I parked near the northern transept of the basilica, just as the sun was setting all golden through the western portico. The glory was such that one understood possible temptations to idolatry, since Monreale's mosaics cover more than seventy thousand square feet [*sic*], and all seemed aglow. I recall thinking: "This must be the most beautiful building in the world!" I caught myself, however, and recalled, "There's always Chartres. Yes, this and Chartres!"

At that moment I heard a familiar voice that I couldn't identify. I turned around and saw Bill Lynch. He had said something like: "C. J., welcome to the most beautiful building in the world!" To which I snobbishly replied, "Well, Bill, there's always Chartres, remember?" "Yes, this and Chartres." (Later, I remember proposing that Ravenna's mosaics as well as Chartres's stained glass were superior even to Monreale, and I found Bill, George, and Max in agreement.)

Fortunately, I kept enough presence of mind to remember my agreement to meet George and Max at eight o'clock. I asked Bill to come along with me to meet "two of the most delightful and learned men in the world." Once he came to know them, he warmly agreed, and they felt the same about Bill.

The next day we all went to Monreale and deepened our grasp of the stunning mosaics, this time with the aid of a leading authority on Monreale, Monsignor Callisti (his name in Greek happily means "most beautiful"), whom I had met the previous evening after seeing Bill Lynch. I had spotted him administering baptism amid all the appropriate glory of mosaics at sunset. Admiring his liturgical style, I told him so in the best Latin I could muster. Then I asked if I could bring my friends to see Monreale under his guidance on the following day. He was delighted to meet people who love his basilica, and said so. He had some problem with my name, concluding that it must be "Gaspar" (like one of the Magi) since obviously no one could have such a bizarre name as "McNaspy." Until Monsignor Callisti went to the heavenly basilica, in later visits and all exchanges of cards my name remained Gaspar.

As our Auntie Mame would say, sharing friends is surely one of the greatest of joys, and I discovered this once again in Rome, when I had the joy of presenting Max and George to Abbot Primate Rembert Weakland, who invited them to assist at midnight Mass with him in San Anselmo. When Rembert was made Archbishop of Milwaukee, Max and George were both able to assist at the ceremony—three very wise men indeed.

———

In the summer of 1974, I had the great pleasure of joining my former students and today full-time cultural travel agents Sam and Lily Betty on a trip to Athens and the Greek Isles, together with students from Spring Hill College. We flew from Rome to Athens, arriving in time for the matchless "Sound and Light" program on the Acropolis, the "high city," a symbol of one of our civilization's glories, particularly with its fabulous Parthenon, the Erechtheion, and the several other temples to Victory.

The Parthenon is unrivaled for perfection, or rather was unrivaled until September 26, 1687. On that fateful day, which should forever serve as a warning to us, even before the atomic age, the splendid temple dedicated to the goddess of wisdom, Athena, was very nearly blown to bits by the cultured Venetians. Whether or not they knew what they were doing, they exploded a shell in their attack on the Turks, who had turned the temple-church (renamed for Mary, Mother of Wisdom Incarnate) into an almost total ruin. True, the Turks should not have used the "mosque-church-temple" as a vast powder keg, asking to be blown up. But neither should the enlightened Doge Morosini have taken the risk he did, causing some grave damage to the most precious monument of ancient Greece.

The Acropolis was the most sacred spot of Athens centuries before Athens became Christian, long before Paul preached his famous sermon on the Areopagus, halfway up the Acropolis. It is always a thrill to reread Paul's words near the traditional spot where they were spoken, now marked with a large bronze plaque inscribed in Greek: "Men of Athens, I have seen for myself how extremely scrupulous you are in all religious matters, because I noticed, as I strolled around admiring your sacred monuments, that you had an altar inscribed 'To an Unknown God.' Well, the God whom I proclaim in fact is the one whom you already worship without knowing it" (Acts 17). A nearby modern Greek church is appropriately inscribed "GNOSTOI EN TRIADI THEOI" ("To the Known God, Known in the Trinity").

In the suburbs of Athens, one of my favorite Greek monasteries is at Daphni where the giant image of Christ as Pantocrator, Lord of the Universe, will stir one deeply, as it did our students. Actually, here one is already in the Byzantine world, even more beautifully represented in Rome, Ravenna, and Sicily, and even more fully, despite the ruins, in Istanbul itself (Byzantium, Constantinople).

We set out from the Piraeus, past one island after another, each strongly reminiscent of episodes in world history. Crete was, of course, special, with its pre-Greek ruins of the palace of Minos. It is also the birthplace of El Greco and the great modern novelist Nikos Kazantzakis, and the place where one sees perfect examples of Boustrophedon writing—from left to right and then right to left, all in continuity. Throughout the Aegean Sea one is never, or at least rarely, out of sight of a Grecian isle, each seemingly lovelier than the one before.

But nothing prepared me for Thera (or Santorini, as the Italians call it). Sailing into the island harbor (really the mouth of a volcano that erupted around 1,623 B.C.), one has an experience comparable to visiting the Grand Canyon. Many scholars believe that this cataclysm is the very same one that shattered the Minoan civilization. Somewhat imprudently, I took the donkey ride up to the crest, and I did enjoy the view thoroughly. But the Greek guides, shocked at my total ineptitude—I failed even to put my feet into the stirrups—kept shouting unintelligible words that did not sound like Plato.

Dawn over the island of Patmos was another truly unforgettable experience, whether or not Patmos was the island on which the author of the Book of Revelation received the marvelous visions described there. Scholars believe that Christianity as such was offensive to many at the time, but that the eschatological cast of John's teaching made it particularly subversive. Patmos is a small, rocky island, and Roman authorities often banished dangerous individuals to such islands. In any case, it was awesome to say the least, and I enjoyed every moment that we had there.

Another unforgettable place in Asia Minor, familiar from Paul's epistles is, of course, Ephesus. The Gospel of John is thought to have been composed at Ephesus, which was a Greek settlement that was retained, under the Romans, as a capital and terminus of the Aegean trade route. One is constantly aware of traditions that place Mary there and, of course, of the great ecumenical council of Ephesus in 325. Finally, there was Rhodes, yet another important Greek island, with the famous Hospital of the Knights and the Castle of the Grand Master of Malta.

Whether Malta counts strictly as a "Greek island" or not, it surely merits a place in the Book of Acts, where the inhabitants are called "philanthropic" or "kindly" beyond measure and where I seem to have met none but the most amiable people. Even today, following the tragic destruction during World War II, Malta offers an unlimited number of prehistoric treasures, temples, Stonehenge-like structures, and the amazing hypogeum where numberless people were buried in community. Somehow, if Sicily is the bridge between Italy and Africa, Malta, with comparable cultural diversity in a much smaller space, seems a bridge between Sicily and Africa.

Chapter Thirteen

Around the World

In Eighty Slides

Once again, as in chapter 9, I have resorted to the logic of geography rather than to the simplicity of chronology to gather together recollections of international travel that occurred over the period of a decade and a half, spanning my years at *America* and at Loyola University, in the 1960s and 1970s.

Sometime in the summer of 1967, Jesuit Missions' Jim Cotter came to *America* House to invite me to participate in the East Asian Jesuit Secretariat Conference, to be held in Hong Kong, April 16–20, 1968. Why me? I wondered half aloud, then aloud. Jim lamely suggested that it was because I always seemed interested in the foreign missions, though I had never seriously thought of applying for one. I made no more protest, however, afraid that this dream would vanish into thin air. My boss approved, though I suspect he was as surprised as I was. He was probably wondering too, "Why C. J.?" though he was courteous enough not to say so.

Once it was clear that all travel expenses were taken care of, I was able to do long-range planning. Since Hong Kong and New York are almost polar opposites, I was happy to discover that I could go one way and come back the other, thus making the journey a "round-the-world" affair. This trip gave me my first opportunity to see Japan, where my fellow theologians from St. Mary's days were still active, as well as other friends. Once the list of seventy or so participants was made available, I discovered a number of unexpected friends on it like the Canadian Jean Desautels (with whom I had been in tertianship, later assigned to the Vietnamese mission) and several American Jesuits like Alden Stevenson, Joe Sheehan, John Doherty, Coleman Daily, and Walter Hogan.

Others were almost legendary, especially Horacio de la Costa, a Filipino Jesuit, whom I always closely associated with my Filipino companions at St. Mary's, but who had studied theology elsewhere. Horacio had written the authoritative history of the Society in the Philippines and was later to become Assistant to Father Arrupe for East Asia, a man of the rarest brilliance combined with charm and accessibility. Indeed, when he died of cancer, unexpectedly, before the General Congregation that elected Father Kolvenbach as superior general, many of us had hoped Horacio would be the first non-European superior general.

Horacio was probably the best known member of the conference, which was made clear when he was elected chairman during the first session, almost by acclamation. Getting to know Horacio at firsthand during the conference was a splendid preparation for the many months that we were together at the Jesuit Curia in Rome, where he, Vinny O'Keefe, and I almost daily shared our latest favorite discoveries in P. G. Wodehouse or Ogden Nash. In Horacio's case, wisdom was never second to wit.

I recall vividly a critical moment in the last session of the conference, when it appeared that no solution to apparently conflicting motions seemed likely to be forthcoming. I heard a Japanese colleague whisper audibly: "Now, let's see you get out of this mess, Horacio!" Horacio miraculously did.

Happily Jim Cotter had thought up something I could do apart from enjoying myself; namely, help in the "Englishing" of final documents drawn up by Jesuits whose first language was not English, especially the Indonesian participants. One paragraph that I believe I practically wrote went this way: "The Church is the church in the world. As the world is a codeterminant of the life of the church, so the world too is a codeterminant of the theological thinking of the church. Therefore it should be normal that the church in every culture find the expressions of its thinking and in that way be able to reach the people of God and be understood by them and integrated in their life." While hardly original, this fairly elaborate statement seems a development of the constant theme of my effort at studying Christian humanism and is surely an echo of much of Youree Watson's thinking also.

A particularly moving statement from the Asian-born missioners to the rest of us reads in part as follows:

> We believe that you have asked with sincerity that we speak with sincerity—a spirit of loyalty to the Society of Jesus which is our common mother, a spirit of mutual respect and esteem, a genuine love that binds us together in the brotherhood of a common ideal, a common task, and a common hope. . . .
>
> You have come to our countries from many lands and many nations. You have come leaving father and mother, brothers and sisters, homeland and native air. You have come often at great personal sacrifice, sometimes bringing with you great resources which, like yourselves and your lives and your efforts, you have placed, in your surpassing love for Christ and His Church, at the service of our peoples, seeking to share in the building of God's reign and kingdom on our shores, on this "distant side" of the earth. . . .
>
> For all this we and our people shall ever remain indebted to you, and your names shall ever be found written on the tablets of our gratitude. In these last few decades you have seen as we have seen, we think, the coming of a new hour in the individual histories of our countries, as well as in the history of all of Asia. We have been witnesses of the awakening of "new peoples," or the awakening within the older nations among us of a new spirit, a new consciousness, a new thrust into the future, as the age of colonialism moves into the past and the present moment confronts us, a moment when the nations of Asia are striving to come into their own, to find their place in the world of today and of tomorrow. This moment has been called the hour of the awakening of Asian and African man.
>
> We, your brother Jesuits, are Asians. We are proud that we are Asians. We belong to the Catholic Church, we belong to the Society, but we belong to our peoples also. We wish to make ourselves more fully one with them, at this moment of history above all moments, sharing their longings and their aspirations, their fears and hesitations, their dreams for our lands and our peoples, and their traditions, their way of life, their ways and their customs, their songs and their sorrows, their

search for identity, their recovery (in some cases) of that personality which the colonial rule, with greater or less success, tried to substitute for another one made to the image and likeness of a foreign model. If we are to effectively bring Christ and the Gospel to our people, at this moment of national and cultural reawakening above all, we cannot wish to be other than this, we cannot wish to be otherwise....

The Hong Kong Conference proved to be spiritually helpful in ways I had never foreseen. Up to that time my interest in missions had been more or less speculative, with no suspicion that some day I might feel the call personally. One of my reasons for this feeling, so far as I can surmise, may have been the fact that during my mother's lifetime, I felt that as her only son my departure for the foreign missions, especially in the Third World, would be much harder for her than for me. In fact, when I accepted the invitation in 1960 to work on the staff of *America* magazine, she found it much harder than I could have imagined, since by that time she had retired from teaching and was living with her sister in New Orleans and obviously hoped I'd remain in New Orleans for the rest of her lifetime. Even after her death in 1973, when I was almost sixty years old, I felt that it was too late to volunteer for a mission in the Third World, never dreaming that Paraguay was soon to be my "fourth career," as the phrase goes. In any case, the Hong Kong Conference papers, to which I had made a small contribution, were to have a much greater influence on me than I on them.

———

I'm not sure when I first heard of the Angkor Wat but am almost certain that it is one of those elm-like things that are "immemorial," at least in my experience. It may have been in my favorite childhood magazine, *National Geographic,* which now seems immemorial too. The Angkor Wat, in any case, seems to be one of those constantly recurring themes, like the pyramids of Egypt or those of Mexico, different as they are from one another. The Angkor Wat is, of course, in Cambodia and was built by the Khmers, who had conquered the country in the eighth or early ninth century. In any case, I've seldom looked forward more eagerly to seeing a great human monument, or come so close to missing the offered opportunity.

Not even the Taj Mahal had so captivated my imagination even since childhood. Air France was the line that promised to get me into the Angkor area, not terribly far from the modern Cambodian capital of Phnom Penh, but I was naive to trust Air France, or any other airline, in those troubled days. Yet the plane did arrive, hours late of course, and gave me the opportunity to hire a pedicab to drive me all through the part of the jungle that included Angkor Wat, Angkor Thom, and a dozen or so other temples. Obviously very little time could be allotted to any of these wondrous places, gates with giant Buddha heads, temple upon temple, and finally the two Angkors, among the greatest wonders of the world. Luckily I had done my homework for some decades and had tried to recapture some of the marvels by subsequent reading.

Simple statistics, found in Helen Gardner's *Art Through the Ages,* show that the Angkor Wat is surrounded by a moat two and one half miles long. One of its many courtyards has a half-mile of sculptured reliefs, and the foundations of the central shrine measure more than three thousand feet on each side. The temples comprising this great complex are set at the corners of two concentric walls girding the central shrine. Eight temple towers add to the mysterious awesomeness, together with giant panels illustrating Hindu traditions and giving the impression of a cosmic dance.

After several hours, I reached the entrance to the enormous bridge over the moat. Paying the pedicab driver my few remaining dollar bills, I started across the bridge. It was obvious that I was doing something absurd, going the wrong way just before darkness and with a storm impending, one of those dreadful Louisiana-like summer evening storms. But I don't think an army could have stopped me.

Vendors tried to, offering miniature Buddhas at minuscule prices, all in French. I had no trouble shouting, "Non!" A quarter of a mile further on, I heard tiny footsteps behind me. I turned and stopped, bellowing *"Qu'est-ce que tu veux?"* to the child pursuing me. *"Rien,* monsieur, I just want to come with you." There was no arguing. So I hurried on to the steps of the giant pyramid and began to climb. Then I was suddenly happy as the child turned on his dim flashlight to help us into the relative darkness of the temple. When we reached the sanctuary, he flashed the light on a splendid statue and whispered, "Le Seigneur Bouddha!"

Without him I would never have seen the climactic Buddha of Angkor Wat, nor do I know how I could have climbed down to the moat and across it to safety, as the storm broke. Meantime, I was able to ask the child, *"Comment tu t'appelles?"* He replied pithily, and it seemed to me appropriately, *"Je m'appelle* Pin, monsieur." From the encircling jungle we could hear monks chanting the praises of Buddha. When we reached the exit, I explained laboriously to Pin that though I didn't have any cash with me, if he were to come to the nearby hotel I could cash some travelers' checks and give him something. To my surprise, he declined: *"Non, merci, monsieur, c'était un plaisir de vous accompagner!"* Then, as the storm broke, Pin disappeared into the jungle. I never saw him again.

Almost a decade later I was happily able to tell Pin's story to great advantage on the occasion in 1977—May 8, to be precise—when Regis College (recently elevated to the status of a university) made me a Doctor of Humane Letters, *honoris causa.* The citation read by Regis's president, David M. Clarke, was worded so gracefully and eulogistically that I shall not repeat it here.

The graduation was held outdoors, in the dry but taxing heat of the mile-high city. I had been notified that I was expected to give the commencement address and had planned something that I hoped would be worthy of a cooler day. Suddenly, however, it occurred to me that in such a case one should have recourse to a story, preferably a true one. What simpler, sweeter, more edifying story was in my experience than that of my guide Pin in the Angkor Wat in Cambodia? It was totally fresh in my memory and hardly required even a line or two of notes. So I simply retold it, as plainly as possible, and urged Regis graduates to imitate the youngster who had proven such a good Christian toward me, while remaining perhaps a Hinayana Buddhist all the while.

Somehow, maybe because it kept my remarks to about seven minutes, the members of the English faculty were delighted with Pin and his story and forthwith invited me to join their faculty. A gratifying compliment, indeed.

Even if Pin himself never reentered my life, the same face appeared a number of times during my flights through Indochina. On one such occasion, my eyes met Pin's avatar, hesitantly, several times like characters in an English murder mystery, until finally we were seated next to each other. Being an American, I felt I had to say something, something I don't remember now. Finally we exchanged names, his sounding quite Irish, though I can't dredge it up from a fading memory. I mentioned that I was an American Jesuit from New Orleans. "Jesuit, eh? I have an uncle who's a Jesuit, Irish province." I prepared my soul for some Joycean anti-Jesuit horror stories, which were, however, not forthcoming. He apparently liked his uncle and was not ashamed to give me his name: Father Dan O'Connell. "Not the Dan O'Connell who runs the Vatican Observatory?" I fairly gasped. "Yes, that's Dan, all right, a good chap, isn't he?" I could not have agreed more.

I'm sorry not to be able to remember the young Mr. O'Connell's first name now. But when I reached the Jesuit residence in New York, the "new" place on West 56th, one of the first people I ran into was none other than Father Dan O'Connell, who was occupying my own room, through no fault of his own: I had simply arrived a day early; needless to say, we had a lot to talk about.

———

Our former poetry editor at *America* John Moffit had repeatedly urged me to get in touch with several of his Indian colleagues (monks and others he had been close to), especially Shonu Palit, who took me to meet his former Abbot in Varanasi (Benares) and to visit the great shrines of Buddha. All seemed a revelation, not least when I managed to reach Fatehpur Shikri (Victory City), Akbar's "Brazilia," which seemed untouched by time as did Chisti's mausoleum, all white in lacelike marble. We went on to Sikandra near Agra, where Akbar began his own tomb before his death in 1605. Set within a superlative garden, with azaleas everywhere, the tomb is about one hundred meters on each side, with a similar lacy white marble screen.

The Taj Mahal in nearby Agra was erected between 1632 and 1643 as a tomb and monument to Mumtaz Mahal, wife of Shah Jahan. I felt, while there, that this must be the most beautiful monument in the world, a pearl, a wound, by whatever metaphor it is meant to be described. An Indian poet prefers to call it "a tear that was shed from the eyes of love and romance which we have named as Taj Mahal." So much feeling enters into discussion of the Taj that we may never know who was the architect. I have heard intense arguments for both extremes: too beautiful to be by a westerner, too beautiful to be by an easterner!

In Aurangabad, which I visited briefly en route to Ellora and Ajanta, I saw another magnificent tomb, this one built by Aurangzeb as a resting place for his mother Bibi-Ka Rauza (or more simply "Bibi"), in imitation of the Taj Mahal. As I strolled in the garden, two well-groomed young men approached me and said, "We like to talk to foreigners." "So do I," I countered. Soon some barefoot youngsters, clearly of a lower caste, came near and seemed to enjoy listening, though they obviously understood nothing. Their father followed, embarrassed, and asked the young men if his children were bothering us. That seemed enough to break up the gathering. I asked the young men why they couldn't understand us. "Because they live in a different part of the city" was their less than ingenuous reply. "Won't they ever learn to speak English?" I asked. My escorts shrugged their shoulders. Then I insisted, "Wouldn't it be possible for you to teach them?" Apparently I had had too much contact with the Peace Corps or with Christian missioners.

Ellora's thirty-four caves with their significant paintings and sculptures seem representative of India's principal non-Muslim religions—Hindu, Buddhist, and Jain. Ajanta's thirty caves are fabulous for their representations of the life of Buddha, save for the earliest ones, Hinayana, which do not represent the Buddha personally. Though my guide was Muslim and disapproved of such paintings, he insisted that he had to show them or go hungry. He even offered to write a quotation from Shaid Siddiqui, the Urdu poet: "The people offer their offerings to those sculptures that I have sculpted, but nobody pays any attention toward me, the Sculptor or the God-maker."

In Bombay, especially in the Heras Institute of Indian History and Culture, named after the great Jesuit scholar Father Heras, I visited what I was told was the finest collection of Indian Christian art and had the opportunity to meet Father Heras's estimable successor, Father Adolfo Esteller, who is famed for his computer restoration of the Rig Veda text. He graciously wrote in my diary, in the Devanagari script, the opening line of the text: *Agnim idaipurohitam.* The first word, *agnim,* is unsurprisingly cognate with our Latin *ignis* and venerates the god of fire. This may be the very first recorded word of any Indo-European poetry. One of the most treasured parts of the Institute is Father Heras's own collection of the art of Mohenjo Daro and Harappa, of the Indus Valley civilization, antedating the Indo-European invasions.

In the Bombay area, one sees the Parsee "Towers of Silence," characteristic of the contemporary Zoroastrian cult. The Parsees are renowned for their intellectual gifts and a considerable number of them attend St. Francis Xavier College for that reason. Among the alumni are maestro Zubin Mehta and his distinguished father.

———

From Bombay to Nairobi the flight seemed endless; though I would very much have wished to stop in Karachi to visit Mohenjo Daro and Harappa or other Indus Valley civilizations before going on over the Gulf of Oman and Somalia, I was constrained by exigencies of tickets to go nonstop. Almost a mile high, Nairobi enjoys endless spring and gave relief after the horrors of Bombay. As I landed, in clear view was the glory of Kilimanjaro in the sunset, as missionary priests introduced me to the tropical beauty of Nairobi. Nothing could be lovelier.

This trip was my introduction to East Africa, with its modern architecture—the cathedral and the baptistry, both open and free in style—and endless flowers. We spent the next day fulfilling many a dream, in the Nairobi National Park, where antelopes, elephants, and other marvels of the animal kingdom reign freely. Then on to Mombasa, Ruanda-Burundi, and the world's second largest fresh water lake, the mighty Victoria.

Not yet had the Leakeys consolidated their paleolithic findings of our remotest ancestors, still one sensed, after much reading, in the nearby Olduvai Gorge an awareness of the truly sacral, that humanity had been there since long before Altamira or Lascaux. For some years now, I have always opened lectures on early history with my slides of Lake Victoria, trying to express some of the awe I felt and feel.

Back in the late 1950s, when I was dean of Loyola's College of Music, I received one of the first copies of what later became the famed *Missa Luba,* though I can't recall now which missioner sent it to me. It was interesting to introduce this now famous music on various radio programs at the time, and my association led to the invitation to provide program notes for other African liturgical music being published by Philips Records.

In the intervening years when the opportunity came for me to visit various African countries, such as the Ivory Coast and Nigeria, I was particularly eager to come to know African musicians directly involved in the new opportunities opening up in the light of Vatican Council II. A cantata honoring the recently canonized Martyrs of Uganda was surely important, though a bit too difficult for general usage. Father Charles Mondah, in Abidjan, was most gracious in offering copies of his many compositions, most of them using parallel thirds (typically African). The Jesuits in Abidjan provided me with a jeep and a polyglot driver, who spoke French with me and several other languages with villagers who helped us in our search for Father Anou. After several false starts, we finally found him, using an improvised drum to accompany his singing of the Holy Scripture. I didn't understand what he was singing until two names came out clearly in the same musical phrase—Jericho and Jerusalem—which gave me the clue that he must have been singing the Parable of the Good Samaritan. He was startled when I suggested as much, thinking I knew the language, and seemed almost relieved when I explained how I guessed correctly. When I asked to photograph his group, the parents objected, insisting that the children were not properly clothed. Once they were hidden behind the adults, however, there was no problem.

The visit to Ibadan (Nigeria's second largest city, with well over a million inhabitants) was happily negotiated with the help of a long-time friend, Father Hugo Nacciarone, who was able to drive me from Lagos to the large seminary in Ibadan. There we met seminarian Thomas Ilesanmi, now ordained and a professor in the same seminary, and highly respected for his skills in liturgical music. I was particularly impressed by his skills in improvisation and the ability to create music of value using random collections of wood and metals. It did not surprise me, many years later at a meeting in Asia, when I met a number of his students and found their esteem of Father Ilesanmi every bit what I had hoped it would be.

Isle de la Gorée is surely one spot on earth that must have few rivals when it comes to human tragedy. It was pointed out by the priest who accompanied me as the principal port from which slaves were sent away from West Africa to America and other points west. My guide added that the prison on the Isle de la Gorée emitted a foul odor, even after more than a century. The thought of such indignity inflicted by those who call themselves human, and suffered by innumerable other humans, still shocks me after fifteen or more years. When President Senghor, back in the LaFarge Lounge of the *America* residence, had invited me to visit Senegal, he had of course said nothing about this place.

What were to be my last days in central Africa passed rather uneventfully, as I hopped from Nigeria to Ghana, to Sierra Leone, to Liberia (where my dear colleagues James and Kathleen Gaffney had served as university teachers and where their two lovely daughters were born), and finally to Dakar in Senegal. Dakar was a fascinating city, almost entirely Muslim (over 80 percent), as I found corroborated by my cabdriver, himself a Muslim. He proved friendly and not at all embarrassed when I asked him how many wives he had. He replied that he could only afford to have two, according to the prescriptions of the Prophet, since he was a rather poor man. His matter-of-fact manner gave me a new perspective on Muslim plurality of wives.

––––

It was while I was still an associate editor of *America* that the first opportunity came for me to visit the Soviet Union. When Rabbi Arthur Schneier proposed the fascinating idea of a goodwill tour to the Soviet Union (titled "Appeal of Conscience Foundation"), he arranged funding for six or seven people of some standing, representative of Judaism, Catholicism, and Protestantism.

This committee, the personnel of which changed every year, would have Rabbi Schneier as a sort of anchor person each year, providing both unity and diversity. Arthur was free to choose the personnel from among his friends, people he could trust and who would trust each other and inspire trust in officials and religious people in the Soviet Union. Thurston Davis was the obvious choice for the first group, representing Catholics; Dan Flaherty, with his wisdom and diplomatic skills, would make an ideal choice for the second group. Both of them were able to suggest me as the Roman Catholic for the third group, helping me to be prepared in skills other than linguistic (since I already spoke some Russian).

Arthur, John Mosler, former Secretary of State under President Richard Nixon William Rogers and his wife, and I met in Washington, D. C., at the Soviet Embassy, our main function being that of assuring the Soviet ambassador there that we were not preparing some nefarious scheme. He proved quite friendly and even admitted some of the more obvious limitations of his own country. All of us were eager to help bring about the success of Arthur's enterprise.

After a blessedly uneventful flight, we arrived at the Moscow airport fairly late at night, which expedited customs, allowing the officials to wave us through without opening a single bag. We were lodged that cold March night in the Hotel National, overheated at least by U.S. standards. Our first impression of the Russian people was of their energy and ubiquity.

Our official guide, Marina (she never gave us her surname), was an English graduate student, majoring in Yeats (whose name she pronounced "Yeets"). I tried to be helpful and explain how we in the West pronounce the name, but suggested that she save that information until she herself was a teacher, since correcting one's teachers would not sit any better in Russia than in America. We both laughed at our innocent complicity.

Having secured the phone number of the international Catholic chaplain, I called and asked if he would receive me that evening. "Come for dinner," he urged. I grabbed a taxi and quickly reached the large apartment complex where the chaplain lived. As we walked quietly into the house, I asked in a whisper whether the place was bugged. "Of course, Father. Everything here is bugged." I was prepared for that contingency and made small talk under the watchful eyes of the unsmiling cook. The only important topic had to do with my offer to celebrate Mass on the coming Sunday for the international community. Late that evening, the chaplain offered to call a taxi for me, but I felt I didn't need one, being at home in the Russian language. As I went downstairs I discovered to my dismay that traffic was so heavy I couldn't distinguish one bus line from another.

Spotting a young soldier with his clarinet, I presumed he'd be friendly, as indeed he proved to be. He offered to get me a taxi, since at that late hour all buses were going the wrong way. He tried and tried, as we chatted about music, especially New Orleans jazz (which he seemed to know and love). After almost an hour he said, "Let's take the next bus the other way and go to a taxi stand that I know." Before I could grab coins to pay the fare, he had done everything necessary. It was zero weather, and we snuggled onto the bus laughing like kids.

Arriving at the taxi stand, my companion led me out and explained in my presence that the fare was one dollar, no more. I clasped his hand and entered the taxi. In less than an hour we were in Red Square at Hotel National. My driver wanted the ubiquitous tip, which I felt I could manage. Going upstairs to my room, I suddenly realized that I had never asked the young musician-soldier his name. So I wrote in my diary the one word, which still means a great deal to me: "IVAN." Throughout the Afghanistan-Soviet war, I wondered every night whether my buddy Ivan was still alive. I shall of course never know.

I recalled that we had left New York without a visa for intervening stops and that one was needed for Czechoslovakia. So, at Marina's advice I sallied forth in quest of a photographer. On the crowded streets one was always jostling someone or being jostled. Two university-aged youngsters, in their fresh jargon, asked me something that my Russian couldn't handle. "Sorry, I'm a foreigner," I managed to exclaim. "Foreigner? What country?" "The U.S.A." was my obvious answer. "We like the U.S.A. and American jazz," they assured me. "Shall we have some tea?" I asked. They were delighted by the invitation. A friendship was starting, and when I returned to my hotel room they accompanied me for a shot of scotch.

One of them was named Traisman—obviously a Jewish name, as I remarked. "No, no. I'm pure Russian," he insisted. I told him I was traveling with a rabbi. "Are you Jewish?" he asked. "No, but I'm traveling with a rabbi," I repeated. I offered him the yarmulke I had brought along for possible Jewish ceremonies. He laughed nervously, put it on, and went to the mirror, at which he stared for several minutes. In this atheistic country, was he accepting silently the God of Abraham? I wondered.

That night Arthur and I went to Moscow's only synagogue to help celebrate Rabbi Levin's seventieth birthday. Arthur offered to help me say something in Yiddish, but rather proud of my Hebrew (which I had studied for several decades), I declined, and when invited to the pulpit roared out in Hebrew: "Hinne ma tov u ma na'im, sheveth achim gam yahad!" ("Behold how good and agreeable it is for brothers to dwell together!") The congregation, most of them ancient and bearded, roared out their applause at the thought that a "goy" could greet them in the Holy Language.

Though Arthur and Rabbi Levin invited me to stay for the dinner, I felt that this would be more trouble for them than necessary. Besides, I wanted to walk a few miles in the midnight Moscow world, unthreatened and safe. I wondered how many U.S. cities would be equally free from danger. The next day my two young friends came to our hotel again, as planned, and I invited them to accompany me to the Pushkin Museum in the Cheka limousine our group used. They showed some fright at the idea; so I didn't push it, but suggested that they take a metro to the museum, while I used the car I had hired. All went well, and we loved the museum.

At one point I decided to quote the last stanza from the poem that concludes *Doctor Zhivago.* They were stunned and said as much. "I thought you were forbidden to read *Doctor Zhivago,*" I taunted them half jokingly. "We are, but we have our underground press, our *samisdat.*" The next day, as if to prove it, they brought me a carbon-copied poem, which I read happily and even published in the *New Orleans Review* on my return to America. It may be the only forbidden poem by Yevtushenko published in New Orleans. I still have the original, now faded with years.

When Sunday arrived I first asked Marina to escort me to Novodyevichi Cemetery, where the graves of Gogol, Chekhov, Mayakovski, Scriabin, Prokofiev, and other Russian giants are revered. We spotted a group clustered around a grave we couldn't identify.

It turned out to be that of Stalin's wife, another tragic victim of his brutality. I wondered what was going through their minds.

As we went on toward the embassy for Mass, Marina asked, "Sir, may I ask a stupid question?" "Marina, if you ask it, it can't be stupid." She laughed at my effort at gallantry, then explained, "How is it that you and the rabbi and your other friends can be so intelligent and still religious?" "What's the difficulty, Marina?" "Well, the conflict between science and religion," she stammered and stopped. "May I ask a question, in turn, Marina?" "Surely." "Marina, did you see the TV account of the U.S. astronauts as they went behind the moon on Christmas night?" "Of course." "But did you hear what they read as they rounded the moon?" "No, they didn't let us hear it. What did they read?" "The opening of the Bible: 'In the beginning God created. . . .'" She was visibly troubled, and we did discuss the topic later, when there was no chauffeur to spy on her. She admitted she had never even seen a Bible, much less done any serious reflection on religion.

The Mass at the embassy proved very touching. A number of Hispanics took advantage of my being there to go to confession or discuss problems, and a cordial Australian told me he had several of my recordings in the "Music for Everyman" series. This was a pleasant surprise indeed.

Our guide in Stalingrad (now St. Petersburg) was also an English major in the university, and we found it somewhat easier to chat with her than with Marina. Her name was Gallina, and about the only matter she seemed unwilling to touch was the Museum of Religion and Atheism. When Arthur and I suggested visiting it, she showed reluctance: "I really don't know anything about it, having never even been inside." "Even so, we want to see it," we insisted. She stayed outside, while we went in and very soon realized why Gallina was too embarrassed to want to join us. In this gorgeous imitation of St. Peter's in Rome, all was turned into antireligious propaganda, the Last Supper being explicitly treated as a celebration of cannibalism, to take one example.

We didn't stay long, nor did we say anything about our experience, nor did Gallina ask any questions. As we drove along Stalingrad's most famous thoroughfare, Nevsky Prospekt, I asked to stop at what had obviously been a Catholic church but had not been open for some years. The inscription was in Latin:

"Domus mea domus orationis" ("My House a House of Prayer"), which I translated, though resisting the temptation to give the rest of the quotation, out of sensitivity for Gallina's feelings. We spent whatever time we could at the stunning Hermitage, with its eleven Cézannes and enough post-impressionists to rival the fabulous Barnes collection in Philadelphia. My favorite statue in Stalingrad is dedicated to Peter the Great, and the dedication is worded in the most lapidary Latin: "Petro Primo Catharina Secunda" ("To Peter the First, Catherine the Second")—the nominative case indicating that Catherine did the dedicating, done with the unique clarity and pith so easy to accomplish in Latin.

It seems to happen more often than not that the farther one is from home the greater the chance there is of bizarre encounters. In Moscow and in Stalingrad, we repeatedly ran into the head of Dropsie University, Dr. Katz, a distinguished Talmudic scholar and longtime friend of Rabbi Schneier. It so happened that Dr. Katz often went in quest of exceptional Talmudic manuscripts, as did Arthur Schneier. To anyone who knew these eminent scholars, such a coincidence would appear normal. Not so to the KGB, to whom only conspiracy seemed unsurprising.

Our last night in Stalingrad, I was chatting with some friends when suddenly Rabbi Schneier rushed to our table, apologized and asked if I could help him for a moment. "Of course," I assured him and left the room with him. Arthur was clearly embarrassed. "Do you remember Dr. Katz, my friend from Philadelphia? He's been arrested by the secret police and ordered out of the country before midnight!" "Why?" I asked. "They claim he's spying against Russia and have given him the third degree. He's perfectly innocent, of course, but they're apparently trying to scare us through him. What makes it most uncomfortable is the fact that the only way he can leave the country by midnight is by the eight o'clock train to Helsinki." "How can I help, Arthur?" I asked. "Could you pay his hotel bill, and let me repay you tomorrow?" "Sure, but I don't see the problem, Arthur." "It's the Sabbath, C. J.," he explained, "and we can't conduct any business. If it's not against your conscience, I imagine you can do it for us." "Absolutely delighted, Arthur! Anything else I can do?" I was obviously happy to be able to be of some help to such a wonderful friend.

The next morning our flight seemed fogged in, which frightened us, since we were to meet our connection in Moscow, the only legitimate flight out of Russia, and we couldn't forget Dr. Katz's terrifying experience. Fortunately the plane to Bucharest was delayed in our favor, and we were swished through customs, with not so much as a bag being opened. Seldom have I appreciated a flight more than this escape from the USSR. At that time, Romania seemed a comparatively free country, unlike what came to light in the late 1980s. The service and food were better, the Hotel Athénée Palace almost modern, its first-class restaurant superior to the finest in Russia, with a delightful orchestra performing Georges Enesco's *First Romanian Rhapsody.*

The next day we enjoyed the first kosher repast of our journey, which meant that at last Arthur could have a decent meal with no disadvantage for us. He had eaten not a bite of meat those first two weeks, though he offered his portion to one or other of us gentiles, with no hint of sanctimoniousness. Bucharest had been his ancestral home, and he was enthusiastically received by the Jewish community, as indeed were we. I met Tad Szulz, one of my favorite *New York Times* writers, and we shared experiences. Bishop Antim, the official Roman Catholic hierarch, was quite hospitable and proudly showed us his library, including both the Latin and Greek patrologies. It was a joy to meet the Communist minister of culture, far more open and liberal than any counterpart in the Soviet Union (at least at that time). I spoke enthusiastically of my favorite Romanian writer, Mircea Eliade, and the minister agreed that he was a great man and had been his schoolmate in the university. Though he personally had to be an atheist to be a member of the government, he admired Eliade's works; he seemed happy when I mentioned having known him when I taught at Boston College.

Our next stop in the "iron curtain" countries was a very brief one in Budapest. Then we went on to Prague, where we were met by the U.S. embassy staff. It is surely one of my favorite central European cities, especially with all its Mozartean reminiscences. A special memory was that of the Prague Jewish Community, approximately one thousand years old, with a Gothic synagogue of some seven hundred years old. Our first important meeting was with the great theologian Dr. Hromadka, then eighty but still full of energy. He had hung a picture of Pope Paul on his wall and spoke warmly of Father LaFarge and reminded us of him. He also mentioned that he was less optimistic about the USSR than he had been formerly. We visited Bishop Otcenasek in his mother's kitchen. He was not by any means the only Jesuit bishop that we met during this troubled time.

Shortly before we reached Prague, a young student named Jan Palluch had immolated himself in front of the imposing equestrian statue of King Wenceslaus on the square in front of the House of Parliament, a square now famous thanks to the television coverage accorded Prague's liberation. When we were there, the powerful Soviet presence was felt everywhere and thus this young man's self-immolation was all the more impressive.

Musicians think of Prague as almost as Mozartean a city as Vienna or Salzburg, and it was not surprising that Milos Forman chose it for the filming of *Amadeus*. After all, one of Mozart's finest symphonies is named the *Prague,* and Prague was chosen for the first performance of his masterpiece, *Don Giovanni.* I was touched by an anonymous woman's cheering shout: "Congratulations on Apollo XI!" Strange how even the slightest recognition cheers one far from home.

Since we hadn't tasted what we thought was an interesting meal since we had left New York, my friend John Mosler suggested, "Comrade C. J., what do you say to a good meal?" "Great!" He hailed the first available taxi, found that the driver understood English, and ordered, "Take us to the best restaurant in Czechoslovakia." "That's about forty kilometers from here," the driver protested. "No matter. Take us there, and wait for us." He must have sensed that my friend was a multimillionaire. On the way, John asked the driver: "Where did you learn such fine English?" "In a Russian prison." An ominous silence took over. The driver assuaged our anxiety by explaining, "I was a political prisoner and had to do something not to go crazy. Learning English seemed a desirable option."

As we drove over the Moldau, I caught myself humming that melody from Smetana's *Ma Vlast.* John then asked the driver: "Where are the Russians now?" "They're here, but you can't see them. They're hiding in the hills, and if we make a false move, they'll take over openly." The restaurant was all the driver promised, with a U.S. flag over our table. I have no idea how much John paid the driver.

Vienna was our next stop on the way home, and this time I found it much enhanced by the learned and kindly guidance of a fellow Jesuit and former student Leo Nicoll, who had already spent some years working on his doctorate in central European history. Leo seemed to know every stone, or at least every building, in Vienna, especially those with a musical or musicological meaning. He took us for supper to the restaurant made famous by *The Third Man* theme. The next day he showed us the text of the Treaty of Westphalia, various homes where Beethoven had stayed in Grinzing, the elegant cemetery where so many famed Viennese are buried—from Schubert and the Strausses to the adoptive Viennese Beethoven, Brahms, and so many others— plus the cenotaph of our beloved Mozart. On subsequent visits to Vienna, Leo was no less a host, especially memorable being the bicentennial of Beethoven, when Leo had long ahead of time arranged for good tickets to Karl Boehm's immortal performance of the *Missa Solemnis* (on December 15, 1970).

On another visit I served as chaplain-cicerone for Loyola's traveling chorale, trying to share with my students some of the learning Leo had accumulated. Some years later, while visiting Vienna again, I suggested to Leo that we try to get into Budapest. He agreed, and we went to the travel agency to see what we needed for the journey. Leo's passport did not picture him in clerical garb, whereas mine did. Leo had no problem and was able to get the visa to Hungary immediately. When the agent saw my passport, he shook his head sadly and said, "It'll take at least three months for you since you have a clerical collar on." This infuriated me, but I was determined to fight the system. "The only hope you have is to go right to the Hungarian Embassy," he assured me.

We followed instructions, but were prepared for trouble. Indeed, at the Hungarian Embassy I got the same frustrating reply. In anger, but hopelessly, I raised my voice, "Can't anyone in this embassy do anything?" He shrugged his shoulders. "May I speak to the highest official possible?" I pleaded. A dapper gentleman entered the office half smiling. "My dear sir," I begged, trying to sound threatening, "Are you going to deprive me of my right as a human being to visit the great city that nurtured Liszt, Bartók, Kodaly, Petöfi, and so many other giants of humanity?" Whether the dapper man was impressed or not, he changed his tone: "Leave your passport with me, and come back in two hours. I'll see what I can do." As obsequiously as I could, I thanked him in advance, hoping against hope.

Two hours later I had my passport back, plus the visa. Overjoyed, we went to the railway station and managed to get on the "Vienna Blood" or "Blue Danube" or whatever the famous Vienna-Budapest train was called. Only when we reached the border did our fear recur. Some eight armed guards came on board and gave us a sort of third-degree. After an hour or so, barbed wire fences and gates opened, and slowly we pierced the Iron Curtain.

We had planned to stay at the hotel where all tourists stayed, and where the chef was a Jesuit brother (in those days thoroughly underground). We asked to see him to compliment him; he bowed appropriately, asking how everybody was. "Fine," we smiled knowingly. "Regards to everybody," I added. Then I called the family of one of the refugees from the Communist regime whom I knew in New York.

His brother-in-law came to our phone booth in a taxi, and surreptitiously we went to visit my friend's mother. Leo spoke German to the family, while I did my best in Russian and French, since neither of us could handle Hungarian. The youngest person in the family considered his uncle a hero, since he had escaped to America, and offered me his silver Saint Stephen's medal. I felt I couldn't accept it. He insisted, and I relented, in turn insisting that he accept my silver ball-point pen (which tourists had assured me was most appreciated in Hungary). We made the exchange, each feeling happy and the grandmother happiest of all. Later, I was able to give the Saint Stephen's medal to the heroic refugee uncle in America.

Much as we enjoyed the visit, we were only given a sense of real safety when the barbed wire gates at the border opened, after what seemed a minor eternity, and we could enter the free world. Before leaving Budapest, however, we had visited the grave of the mother of a priest-friend, Hajtas Ference, working in New Orleans, who was not at that time allowed into his country. Happily things have improved in the past few years.

Chapter Fourteen

With Jesuit musicologist T. Frank Kennedy (left) *and our driver, searching for Jesuit Reductions in Bolivia.*

American South
and South America

Loyola University, New Orleans, 1970–80

Toward the end of the 1960s, the world appeared to be coming to a thunderous end. It seemed the perfect time not to be teaching, yet it was exactly the time when Father Tom Clancy wrote me a charming letter, urging me to return to Loyola. He was academic vice president at the time and felt that I might be if not the perfect person, at least a satisfactory person to help bridge the world of faculty and students, Jesuits and laypeople. As an inducement he announced that I should be appointed "university professor," a title held by few university scholars.

At the time I felt less like leaving *America* than I had felt in years. Don Campion was the recently appointed editor-in-chief and could not have been more ideal. But the challenge in the tone of Tom's letter captivated me. I knew that as an old friend he wouldn't allow me to be devoured by wild beasts. And on second thought it seemed, in some ways, the right time if ever to return to teaching. The people at Loyola—the Jesuits, at least—seemed pleased at my appointment. My only fear was that they might expect too much and feel let down. One person in authority, whom I'm not inclined to name, may have thought he was reassuring me when he announced that he had put all the toughest students in my class.

The following night I slept not a wink! Interesting, in retrospect, how small matters become disproportionately great: I was almost literally scared to death. Even such a tiny decision as how to dress for class kept me awake. If I wore a clerical collar, wouldn't that seem cowardly and ultraclerical? If I wore a tie, wouldn't that look phony? If I went without coat and tie, wouldn't that seem even phonier? By the time classes started, I hadn't made up my mind, and that meant neither tie nor coat.

I arrived at the classroom in time to see smoke festooning the "No Smoking" signs and an entire back row of students visibly brandishing newspapers, so as not to be caught paying attention. I had to improvise and hope to avoid crucifixion. So I strode (sort of) to the blackboard, trying to appear unafraid. I announced that there were several dark secrets in my background: one was my name, which I spelled out, making it easy for them to laugh at it. Next I explained that it meant "Son of the bishop!" adding, "I've been called something like that, too." Finally came the *deus ex machina* that broke through the ice, so to speak, as a good Cajun voice bellowed out: "Any connection with the McNaspy Stadium at USL?" Silence, followed by this response: "I suppose you can tell by looking at me that it's not named after me." Laughter. "But it was named after my father, who was a great athlete, and . . . to whom I was . . . a great . . . disappointment." Not really true, but a fair bit of self-mockery for the spur of the moment. Somehow, from then on the class and I seemed friends, and the chap with the worst reputation became the friendliest. From 1970 to 1980, all seemed peace and reconciliation.

There were exciting courses, too, which New Orleanian Don Gelpi, Bostonian Frank Sullivan, and I worked on together, Don being more philosophical, Frank more theological, I more interested in the arts, yet it all seemed to fit together at the time. Another delicious course (for me, at least) was one suggested by Ransom Marlow, a study of genius in arts and sciences, open only to very good students from the upper classes. A touch of spice was added by a senior student, Sidney Bezou, who had never had the chance to go to college when he was younger, staying out in order to work so that his siblings could take advantage of it. I've never enjoyed a student more than I did Sidney and his lovely wife, Brenda. No one could give a better example of enthusiasm and appreciation of everything true and beautiful. By the time Sidney graduated, I was already in Paraguay, but I appreciated the good news all the more.

Another type, of course, I particularly enjoyed—and still do—is designed for music majors. Called "Music as Value," it is an attempt to bring together in informal synthesis values found in music as well as those in theology and philosophy. Obviously, no one textbook would fulfill all these expectations, but I try to provide interesting readings from Suzanne Langer, Jacques

Maritain, Étienne Gilson, Walter Wiora, Gabriel Marcel, and other important aestheticians.

One of the great joys of such a course is the freedom to illustrate insights with slides and cassettes, and especially with live music, such as can be provided by the finest students—persons like Brett Duggan (several times winner of the international Bach contest, and now a fervent Benedictine at St. Joseph's Abbey), Ruth Myrick Lapeyre (as splendid in her Bach as in her Puccini), Leah Chase (mistress of spirituals and cantatas), Logan Skelton (a superlative pianist, today with a doctorate), and ever so many other students and younger faculty members.

A sure-fire class comes every semester when I play a tape made some thirty years ago by Mrs. Percival Sitges as a birthday present for her husband, capturing incredibly the beauty of a mockingbird doing an *obbligato* to familiar works by Chopin, Schumann, Debussy, and Mozart. By now countless people on three continents have heard this incredible tape, and Mrs. Sitges is always happy to learn of their enjoyment and amazement.

———

In mid-April 1972, during my "Music as Value" class, while showing slides of the Holy Land, I was interrupted by a familiar voice—that of Denis Pontiff: "Hey, Father, can I go with you on your next trip?" The expected laugh followed immediately, giving me time to work out a repartee. "Only if you can be ready in an hour, Denis." The students howled again, until I could assure them that I was, in fact, about to leave for London, that very afternoon.

"I've been invited to the Bach Festival at Oxford, but I'll be back within the week. A good friend, Richard Yardumian, is presenting the first European performance of his new mass, *Come Creator Spirit,* and his patron invited me to be there. Vaughan Williams will be there, too, and William Walton, also. You all wouldn't want me to miss that, would you? And they're paying my way." A loud gasp reassured me.

This particular Bach Festival was exceptionally wonderful, including not only Bach's *Saint Matthew Passion,* but Schuetz's as well, plus a number of cantatas and the entire *Well-Tempered Clavier,* performed by Henning Wagner on the harpsichord, clavichord, and chamber organ (according to which he judged more appropriate for the different preludes and fugues, since Bach left the options open). Not until 1985 was I so fortunate as to hear the entire forty-eight preludes and fugues, performed live here at Loyola at the beginning of the Bach Year by our eminent alumnus Sean Duggan, a Benedictine monk whom I have already mentioned several times.

An unexpected treat was arranged for me by the Yardumians—having dinner with them and Sir William Walton on his seventieth birthday. The many times I enjoyed his stunning *Belshazzar's Feast* I never dreamed of such a serendipitous delight.

The following day, before flying home by way of Miami, I ran into fellow Jesuit Peter Levi quite by accident on Oxford's High Street. He told me then that he was going to do the invocation in Westminster Abbey's Hall of Poets for Gerard Manley Hopkins, on the forthcoming occasion when the following inscription would be dedicated:

A.M.D.G.
ESSE QUAM VIDERI
GERARD
MANLEY
HOPKINS
S.J.
IMMORTAL DIAMOND

When I boarded the plane, I found myself seated next to a handsome couple who seemed somewhat heavily dressed for landing in Miami. Casually I made this observation. The lady assured me they lived in Miami and could change their clothes there but had been visiting relatives in Soviet Armenia, where it was chilly even in late April.

Armenians are the most patriotic of people. Proud of my own Armenian connection, I mentioned that I had been a guest of Richard Yardumian during the Oxford Bach Festival, but went on to assure them that I knew the litany of famous Armenians: Saroyan, Mikoyan, Agagianian, Yardumian, and others. The lady immediately added, "And Yepremian?" They both laughed. The couple to whom I had been speaking were indeed Mr. and Mrs. Garo Yepremian, the place kicker for the Miami Dolphins and his wife. I showed Garo *The Penguin Book of Russian Verse,* which

I was reading, and asked him to autograph it. He did it modestly and graciously and altogether legibly, with no hint as to how little Armenians love Russians. Once again I hoped my dad was delighted. Needless to say, when I got back to New Orleans, I showed it proudly to Denis Pontiff and other friends.

It was a special privilege of mine to be a member of the Board of Georgetown University between 1970 and 1980, a privilege in the literal sense since I never knew how it was that I came to be elected. The excitement of the District of Columbia is so multiple that it's impossible to know where to start. In my own world, in some ways a small world, D.C. spells Georgetown, since most of my best D.C. friends have always been associated with the senior U.S. Jesuit University, and over the years I can think of Gene Geinzer, Jim Walsh, Otto Henz, Paul Cioffi, Dan Gatti, Bob Drinan, Bill McFadden, Harold Bradley, Leo O'Donovan, Dick McSorley, Phil Land, John Breslin, Jerry Fogarty, Lasdislas Orsy, Dick Currie, Jack Haughey, Terry Toland, Walter Burghardt—a truly remarkable group of men.

Even if one weren't forbidden to make sultry revelations, I have none to offer. The quality of the persons I've known both on the board and on the faculty make bad news rather absurd. At the very middle of my term, in 1975, came my sixtieth birthday, which was given a triple celebration by some of the friends just mentioned. Gene Geinzer, who has since gone successfully into a third career at Loyola of Chicago, prepared the three festivities in a masterly way.

One gift I must recall with particular gratitude was that of Joe Sebes, who is now enjoying the heavenly festivities. It was a copy of his Harvard doctoral dissertation, published by the Institutum Historicum in Rome: "The Jesuits and the Sino-Russian Treaty of Nerchinsk (1689)"—basically a critical edition of the diary of a distinguished Jesuit musician Thomas Pereira, who, with another Jesuit, Father Francis Gerbillon, made remarkable achievements in working out the first treaty between Russia and China. Both were unique in being Westerners, priests, Jesuits, as well as men completely trusted by the Emperor of China when he was negotiating with the great rival emperor of Russia. Anyone interested in this important matter, but unable to devote the necessary hours to it, may do "second best" by securing and reading closely Father Sebes's splendid essay "China's

Jesuit Century" in the winter 1978 issue of *Wilson Quarterly.* It is a work of rare quality and high synthesis.

Midway during this second, longer stay at Loyola, the Vietnam War ended, and the mass immigration of refugees began. I was fortunate to be sent to Fort Chaffee by the U.S. Catholic Bishops at Archbishop Joseph Bernardin's behest to write a story about the immigration. "We've run out of refugees. I think I'm going to cry!" sobbed Sister Sheila McGinnis, a medical missionary. The 135,000 refugees from Vietnam, landing suddenly on American soil just before, had already been placed and found sponsors to help them enter a totally new world. Meantime, an epic of almost unprecedented scope was taking place within the U.S., quietly, unknown to me and to millions of other Americans. Immigration here is nothing new. Even the American Indians had long ago been immigrants to a new world, somewhat like the later Spanish, Portuguese, French, and British. Only the blacks had come with no regard for their wishes, or against them. Around 1820 began an avalanche that brought forty-six million immigrants, 77 percent of them Europeans. But the 135,000 Vietnamese of the summer of 1975 came almost overnight, with few fellow Vietnamese to welcome them. The U.S. Catholic Bishops' only purpose was to help refugees because they were refugees. No questions asked, regardless of whether refugees were Catholic, Buddhist, Hindu, or Muslim. California welcomed the most, 10,135; Texas next, 4,547; Louisiana third, 3,358; then Florida, 2,569; Virginia, 2,494; and Pennsylvania, 1,593. My story about the immigration was underwritten by the LaFarge Institute of New York City and published in booklet form in 1975.

Also in the middle 1970s, the important liturgical publishing house J. S. Paluch did me the surprising honor of asking for three years of weekly "homily hints." It proved perhaps the easiest and most fruitful task I could imagine. If one follows the suggested three-paragraph plan—all three paragraphs being quite brief—the work is made simple, and I am endlessly happy to realize that these simple thoughts can help busy parish priests to produce brief, clear homilies, Sunday after Sunday.

———

My several visits to Mexico, and consequent efforts to get a working knowledge of Spanish, led to other invitations during this period. One was with Father Elmo Romagosa to Guatemala. We left New Orleans by a four-motor prop plane, which, about halfway to Guatemala, lost the use of one of its motors. After another hour or so, a second motor faded out, and the pilot walked back into the cabin to cheer us up, assuring us that Latin American planes needed a siesta from time to time. Finally, an hour late, our maimed plane landed in Guatemala City airport, where we were greeted with marimbas and assorted refreshing drinks.

The next day we saw most of lovely, vernal Guatemala City and visited some functionaries. That evening my old classmate Father Jorge Toruno invited us to dinner at the home of his nephew, who was the rector of the national university, while he himself was rector of the Universidad de Landívar. I had read Father Landívar's great Latin epic, *Rusticatio Mexicana,* years earlier, thanks to Ernie Burrus, who had arranged for Landívar's reburial in his native Guatemala from his temporary grave in Italy. Many of the Latin American Jesuits had been exiled to Italy at the time of the Society's expulsion from the Bourbon empires. Rafael Landívar, perhaps the outstanding Latin poet of Latin America at the time, was one of many exiles.

I had made it a point to memorize some lines from the epic, especially the opening couplet: "Salve cara parens, dulcis Guatimala, salve,/Delicium vitae, fons et origo, meae" ("Hail, dear parent, fair Guatemala, hail,/joy of my life, its fountain and source.") When I hailed a taxi and asked the driver to take me to Landívar's monument, he started the first line of Landívar's epic, which I continued, each of us proud of at least that minor achievement. I feel especially proud of Landívar's exceptional poetic talent, and perhaps even more so of his great nonmacho appreciation of the leading light of Mexican literature at the time, Sor Juana Inéz de la Cruz, whom Landívar praises both in his epic and in the appended notes, where he refers to her as "schooled in every branch of learning and worthy of a place among the Muses on account of her elegant poems published in three volumes." Ernie Burrus assured me that another famous Jesuit poet, Father Alegre, was equally appreciative of Sor Juana Inéz de la Cruz. The recent publication of the Metropolitan

Museum of Art with an introduction by Octavio Paz, *Mexico: Splendors of Thirty Centuries* (1994), is no less fond of the great nun's work. I had heard of her during my first visit to Mexico and even at that time had copied some of her poems.

Another wonderful entry into South America came while I was still working at *America* in New York, and a diocesan priest whom I had known since his childhood, Father Willy Todd, brother of Jesuit Brother Terry Todd, came to see me. Willy wanted to visit Peru (still something that could be enjoyed without too much danger), but he wanted to do it with someone who knew Spanish. I was delighted, of course, to accompany him, having never seen the other capital of Spanish America, and of the Inca, Quechua, and Aymara worlds.

At the time, the only Peruvian Jesuit I knew was Santiago Izuzquiza, originally from Spain, who had studied English with me at Grand Coteau. "Santi" could not have been more generous with his time, and we particularly enjoyed getting to know Jesuit Bishop Luis Bambarén, recently appointed as "Bishop of the Slums" (that wasn't his official title, of course!). We particularly enjoyed going with him on his truck to a new barrio, where he gave a magnificent sermon on the importance of making a barrio a community rather than a slum, and how to do it. A truly model bishop.

Willy and I particularly hoped to visit the ancient Inca and colonial places in Cuzco, Sacsahuamán, and of course "the lost city of the Incas," incredible Machu Picchu, discovered by U.S. congressman Hiram Bingham in 1911. It is almost surrounded by the Urubamba River, two thousand feet below, a river that begins near the Pacific, whose water empties into the Atlantic via the Amazon. Long safe from invaders, Machu Picchu has enjoyed much speculation as to its whole meaning and is now reckoned one of the wonders of the world. Today it is all too accessible.

The Incas are often compared to the Romans in their engineering skills, their network of highways, their disciplined army, and their willingness to adapt cultural advances from other civilizations. Most of all, there is their enormous contribution in architecture—from Sacsahuamán overlooking Cuzco, a true wonder of the world, to Machu Picchu, its rival. A good friend of mine from Paraguay, patron of the arts and until recently ambassador to the Court of St. James, Anthony Espinosa, did his

dissertation at Harvard on the marvels of Sacsahuamán. Willy
Todd and I offered a curious contrast to our hosts—Willy a giant
and I almost the opposite extreme. Some suggested that Willy
was actually a boxer and I his manager!

At about this time of my life I developed a certain curiosity
regarding variations in "toasts" and made it a point to ask people
I met how they would propose a "toast" to someone in their
own language. In Cuzco this resulted in a fascinating exchange.
I asked a taxi driver how this was done in Quechua. After a
moment of reflection, the driver suggested "Salud!" No, I
protested, that's Spanish. How do you say it in Quechua? The driver scratched his head and suddenly felt enlightened: "In
Quechua we say, 'Ave María Purísima'!" I asked no more.

Early in 1974, I began a half-year's work in Rome assisting
Father Gordon George in the Jesuit Information Bureau, the happiest period I ever spent there. During those months at the Jesuit
Curia, I made a phone call one morning to a special pal of mine,
Brother Redín, with a voice full of surprise. In my best Spanish I
announced, "Brother Redín, this is your twin brother." "I haven't
any twin brother," the dear brother solemnly responded. "Oh yes,
you do. Turn to your copy of the Roman catalog and see who
else was born on March 22, 1915." He was astonished to find that
I had been born on the very same day as he had—same date,
same year. From that time on, whenever we met, we addressed
each other as "twin." In fact, several years following this first
coincidence, I happened to arrive, yes, on March 22. I went
straight to Brother Redín's room, knocked, was admitted and
immediately cried out in Spanish: "Happy birthday, dear twin!"

When I first noticed I had an "identical twin" at the Roman
Jesuit curia, I had been doing some trivial research. One of my
discoveries was the fact that in South America both assistancies
had Jesuit secretaries who were "identical twins." There were
two Herberts in the curia: Herb Dargan, Irish born, Hong Kong
province, and Herb de Souza, born in Karachi (but not in
Pakistan, since his family had left Karachi before Pakistan was
formed). The oldest Jesuit in the curia at that time was Brother
Giovanni Barlasima, then eighty-one, with sixty years in the
Society and fifty-two years working in the clothes room. Rufo
Mendizabal completed seventy years in the Society on
November 12 that year. Father Dezza had attended five General

Congregations, a sort of record; he has since attended at least two others. Brother Edwin Amran, who also worked in the curia and was a genius at handling radios, was an Egyptian Jew from a Sephardic family, with a Spanish passport.

One of my main trivia in this research had to do with the use of beards in the Society, since some younger men wanted to wear them, while older men were opposed. It was fascinating to discover that the first ten fathers general were men who wore beards, while the great patron of the arts Father Oliva, the eleventh, was clean-shaven. So many bizarre tidbits turned up, in fact, that I wrote an entire article—of no importance whatsoever—on this timely subject.

Ms. Elena Bartoli, the soul of hospitality, appropriately directs the Jesuit Guest Bureau in Rome, and she always seems to come up with fresh ideas on how to be of service to Jesuits' friends. She is, as a consequence, probably better known personally to friends of Jesuits the world over than is any single Jesuit. During this period, when I also had time to reread all of Virgil (in the original), Elena came up with one of her genial (in both senses) ideas: for us to collaborate on a modest guidebook geared to Jesuits and their friends. Elena did the first thirty pages—all practical and sensible—leaving the remaining twenty-five for me to do, describing the points of special Jesuit interest. The tiny volume mentioned earlier—*Rome, A Jesuit City Too*—appeared in record time, with a clever, colorful cover done by André Bouler of rue de Grenelle in Paris. When I phoned André with our request, all he needed to know was when we wanted it. "As soon as you can get it to us," we replied. Within a week it was in our hands. The booklet has since gone through several editions, in at least English and Spanish, increasingly our Society's two almost universal languages.

———

On my way back from Rome and work in the Jesuit House of Writers, I was more than delighted to keep two promises: to visit the Hennessys in London and the Kenningtons in Nottingham. Both couples had visited me in Rome—the Hennessys to ask my help regarding the Americas Society's forthcoming exhibit of the arts of the Jesuit Reductions in the

Paraguay area, the Kenningtons to share some of our favorite cathedrals in northeastern England.

I stayed with the Hennessys in London for some days, planning the exhibit "Paradise Lost: The Jesuits and the Guaraní Missions 1609-1767" to run at the Americas Society Art Gallery on Park Avenue in New York from October through December 1988. The Hennessys, supported by David Rockefeller and Ambassador George Landau, wanted me to select some fifty polychrome wood carvings and altar decorations from the Bogarin Museum and a few private collections in Asunción. They guaranteed the financing of the exceptional project, while Father José María Blanch (who had done photographs for my book *Lost Cities of Paraguay* and other exhibits) helped me to choose the finest works available; for example, *El Niño Jesús Alcalde* from the mission of San Ignacio Guazú. The exhibit proved to be one of the most satisfying single projects I was ever involved in.

My nephew Henry Kennington had arranged to drive down to London to pick me up for the journey to Nottingham, where Ivis was keeping the home fires burning. We drove out of London in a rainstorm that turned into a rare hurricane, as we learned from the radio. When we reached Nottingham, Ivis was relieved to find us safe and sound.

The next day we drove to Durham, my favorite Norman cathedral (that gives the impression of "rocky solidity and indeterminate duration," in the words of Samuel Johnson), high on a commanding spot over the Wear River. Durham is closely associated with two eminently English saints—Cuthbert and Bede—and the inscription over Venerable Bede's tomb is unforgettable: "Hac sunt in fossa Bedae Venerabilis ossa" ("In this grave are the bones of the Venerable Bede").

Anyone who has traveled at all knows at least the name of Stonehenge. It used to be almost as easy to reach from London as is Salisbury Cathedral, with its incredibly graceful 404-foot spire, England's tallest medieval structure. Today, as I hear, Stonehenge is hemmed in to protect against vandals, though it used to be a sort of secular shrine. It was built between 1800 and 1400 B.C. as part of the sun cult, focused on the solstice days of summer and winter, when the movement of the sun appeared to stop and reverse its direction. A few days before June 21 (sometime in the mid-seventies), I luckily happened to be in London, visiting English Jesuit Francis Walker (who had taught at Loyola), T. Frank Kennedy (recalled earlier in connection with our discovery of music by the Italian Jesuit missioner Domenico Zipoli), and Clyde LeBlanc (artist and fellow explorer of Constantinople, Rome, Chartres, and other marvels). I forget who pointed out the fact of the forthcoming solstice and made arrangements for a car to be used on that day.

We reached Stonehenge in time to see the sun lining up between the main pillars of the sarsen circle. Ahead of us were several dozen "druids," clad more or less like Ku Klux Klansmen, and praying in loud midwestern U.S.A.-style accents. It was all too exotic for words, and we had difficulty controlling our laughter. Even so, every time I've managed to visit Stonehenge I've been more stunned by its unique quality and an increasing sense of what it cost in human labor, at a period long before the wheel was in use, to transport the many-ton bluestones from far away Preseli and then to hoist them to their height as lintels. Nearby in Avebury, we visited the great set of concentric stone circles, hailing from the same period but larger in extent, each about 320 feet in diameter, some weighing forty tons. Again, we were awed.

Unfortunately, my three sensitive companions were not with me years later when I was visiting the island of Malta, with its rather recently uncovered temples and hypogaeum (underground tribal tomb). Paradoxically, the constant bombing of Malta by Nazi aircraft led to the happy discovery of architecture rivaling that of Stonehenge in quality and probably surpassing it in age.

———

In 1977, an old Jesuit friend and former student, Jack Vessels, dropped in on me at Loyola in New Orleans and gave me a surprising invitation: "C. J., how about learning Portuguese and spending some time with us in Brazil?" I hadn't the slightest idea of what I might be able to do to make the venture worthwhile, so I said as much. "Well, since you know Spanish," he said, "Portuguese shouldn't be too hard. I'll line up a series of lectures for you to give on subjects that you're interested in, and we'll find some way of paying for your travel." I suspected that Jack had something up his sleeve. It turned out that he was hoping for some free or almost free publicity for the Brazilian mission that he, Harold Rahm, and Edgar Tiblier had started some years earlier. My response was tentative at best.

Happily, however, I met a student on campus who wore a São Paulo T-shirt. Without asking his name, I simply went right to the point: "Will you teach me Portuguese, and I'll help you in your English?" It turned out that his English was already better than my Portuguese would ever become. He finessed, assuring me that his mother was perfect in Portuguese and would surely love to teach me for nothing. The last phrase was decisive! Mrs. Hilda Stappers (nee Barbosa) proved to be not only quite competent but also no less charming, one of those rare people who seem to prefer to help rather than to be helped, always giving the impression that you are conferring the favor.

We met every day for half an hour or so, taping our entire conversations and using the splendid Georgetown Brazilian-Portuguese cassettes as well. Realizing that my memory was in decline, I determined to do many times as many repetitions as I had had to do forty years earlier when I was trying to consolidate my French. Finally, Hilda seemed satisfied, and other Brazilian friends assured me that I could at least read lectures in Portuguese satisfactorily.

My former student and great friend John Joyce, who seems to know more about the history of New Orleans jazz than anyone else I've met, completed a superb tape on the subject and assisted me in composing a text for it, which Mrs. Stappers helped me translate into Portuguese. George Hutzler provided me with a splendid set of slides on Scythian art, with a text that Hilda and I put into Portuguese; and several other rare lectures were lined up, mainly with the support of unusual slides. Jack Vessels made a monumental act of faith in his old teacher and arranged lectures in Rio, São Paulo, Salvador, and other educational centers. People were more than ordinarily charming, even by Latin American standards, apparently delighted to find a "Yanqui" interested in arts and languages, especially one from New Orleans who could speak some Portuguese.

This was to be my first Christmas south of the equator, south indeed of the tropic of Capricorn. Some people insisted on singing the commercial "White Christmas," though everything was totally green. I was grateful that at least there was no artificial snow. The cribs, or *nacimentos,* had plenty of straw, the usual floor of chapels in poorer sections, especially at Vila Brandini. Downtown São Paulo was already festooned with tickertape, as Bob McCown and I filmed it.

We spent time with that great Jesuit missioner Harold Rahm, whose work would require at least a volume to describe, and who has a miraculous way of celebrating Christmas: providing even a live baby to squall at the moment of Jesus' birth! This time the baby went to sleep, however, when placed in the crib. At the "Gloria" the multitude sang (as often in Latin America) the tune of what we call "The Battle Hymn of the Republic." Father Casimiro Irala, a tremendous musician and even greater person—whom I had known from a meeting of Jesuit artists in Guadalajara and who was, in fact, the first Paraguayan Jesuit I ever met—did much playing of his guitar and singing with and for the people. The last blessing included *"Pa'`e Noël,"* with "Jingle Bells," and a "Happy Birthday, Dear Jesus" and "Happy Birthday" to all the newborn of the village. The word that came to mind spontaneously was "A Charismatic Christmas." That night, for the first time, I saw the Southern Cross and Alpha and Beta Centaurus. God had blessed my astronomy hobby.

I got my first taste of the size of Brazil as we flew from Miami to Rio. When we entered Brazilian territory, the pilot announced that hopeful fact, and I attached my seat belt anticipating an imminent landing. Five hours later we arrived in the airport! Tom Cullen, an expert in physics and a fine musician, was there to meet me, together with Andy Whitman, a fellow member of the New Orleans Province and a former student. Andy had been one of the founders of the splendid Clavius Group, a mathematics society that was one of the inspirations for our Jesuit Institute for the Arts. When Andy presented me to the rector of the Pontifical Catholic University (PUC), using Portuguese, and I replied in the same language, both were visibly delighted, though I could detect in Andy's smile his pleasure in being able to present a fellow American who knew the difference between Spanish and Portuguese.

Since Andy is known as a perfectionist, I became even more delighted, principally because I had not let him down. Tom

Cullen, who is since deceased, was specially responsible for my very favorable first impression of Brazil. He took out almost two weeks to show me the glories of Rio and vicinity, and everything interesting in a musical way. Thus I was able to meet musicologist Cleofa de Nattos, whose study of Padre Mauricio is reckoned definitive. I'm ashamed now to admit I had never even heard of two real giants of Brazilian music, Padre Mauricio of Rio and Carlos Gomes of Campinas (although I recalled that Hilda Stappers had mentioned the latter). Ask ten North Americans to name a Brazilian composer and all ten will name Villa Lobos, probably pronouncing Villa as if it were Spanish! Yet among musicians it is well known that Carlos Gomes has several operas of world renown, and New Orleanians should be grateful that Louis Moreau Gottschalk is renowned throughout Brazil and, when he died, was even given an imperial funeral by Brazil's Emperor Pedro II.

A surprise came one evening when Tom Cullen invited me to hear a great Hamburg string group perform Brahms's Second Quartet and his Viola Quintet. The latter had long been one of my favorite pieces of chamber music, but I had never heard it in person, though I had just missed the chance to hear it done by the Budapest String Quartet when it was performed in Rome on my first Easter Sunday in the Eternal City. Another delight was offered by Tom when he discovered that I admired Lucio Costa's work, despite his allegedly leftist tendencies. Maestro Costa was kind enough to show me all his photos of the Jesuit Reductions and to express his appreciation for the many contributions of Jesuits to the history of art in general, not merely that of the Reductions. He described the Jesuits, to my great delight, as bridges, even "many channels" linking the arts and other values.

Yet another surprise was in store: the extraordinary Russian film by Andrei Tarkovsky on the life of the great icon painter Andre Rublyov (ca. 1350–1430), a monk of the Trinity-Sergius Monastery near Moscow, especially renowned for his *Icon of the Trinity,* now in the Moscow Tretyakov Gallery. Rublyov was an almost exact contemporary of the Florentine Dominican Fra Angelico, with whom he has much in common. When in Moscow long before, I had asked my guide Marina if she had seen the film on Rublyov, and she sadly admitted that they were not allowed to see it in Russia, where it had been made! I had to wait to see it in Brazil, though I now have seen it again at Loyola in New Orleans.

Not far from Campinas, where our Centro Kennedy houses the work of Brothers Hollingsworth and Coco, is the city of Americana, named after the American Southerners invited by Emperor Pedro following the American Civil War to help Brazilians with modern agricultural methods. My wonderful experience there on July 4 is recounted here in chapter 1.

One of the best features of this particular trip was the fact that I was accompanied by my old buddy Jesuit Brother Filmore Elliot, then a missioner in Brazil, later a dedicated nurse at our Ignatius Residence for infirm Jesuits in New Orleans, and most recently launching into a variation on his earlier work as a hospital chaplain in Tampa. Filmore has outlived both his Jesuit brothers, Clyde and Larion.

The day after the Americana stop, Father Irala and I set out for Belo Horizonte, by night bus, guaranteed to be a "luxury" bus with good heating. It turned out to be one of the most miserable nights of my life since the heating did not work, and the altitude of the hills between São Paulo and Belo Horizonte makes the winter cold unspeakably uncomfortable (July is, of course, winter in that hemisphere). But the sunny morning in Belo Horizonte was golden. We enjoyed the church at Pampulha with the great Portinari art and that of Oscar Niemeyer, which we found utterly delightful. The Brazilian state here is known as Minas Gerais, or General Mines, and the main city Ouro Preto or, "Dark Gold," today meaning oil rather than gold.

The art historian Father Massote had urged us wisely to spend as much time as we could afford with the great works of Aleijadinho (nickname for the supreme Brazilian artist, meaning the "beloved maimed one"). His real name was Antonio Francisco Lisboa, the mulatto son of a Portuguese and a black slave. In Congonha, Aleijadinho is best known for his chapels of the mysteries of the Passion of Christ and for his twelve prophets, the former in polychrome wood, the latter in what is called "soapstone." My own set of slides is fairly successful, but no match for the many of Father Massote, nor for the pictures in the extraordinary volume *Aleijadinho* by Germain Bazin, curator of the Louvre, who has helped the whole world to get to know the superlative Brazilian master. Aleijadinho is now a national hero, and as you go along the roads in Minas Gerais, youngsters are eager to show you a house "where Aleijadinho lived," almost anywhere in the area! In any case, he is certainly one of art history's supreme heroes, having overcome every conceivable handicap.

On July 12, following Father Irala's suggestions, I flew to Foz Iguazú, the giant waterfall made famous in the film on the Reductions, *The Mission.* I stayed overnight with the Society of the Divine Word missioners (S.V.D.s) and met a most extraordinary person named Father German. He had been crippled in an automobile accident, but as a model of patience, gradually overcame his handicap, and some ten years later was in perfect strength. Crossing over to Argentina by boat, I barely missed the first bus going to the land of the Reductions. With unheroic impatience I blamed my luck and waited for the next bus. It was a chilly day and the bus was unheated, but I was at least fascinated by the bus ticket, which read like a litany of Jesuit missions.

The bus being practically empty, I sat in front and joined with the driver and helper quaffing *tereré,* a popular local drink made of herbs and cold water, more out of a sense of duty than of preference. Not far from San Ignacio Mini ("mini" meaning little and "guazú" big, there being a San Ignacio on each side of the Paraná River), we discovered that the bus I had barely missed had crashed into a ravine, killing three passengers and seriously wounding twelve others. I thanked God that I had missed that bus and prayed for those who had not.

When our bus reached Posadas, I was warmly received by the Jesuits in the two missions there. They did me the favor of phoning San Ignacio, whose pastor, Father José Marx, S.V.D., was a good friend of all Jesuits and especially of Father Irala. Father Marx met my bus and invited me to attend the wake of one of the victims of the accident I could have been in. It was very poignant, of course, but the widow and children were most grateful at the arrival of two priests.

Father Marx, realizing it was my first visit to the Reductions, provided me with a special introduction, giving me magnificent books of photographs of the area, and informing me that San Ignacio Mini (so called because it was a few years younger than the San Ignacio in Paraguay) had been built by Jesuit Brother

Domingo de Torres, who had also built the Reduction of Loreto, together with Brother José Bresanelli. Brother José had built Santa Ana, too, and was surely one of the top artists of the Jesuit Reductions. Father Marx explained to me that the main artist had been another Jesuit brother, Juan Bautista Primoli. Both these brothers were from Milan; Bresanelli died in Santa Ana in 1728, while Primoli died in Candelaria in 1747. Today all these names are most familiar to me, though at the time they were almost entirely new. It is interesting, to say the least, that most of these artists were brothers and Italians.

Two German laymen were visiting Father Marx at the time; and every other time I visited, there were Germans there too, though not the same ones. They were listening to tapes of Brahms and Beethoven, which pleased me no end. Then we visited nearby Museo Jesuítico of Don Miguel, which I was to visit many times again and to treat in *Lost Cities of Paraguay* (pp. 99–100).

In a sense, historically viewed, many of the sites I have just mentioned seeing were in (ancient) Paraguay, a country torn apart by the absurd War of the Triple Alliance, fought just after our own Civil War and even more devastating to the losing side. Technically, now, when crossing the Paraná from Posadas to Encarnación (both founded by Saint Roque González de Santa Cruz), one enters the present borders of Paraguay and the Jesuit province of Paraguay as well.

The Jesuit superior was Ricardo Romero, a very kindly, pipe-smoking gentleman and the soul of hospitality. He realized that little remained from Reduction days in Encarnación but that a good deal could be seen in two of the last built Reductions within striking distance. So, he telephoned a taxi driver who could be trusted and who agreed to drive me to these two Reductions—Trinidad and Jesús—with a breathing space in each place, all for ten dollars. Today it would be at least five times as much.

A lot has happened since these first visits, and in the intervening time I've managed to make them principal tourist spots in any guided tour. Jesús was never completed, being even more poignant for that reason. I believe that it was the creation of Salamanca-born Antonio Ribera, priest-son of the leading Spanish architect of the period and the person who built the "New Cathedral" of Salamanca.

Trinidad, far larger and even awesome, seems to have been the masterpiece of Brother Primoli and was much celebrated nationally on TV and radio on the feast of the Holy Trinity, May 25, 1986, when a group of my best friends in Paraguay performed Domenico Zipoli's mass there for the first time in several centuries. It is hardly an exaggeration to suggest that this was the liturgico-musical event in the Reductions area that seemed the most important during all my years in Paraguay. Almost the entire nation had become galvanized to celebrate the rediscovery of the composition and the partial restoration of the Reduction itself.

Even more restoration has been completed since the pope's visit. In fact, so much has been done since my first few visits that it is hard to remember accurately the overwhelming debris covering most of the sanctuary and all of the nave at that time. The extraordinary baroque doors leading from the sanctuary, and the no less exceptional friezes illustrating the glory of baroque musical instruments, provided me with slides that helped persuade several benefactors to underwrite the documentary film on the Reductions that Bob McCown and I were to produce. I feel that if Father Romero had not made this visit to Trinidad and Jesús feasible, our film would probably never have been made, and the general awareness of U.S. Jesuits regarding the Reductions that led us to volunteer for new missionary work there, specifically in Paraguay, might never have been raised.

I was pleasantly surprised too by Paraguay's relaxed style of novitiate and its novices, all of whom make pilgrimages to important historic spots in the Jesuit life of their country. I might even venture to say that I felt "edified" at their attitudes and those of their superiors for allowing this healthy return to the Ignatian spirit.

As the time came to leave for Asunción, I said adieu to the Encarnación Jesuits and went to the bus station. Chance or divine providence placed me near a university student from São Paulo. I showed him a book on the then Blessed Roque González that Father Romero had given me. The student seemed moved and commented on all the great work that the Jesuits had done for Paraguay. This, of course, moved me too. The bus ride seemed very long, despite the agreeable stop in San Ignacio Guazú, where I paused briefly to say hello to the Spanish Jesuit missioners working there. They phoned the provincial in Asunción and arranged for a place for me to stay at his house there.

I dimly recall crossing the Tebicuary River, which roughly demarcates Franciscan and Jesuit missionary leadership, and going past the stunning church in Yaguarón, once Franciscan, today under diocesan direction. Finally, as winter dark fell, our bus reached Cerro Corá, where at the address given me in San Ignacio I met Antonio Rojas, secretary to the provincial, who put me at ease and assured me that Father Provincial Antonio González Dorado would see me as soon as a meeting of all province superiors ended. In my diary I scribbled, "great people, marvelous hospitality," an opinion which I have seen no reason ever to modify.

The next morning the provincial called several people at the main Jesuit high school in Asunción, Colegio Cristo Rey, who assured him they would be happy to meet me: Father José María Blanch, a splendid photographer, with whom I later collaborated on several books; Father Michelángelo More; and the assistant principal, a charming lady, whose name I cannot recall. Visiting the national "Panteón," I was unhappy to find so few suggestions of Paraguay's religious life, though delighted to see an impressive statue of Blessed Roque González.

Back at the provincial's residence, I spent hours discussing (entirely in Spanish, since the provincial spoke no English) the possibility of finding young Jesuits from the United States to participate in the Paraguay apostolate. At the time I saw little possibility and said as much. Happily I was to be proved wrong. At the airport I met two fine United States Redemptorists, Fathers Aschmann and Burke, this being the beginning of a long friendship with Redemptorists in Paraguay. After a quick change of planes at Iguazú, I went on to São Paulo for a grand reunion in our house at Osasco with Jack Vessels, Edgar Tiblier, and Filmore Elliot.

The next day, July 19, had been put aside for Brasilia, a bit like crashing into the twenty-first century. I was deceived on arriving near Goiania, a city of more than a million inhabitants; since like most "Yanquis" with our ignorance of Latin America I had never heard of it, I took it for Brasilia. Twilight was incredible. Friends showed me the city at that bewitching hour, especially the bluish glass of the cathedral which I found otherwise cold. The Centro Cultural de Brasilia, run by Jesuits, proved hospitality itself. Fathers Cristóbal and Iglesias I had known at St. Mary's College in Kansas and José Aleixo at Woodstock College; Urbano Rausch, a teacher at the university, I met here for the first time.

It was fascinating to discover the *Vestibulario,* a list of those who managed to make it into the university. Brazil has so few surnames that it is common to give lists of names stressing the bizarre "Christian" names, such as Emerson, Lindberg, or Eisenhower. I missed my afternoon plane, but thanks to Iglesias my confusion turned into a felix culpa. This gave me a chance to see the hidden truth about gorgeous Brasilia—the tragic "satellite cities," slums that aren't the result of decay but that seemed to start that way. There you meet the real heroes, the brothers, nuns, and priests who identify with the poorest of the very poor. I particularly enjoyed meeting Brother Gabriel, a Christian Brother, and singing with him the great hymn "Honneur à toi, glorieux de La Salle," which I had learned in Lafayette back in grammar school.

My next stop was Salvador, Bahía, where a New England Jesuit friend, Ron Collavecchio, was all that one could expect of a host. The statue of Father Nóbrega, the Jesuit founder of Salvador, dominates the plaza facing the cathedral, once the Jesuit church. The Church of St. Francis can hardly be matched for sheer glory, paradoxically all of gold leaf. Bahía in 1576 had sixty-two churches and forty-seven sugar mills, historians tell us. A co-worker with Nóbrega in the missions was Anchieta, a sort of Saint Francis Xavier of the early days of Brazil; he is sometimes called the Father of Brazilian literature of the New World, as famous as a geographer and historian as he is as a devoted missionary.

A unique coincidence occurred in Salvador when I went to see the U.S. cultural attaché, offering to give a free illustrated lecture on New Orleans jazz. Salvador, with its strong Latin-black traditions similar to that of New Orleans, seemed to become almost instantly my favorite Brazilian city. The attaché beamed and asked if I knew what group was going to perform in Salvador the next day. I had no idea. He glowed with satisfaction and announced: "The New Orleans Preservation Hall Jazz Band!" A preparatory illustrated lecture the previous night would be much appreciated, he insisted. He proved right. Thanks to some Brazilian

Jesuits, I had come to know a number of young black musicians and succeeded in securing enough complimentary tickets to get them in free. The giant auditorium was quickly packed.

Afterward, I urged my young friends to come backstage. There we met my older friends from New Orleans, several of whom actually remembered me. They seemed pleased, especially as I was able to introduce them in a blend of Portuguese and English to their fellow black musicians. The leader of the group was fairly exhausted, having been flown from continent to continent almost mercilessly, performing New Orleans's native music. He asked, "Say, Father, I know what town we're in—Salvador—but tell me what country this is!" One could talk on and on about Salvador and never exhaust the subject.

Recife and Olinda are both fabulous cities, whether one of my special heroes, Archbishop Helder Câmara, is present or not. I was particularly happy to meet a California Jesuit, Father Azevedo, and the Canadian rector of the University, Bernard Morissette. Brother Freitas helped me get to Carmo and to the seminary founded in 1551, where the first Jesuit missioners, Nóbrega and Antonio Pires, worked among the Indians. In 1576 Anchieta founded a college, where that master of Portuguese prose, Father Vieira, was to teach.

When time came later for the making of our documentary film on the Jesuit Reductions of Paraguay, my journey to join the brothers McCown, Bob and "Hooty" (James Hart), began in Baltimore of all places. To my surprise, Loyola of Baltimore had offered me an honorary doctorate, to be conferred on May 30, 1978. Apart from the usual niceties observed on such occasions, Loyola's president, Father Joe Selinger, delighted my local relatives and me when he read, "Baltimore has a place of honor in his family history, because his grandfather, James McNaspy, was born here, and we are delighted that Father McNaspy now has a place of honor in Loyola's history."

At the dinner following the ceremony, Father Selinger (since deceased) was especially kind to my Baltimore relatives. My close Washington friends Mr. and Mrs. Vincent MacDonnell were at the ceremony, too, and drove me back to Washington for the night, then to the airport for the flight to Miami. In Miami, Father Tom Griffin, an old student and buddy of mine, met me and drove me to the Gesù residence, where other old pals like Don

Pearce and Harry Martin always made a visit something special. Tom Griffin got us to the airport for our Rio flight. This was only the beginning of what was to prove an outstanding experience.

The slides I had made of the Reductions of Paraguay stirred the generous interest of such good friends as Father Dan Flaherty of Chicago and Father Harold Bradley of Georgetown. Obviously, documentaries cannot be made without money, and the one in question, thanks principally to the skills of Bob McCown, was actually done with perhaps one tenth of the money estimated by other experts in filmmaking. No one thought it could be done for under two hundred thousand dollars, whereas the actual cost was only twenty thousand dollars, unless one counts "contributed services"—the hundreds of hours spent by Bob piecing it all together, and the time I spent on the script and Father Irala on the music, plus Roger Wagner's generosity in allowing us to use his group's performance of Zipoli's "Gloria."

Moreover, the Paraguayan Jesuits were infinitely generous in putting us up and lending us a jeep, with no charge save for the gasoline. In any case, whatever success the film has enjoyed— including the Golden Eagle Award as an outstanding cultural documentary—may be attributed in great part to the cooperation of brother Jesuits. Father González Dorado, Paraguay's provincial, was most hospitable and expressed his appreciation of our work and efforts.

From the day we sallied forth on our filming in the unpaved jungles of Paraguay, across the Guairá Falls, with dangerous forays through the south of Brazil, we were never far from drama or blessed with feelings of over-confidence. True, there were many hours of sheer beauty, as one flew by helicopter over Iguazú Falls, and back and forth over the colossal Paraná River. Our friends back in the New Orleans Province were not rash when they wondered aloud how three eccentrics named "Mac" could ever be recovered from the jungles. We may have wondered the same, at least from time to time. Would it be arrogant to suggest that our guardian angels were willing to work overtime?

While preparing the script of our documentary film, I ran into countless surprises, not least an idyll (or diminutive epic) written about the Reductions by the important English Romantic poet Robert Southey (1774–1843), who had been named Poet Laureate by George III in 1813. It is no secret that poets laureate are by no means always synonymous with "best poets" of the period, though they always seem important enough, as witnessed in the choice of William Wordsworth, Alfred Lord Tennyson, Robert Bridges, John Betjeman, and a host of others. Robert Southey, in fact, seems far superior as a historian. Yet in both capacities he seems to appreciate highly the Jesuit Reductions.

In his diminutive epic, titled "A Tale of Paraguay," we read in canto 3:

> Loyola's sons, now long endeared
> To many a happy tribe, by them conveyed
> From the open wilderness or woodland shade,
> In towns of happiest polity to dwell

And further on, in canto 4:

> For in history's mournful map, the eye
> On Paraguay, as on a sunny spot,
> Many rest complacent, to humanity
> There, and there only, hath a peaceful lot
> Been granted. . . .

In his masterpiece of historiography, *History of Brazil* (part 2, pp. 307ff.), Southey writes,

> The Jesuits opposed the Indian slave trade with the zeal of men who knew they were doing their duty; never had men a better cause, and never did men engage in any cause with more heroic ardor. . . . Europe had no cause to rejoice in the establishment of the Jesuits; but in Brazil and Paraguay their superstitions may be forgiven them, for the noble efforts which they made in behalf of the oppressed Indians, and for the good which they effected. . . . It was their fate to be attacked with equal inveteracy by the unbelieving scoffers and philosophists on one side, and by the all-believing bigots and blockheads of their own idolatrous Church on the other.

Such quotations could be multiplied almost endlessly.

Everyone who has read *Candide* recalls Voltaire's fairly cyn-ical treatment of Jesuit missioners. Fewer, however, have read Voltaire's more considered evaluation in chapter 154 of his *Essay on the Morals and Spirit of the Nations:* "The conquests of Mexico and of Peru are prodigies of audacity; and the cruel-ties practiced there, the entire extermination of the inhabitants of Santo Domingo and some other islands, are excesses of hor-ror. But the establishment in Paraguay by Spanish Jesuits alone seems in some ways the triumph of humanity: it seems to expi-ate the cruelties of the first conquerors. The Quakers in North America and the Jesuits in South America have given a new spec-tacle to the world." A bit oversimplified, though broadly true.

Sometimes rivalries between religious orders can be less than edifying, often in the name of loyalty to one's own group. Franciscan Bishop Cárdenas in Asunción is often cited as a dised-ifying instance of such rivalry, though the life of Franciscan mis-sioner Father Luis de Bolaños is at least as edifying as anyone's can be. If one were to have asked Jesuit St. Roque González de Santa Cruz who his best friend in another religious order might be, he would surely not have hesitated to name Luis de Bolaños, who saved his life and the lives of some of his companions more than once.

A very famous Capuchin Father, Florentin de Bourges, could not have been more favorable to the Jesuit missioners of the Reductions. On his way to Pondichéry, India, in 1716, Florentin arrived in Buenos Aires planning to cross the continent to Chile. He wrote, "I had heard a lot of praise for the Jesuit missions of Paraguay, but now that I have seen them with my own eyes I must say they surpass their fame." He found Jesuit houses "sim-ple, with no ostentation, but the Church is done splendidly, in polished stone—done with such art by the Indians that the Church could be held in honor in any European city. Indians make wonderful Christians—they have no contact with Euro-peans! Older missioners, who said they were 'resting,' were doing as much as three priests together in Europe!"

When the McCowns and I were ready to start back, I had to leave them in Lima, following the superlative performance of a sixteenth century drama in front of the Jesuit church. They went on up to Machu Picchu and Sacsahuamán, which they had never seen before, while I hurried back to other obligations in New

Orleans. After some days, Bob returned to Dallas, where he did campus ministry at Southern Methodist University, spending his free evenings editing our film. Shortly afterward he flew to New Orleans to do some polishing with me at Loyola University's TV station.

One curiosity about the film should be mentioned. On occasion friends have commented how much more athletic my arms appeared in the film, pointing to the map, than they are in reality. The explanation is simple: back in Dallas, Bob had asked Father Earl Johnson to substitute his arm for mine when he needed additional transition shots. It was odd that I never did get to watch our film until it was too late to make any changes that I might have wanted to make. In fact, I didn't see it at all until we showed it in Tokyo many months later, when it had already won the Golden Eagle Award.

Chapter Fifteen

After the rich experience of Japan itself, a rare theatrical appearance in Loyola's production of The Mikado.

Going More Than Halfway

Sophia University, Tokyo, 1979

Japan's magic has caught on almost throughout the world, and I have a hard time remembering when it was that it first captivated me. But my happiest, because it was the longest, experience regarding Japan came during the first six months of 1979, when I was able to spend two academic terms at the International College of the Jesuits' Sophia University in Tokyo. On the way over I was able to stop in Honolulu and visit an old confrere, Vinny Sykes and his lovely wife, Judy, of Japanese descent, Sansei (that is, third generation).

Two close friends, Jesuits formerly of the New England Province, Joe Love and Larry McGarrell, were at the airport to meet me, and at the evening Mass I was presented to the community by Sophia's distinguished rector, Father Yanase, who had been Nobel Prize winner Eugene Wigner's protégé at Princeton. It was New Year's Day and on the following day we went to the Jesuit theologate Kamishakuje, in another borough of Tokyo, where we visited Bill Farge, later my colleague at Loyola in New Orleans. A few days after that, Bob North, an old classmate from St. Mary's, arrived at Sophia on one of his many world tours, together with the surprising good news of my being the recipient of Loyola's Dux Academicus award.

A few days later, I was astonished at the quality of Sophia's Symphony Orchestra in its rendition of the Brahms Second, not only because they did so well, but even more because Sophia has no music department, and its musicians are all strictly amateur. The quality surpassed any expectations. My classes included History of Music, History of Art, and Aesthetics. Since all lectures were in English, and extensively illustrated with slides, I must say that I found both semesters fascinating and found a way to add classes for anyone interested in such subjects. The student who participated most actively was Peter Morton (whose name had been Visochanea Meas in Cambodian).

Peter had suffered during Cambodia's most horrendous days, during which practically his entire family had been wiped out. In the midst of these terrible events, he walked almost aimlessly toward the Mekong River, helping young orphans find their way, until they crossed the river and reached a refugee camp. The Anglican chaplain there accepted him for baptism and renamed him "Peter" because "you are the leader of the twelve" (young abandoned orphans)! When I returned to Loyola, Peter secured permission from his adoptive parents to accompany me. Later he graduated from another university, married a wonderful girl, and is faithful about keeping up with his friends. He is active in lay ministry and refugee work, as one might expect.

That weekend Don Mason invited me to the Sophia community's vacation house, near Lake Hakone and within clear sight of incomparable Mount Fuji. We had managed to watch the U.S. Super Bowl on Japanese television, combining all manner of aesthetic experiences, as well as a Japanese TV documentary on Antarctica. The last weekend of January gave me a fright. The weather, while not exactly cold, was chilly and penetrating. Nothing that the university nurses could give me seemed to help, until at length someone reminded me that often Caucasian and Japanese medicines might not be universally effective. So I went to a Russian doctor, who prescribed the same medicines but with twice the dosage, explaining that very often we Caucasians needed double dosage. The new prescription worked perfectly.

My students, though English was their second or third language, had more problems with English spelling than with content. This I learned during the first test, when such orthographic rarities turned up as Stone Henji, Aclopolice, Colecium, Austraria, Mileapolice, and Cheops, identified as a "famous English artist."

A visit to St. Mary's Cathedral with Peter Morton showed me that the German bishops had been right in insisting that Tokyo's new cathedral be constructed in modern style, according to Japan's finest contemporary architects, rather than in facile pseudo-Gothic. We also did a splendid tour of Kamakura, one of Japan's greatest capitals, with the vast DaiButsu, the great

Buddha. Father Bihari, a Hungarian Jesuit and great friend, invited me to a superlative museum of western art, including works by Rembrandt, Cranach, and Murillo. We also witnessed the formal opening of one of Tokyo's largest department stores, where all the employees bowed solemnly in majestic welcome.

On March 12, I assisted at my first Japanese funeral, that of our colleague Father Heinrich Muller. Quite formal but simple, the service included the placing in the casket of flowers together with a photo of the deceased, and preparation for cremation, which is a normal procedure even among Catholics in Japan, given the paucity of burial space. On Saint Patrick's Day we enjoyed the ordination of young Valentine de Souza, originally from India but ordained for the Japanese province by the bishop of Tokyo. A few days later Don Mason and other good friends gave me a stunning sixty-fourth birthday party, quite impossible to describe. Some days later, Don Mason and Father Pittau (then president of Sophia University, but today first assistant to our superior general in Rome) invited me to lunch on the fortieth floor of the New Otani Hotel.

Then came the Man-kai, approximately a week dedicated to contemplation of the cherries of Japan, and on Sunday, April 1, a special Mass and lecture on the great Brazilian sculptor Aleijadinho (one of my special favorites), at the invitation of Father Lorscheider, brother of a Brazilian cardinal and cousin of another. A very warm reception.

On April 2, I flew to Nagasaki in the rain. There it was perfectly clear, and the hospitality of Father Clarkson and Brother García was simply perfect. Nagasaki is still a bit of Christianity in another land, with the oldest church in Japan (Oura Tenshudo), the Peace Park (Urakami), a Gaudí-style monument to the martyrs, and the Glover Mansion memorial to *Madame Butterfly.* A train through Kyushu brought my good friend Kanji Takeno; we met as planned at Yamaguchi, to visit the young martyrs' shrine in Tsuwano, festooned in cherry blossoms.

The story (true and well authenticated) of little Mori, when threatened with death by starvation and cold, ranks with the finest in hagiography. As her executioner saw her very near death, he played one more trump: "Dear Mori, don't you like cookies." "Of course I do, sir!" "Then deny Jesus and have all the cookies you want." "No sir, I want the cookies Jesus has in heaven. They're sweeter, you know!" These were almost her dying words, as later confessed by her executioner, who thereupon asked for baptism.

On April 5 we went on to Yamaguchi and the Xavier shrine-museum, Xavier being almost a national hero there, and in the evening on to Hiroshima, where I met my musician friend Father Benítez and New Orleans Jesuit Bill Farge. On the following day, with Benítez I visited the enchanted island of Miyajima—more cherries and deer in abundance. A funicular carries you up the mountain, where you choose between two routes upward: one, clearly marked, indicates that you will save eight seconds [*sic*]. The new cathedral is built of the debris from the atomic bomb.

There everyone remembers that when the atomic bomb fell, Father Arrupe, the future superior general of the Jesuits, then in Hiroshima, rushed down into the bomb site to rescue anyone he could. One was his friend (and mine) Jesuit Father Schippers, who often recounted the story of Arrupe's heroism. Up the hill, where the Jesuits have a place of contemplation, lies the grave of Father Tony Achee, a dear friend of many New Orleans Province Jesuits, who had been novice master and later tertian master. His picture is near the chapel door, together with those of "other saints," as the phrase goes.

The next day was Palm Sunday, when we had rain in abundance and a chance to visit Father Flynn in Kobe at the Jesuit school. Back on Tuesday we took a bullet train through Kyoto and its glories (old friends by now) in time for a very special dinner party given by Father Lobos for Don Mason and me, at perhaps the finest French restaurant I've ever experienced. On Good Friday, there was a wonderful liturgy followed by the most recent recording of the *Saint Matthew Passion*. On Holy Saturday in the evening, we celebrated the baptism of one of my students, Takino.

A few weeks before I went on my Nagasaki pilgrimage, on a very rainy day when classes were only half full, I noticed photographers meandering about my class taking pictures. No questions were asked, since we all thought they were simply student photographers. I had invited the students to sit down in a half circle and proceeded to chat with them about aesthetics—more a conversation than a conference.

On Easter Sunday, however, the Japanese version of *Playboy* came out with abundant photos of my class and me—fully clad, of course! The article pointed out what a friendly atmosphere reigned in Sophia International College, easily the finest in all Japan. Word quickly got around that my picture had been in *Playboy.* So, I thought it appropriate to forewarn my sister in St. Louis of this occurrence. I explained the entire story, adding the fine fact that in Japanese *Playboy* is pronounced "Prayboy." How appropriate!

In April we celebrated Father Lasalle's sixtieth jubilee as a Jesuit; he is the great authority in Japan on Christian Zen, but was quick to point out that he thought Father Dumoulin's book the best of all. The modesty of saints. Many of us are looking forward to the forthcoming book on the subject by Loyola's Ben Wren, the fruit of twenty-five years of work.

On Sunday, April 29, I received a visit from Pat and Barbara Berrigan, from Slidell, Louisiana. Since it was the emperor's birthday, after our own Mass we decided to go to the imperial palace. It was a very moving experience, particularly as we saw the future empress, who was an alumna of the Sacred Heart Nuns' university, where several of the sisters were friends and admirers of Sister Mary O'Callaghan, R.S.C.J., whom I have often mentioned.

During "Golden Week," I had the opportunity to show my series "Around the World in Eighty Slides" at the Hatano branch of Sophia, where Jerry Barry, originally from here in Louisiana, served as dean; today he is superior of the Jesuit community in Sophia. Another visit to inexhaustible Lake Hakone, surely one of the most beautiful in the world.

Back to Tokyo and an invitation to visit Don Klugston, our registrar at the International College. He gave me detailed directions to the apartment house where he lived, and fortunately I had the rare good sense to write them out in full. After an hour or so and several changes of metros, I reached the designated apartment house, very proud of myself. Then the trouble started. Don had forgotten to give the apartment number, supposing that I would be able to read the list of names, printed in clear Katakana script. Alas! The name "Klugston" did not fit into my Katakana.

So I stood staring at the mysterious list until a kindly Japanese tried to rescue me. By then I was so panicky as to forget Don's surname. How does one explain one's plight in a strange language, when the fault is entirely one's own? I tried and tried, talking about the International College of Sophia University, where my friend "Don" was registrar. After some time the mystery was solved, and my helper even escorted me up to the floor where Don lived. For once, my ineptitude provided cheery material for many belly laughs.

The next day my student Kanji Takeno announced that he had decided to come to Loyola (New Orleans) with me for his final years of photojournalism. This decision turned out happily, both for him and for me, and later for another Loyola student named Joyce, since he would eventually marry her here in Loyola's community chapel. I was particularly happy when Kanji's father visited me at Sophia. Both of us were obviously eager to make the right impression, perhaps all too eager. Mr. Takeno prepared a Western-style handshake, while I prepared a Japanese-style bow. Fortunately for us, Kanji was ready for the humorous situation and burst into a hearty laugh, which we joined. A sense of humor obviously solves many problems in intercultural relations. During the wedding, years later, I told the story in English, after Kanji prepared his parents in Japanese. Everyone seemed delighted. The point I made was obvious: a successful marriage is one in which each partner goes more than halfway.

As my months in Japan were coming to an end, I felt some need to play the tourist and visit the baroque city of Nikko, following the proverb "He who hasn't seen Nikko hasn't seen beauty." There, among other marvels, are the three famous monkeys, carved in wood on the wall of a temple, one holding hands over his eyes, another over his ears, a third over his mouth. The translation "See no evil, hear no evil, speak no evil" is more than a translation; it is an elaborate series of visual-auditory puns: "Mizaru, Kikazaru, Awazaru." *Saru* means "monkey" while the suffix *zaru* is the negation, equivalently "no" with "evil" simply understood.

Back in Tokyo I had the chance to hear perhaps the most exciting performance in my life of Bach's B-Minor Mass, directed by the renowned Bach expert Helmut Rilling. Since Rilling knew no Japanese and the Japanese singers and instrumentalists knew no German, they turned to Sophia University for a German Jesuit who knew music as well as both languages as a medium of communication.

Another pleasant surprise came when I discovered that the head of the United Nations University in Tokyo was former Rhodes Scholar James Hester, who had been in the Marine Corps with my Jesuit Provincial Bob Dieters and whom I have already mentioned in connection with an audience with Pope Paul VI. Father Yanase, president of the university, invited the three of us to a luncheon in his private dining room at Sophia. We were delighted to learn that our Baptist friend Jim Hester's two daughters had finished at Sophia's International College. The luncheon became a counterpoint of reminiscences.

As a Gerard Manley Hopkins buff, I was invited to speak to the Tokyo Hopkins Society and decided to take as my theme the Anglo-Saxon monosyllables in Hopkins's poetic style. The one slight mishap on that occasion came when I arrived late for the talk, having failed to wind my watch. Fortunately the Japanese scholars laughed when I offered my apology: "Sorry, gentlemen, you see my watch is only a Swiss watch!" They were also gracious enough to publish my talk in their review, *Hopkins Research*. Other articles of mine that appeared in Tokyo included one translated into Japanese titled "Changing Race Relations in the American South" and another in the English-language *Sophia Review* on the Jesuit painter-missioner Castiglione.

Perhaps the high point of my Sophia experience came when one of the founders of Sophia, Father Rogendorff, and two other leading German Jesuit scholars came over to the English-speaking corner of our Jesuit recreation room and formally invited me to remain permanently at Sophia University. The honor overwhelmed me, but apparently not to the point where I retained no residual common sense. After some reflection, I thanked them profusely, but explained that I was much too old ever to master Japanese, and this would mean feeling forever a foreigner from the moment I stepped out of the Jesuit community there. Comparing notes with other Americans stationed in Japan, I believe my decision was correct.

A comparable high point came some days later when the film about the Jesuit Reductions of Paraguay, which Bobby McCown and I had made some months before I left for Japan, finally arrived in Tokyo. The Jesuit community could not have

been more hospitable in their reception of our film, as I registered in my diary for July 5: "Paraguay film for Sophia community: what a reaction!" During the remaining days of the
semester, a number of professors showed the film to their
classes, with almost equal enthusiasm registered.

I was thrilled when the dean of Sophia International College
invited me to give the baccalaureate talk at graduation, especially since several of my students were to be present. I tried to
weave a number of Japanese proverbs into my text, wonderful
words of traditional wisdom taught me by a student, Toshi Doi,
who has now published a number of poems in the *New Orleans
Review.* On July 10, at seven o'clock in the morning, more than
half of the Jesuit community of Sophia gathered at the back door
of our community house to wish me "sayonara"; this was,
indeed, the most surprising and delightful treat of my whole
Tokyo experience, since Jesuits as a group usually do not rise so
early and never without some obligation.

———

The Takenos drove me to the airport, far out of town, and my
plane at length took off for Bangkok. There Peter and Sue
Morton welcomed me and escorted me to Xavier Hall, where I
had a number of friends of different nationalities. That night we
showed the film about the Jesuit Reductions of Paraguay, as
indeed I did on my trip home whenever an English-speaking
audience seemed willing to see it.

Following lunch on the Mekong, with Laos just across, we
met some people from New Orleans, and spent a day and a half
crossing Thailand, elephants and all. Back to Bangkok, then to
the crowded airport for my plane to Jakarta. Unsurprisingly it
was delayed. When it finally took off, I was sitting next to a
Muslim from Bangladesh, who asked if beef was the same as
pork. I assured him it was not. As a devout Muslim, he wanted to
be sure. So I tasted his plate and assured him that as a religious
person I would most certainly not want him to commit a sin
against his conscience. We then listened together to Beethoven's
Leonore Overture #3 and Brahms' *Haydn Variations,* both in a
radio broadcast of excellent recordings. Somehow Europe and
Asia came neatly together in music.

Exhausted, we reached Jakarta, and I went to the Jesuit house there. Since Indonesia is more than 95 percent Muslim, I was assured that I needn't be worried about getting up on time: the *muezzins* would make sure of that! I was more interested in seeing Jogjakarta, Borobudur, and Prambanan than Jakarta, which seemed an oversized, almost featureless metropolis offering hardly any reason to stay longer than necessary. When I reached the ancient capital, Jogjakarta, I felt vindicated.

Father Koengono, whom I had known at Sophia and who had frequently insisted that I come to Indonesia, met me together with Jim Spillane, an economist and old friend from the New England Jesuit Province. Jim took me to visit some friends from Louisiana, the Tillmans, and we spent hours reminiscing about Loyola and USL (where my dad had taught) and old friends. That night Jim urged me to go with him to the great gamelan concert, the actor being one of the finest. Even so, after some four hours of unintelligible beauty, amazing skill, and remarkable complexity, I felt fit for nothing but bed. Jim made sure that I had a cassette of the great gamelan tradition (which, as all musicians know, strongly influenced Debussy).

The next day was Sunday, and I was awed by the attendance and participation of ever so many young Indonesians at various Masses. Apparently, as a rule Indonesian Muslims are not violently anti-Christian, even allowing some conversions. Both the diocesan seminaries and the religious orders are burgeoning with vocations. The next morning I visited the large diocesan seminary directed by Father Koengono and the stunning Prambanan Hindu temples nearby.

But the incomparable treat of Indonesia, Borobudur (the name had constituted our greeting every time we met during those last months at Sophia), was reserved for the following day. Until the present century this greatest monument of Indonesian art was virtually unknown, having been so cluttered with debris that it looked like yet another hill. Though it is a structure of steps, its general outline matches that of a dome, the dome being understood as a *stupa* or skin. There were once 505 sculptured bas-relief figures of the Buddha on the open terraces, all of this designed as a mandala, a symbol of the total human self or of the universe. Clearly one of the greatest works in all Buddhist art.

Philippines Airways Service gave me the chance to be reunited happily with old and dear friends Father Torralba and four other Jesuits with whom I had studied theology, and Father Rey Garcia, a graduate nurse who had worked with lepers before joining our New Orleans Province. As I write this, Rey is at present working in Miami, though always most welcome when he has a chance to visit us in New Orleans. His father had been a doctor but had already died when I visited the family in Manila. According to them, Rey, though only seven years old, had fearlessly faced the Japanese soldiers as they threatened the family. He managed to persuade them that doctors ought to be allowed to live, in order to help other people. No one who knows Rey will doubt the veracity of the story. Manila and other parts of the Philippines are endlessly interesting to anyone who has ever been associated with Catholic missions, especially those of the Jesuits. The fine scholars at the Ateneo in Manila, like Fathers Bulatao, Arevalo, John Carroll, John Doherty, and others, are special lights in today's theological world. I particularly enjoyed meeting Jim Reuter, whose life had been repeatedly threatened and who brought me to meet some of the Muslim rebels, who were willing to negotiate only with him among non-Muslims. Jim is a great peacemaker, indeed, and a hero to many Filipinos—and the principal subject of an article in the *New Yorker.*

Rey Garcia's family drove me to the Rizal Park, Mariangmakiling, and Tagaytai, which overlooks the Taal volcanic lake, while Rey himself was able to show me some of the most tragically undeveloped parts of the country and to help me understand what was ahead after the Marcos disaster. From the Manila airport I flew to Guam, where I met Neil Poulin, also a Jesuit, and several Peace Corps personnel and seminarians.

It proved very exciting to move on to see Brother Terry Todd on Truk, and with Terry's help to cross the vast lagoon over to Fafen Island, where the family of his buddy Francis lived. Toward the middle of the lagoon we stopped, and Terry asked me if I'd like to see the Japanese navy. "Where?" I asked. "Look straight down," Terry directed. There, hundreds of feet below the surface, in clear water one could discern the remains of many Japanese war ships, sunk during the war. Meantime, I realized, the Japanese seemed to have won the war, since almost every car or truck or other vehicle in those islands bore

Japanese trademarks, even at a time before Japanese products had earned their present worldwide reputation for excellence.

On Francis's island we met his dignified father, a veritable paterfamilias, and went to pray at his grandmother's deathbed. The children, meanwhile, seeing Terry and me, felt a bit like the disciples who were unclad and hastily put on vestigial clothes! Back at home, we celebrated the Mass of Saint Ignatius—it was his feast day—with Jesuit Bishop Marty Neylon, whom I had known in New York when he was novice master—a charming person, indeed. I offered, and they accepted a showing of our film on the Jesuit Reductions of Paraguay. It was received most warmly.

The next morning Terry, Fran Hezel, and I drove to the airport. There a total stranger gave me a parcel to give to his son on the next island, Ponape. This informal way of trusting strangers struck me as very beautiful and Christian and proved far simpler than I anticipated. There's an informal system of communications on those Pacific islands that seems to work without a hitch.

We crossed the International Dateline at Majuro, thus being provided with two Saint Ignatius days in one year! I had already been on United States soil, but felt even more so after arriving in Los Angeles, where two wonderful friends, Chuck and Bernice Medinnis, met me and escorted me to their home, where we had a great reunion of several old friends. The following day Bernice drove me to the fabulous Getty Museum and yet another reunion of old friends. I was at last truly back home.

Chapter Sixteen

At Asunción's airport, a Paraguayan farewell from seminarians and friends, including Gisella Von Tümen, patron of the arts (far left); *Jesuits Charlie Thibodeaux* (my left), *and Father Superior Escobar* (far right).

Disappearing
below the Equator

Asunción, Paraguay, 1980–89

It was the Paraguayan provincial, Father Gonzáles Dorado, who
had planted the seed of my becoming a missioner to Paraguay,
or at least of my inviting other people from the New Orleans
Province to do so. If I had my doubts, it was for many of the
same reasons for which I had declined the invitation to enter the
Japanese mission a year earlier, although in this case there was
no language problem. Was it or was it not a divine inspiration?
Was it simply sheer vanity or arrogance? And was it something I
had the stamina for, or just an idle dream?

In such a quandary, a Jesuit has a readily available solution:
to make an Ignatian retreat and in the process, with God's grace,
to try to discern the matter according to God's will. Even the
fact that Father Arrupe, the superior general of the Jesuits at the
time, had asked for volunteers for Paraguay did not clinch the
discernment. Just because something is good doesn't necessar-
ily mean that God has chosen you to do it. The parable of the
foolish person who wants to build a tower without reckoning
expense or feasibility should make one hesitate (Lk 14:28-30).
It did me. Yet, finally, with proper guidance and time and prayer,
I believe I came to the right decision. The decision seems so simple in retrospect, now that I know how much I have come to
love those years and the people in Paraguay. I had hoped to stay
for five years, but stayed for nine, and would probably have
stayed longer save that Father Edmundo Rodriguez, then provincial, saw that my health was deteriorating rather seriously. He
virtually ordered me to come home—which simplified that particular decision.

Regarding my decision to go to Paraguay, I didn't want to
make a general announcement, for reasons that may not be

obvious. There was one special person, however, I did want to tell—Eddie Fernandez, then about to graduate from Loyola and thinking of a possible vocation to the Jesuits. One evening he and I went to the Loyola pub to have a beer. It seemed the right moment to tell him, since I knew he was debating whether or not to become a Jesuit. When I broke my news to him, he hit the table gently, and said quite simply: "If you can go to Paraguay, I can go to Grand Coteau." In the New Orleans Province, to go to Grand Coteau means to enter the novitiate. Plainly this was not the first time he had thought of entering, but it may have been somewhat decisive.

Meantime, I had discovered that three other men from our province had been accepted for Paraguay: Don Bahlinger, Frank Renfroe, and Charlie Thibodeaux. All were good friends and ideal persons to make a support group. Further, they had all been students of mine back in the juniorate and were always considerate and friendly. They were also more robust than I— which added to my feeling of security. Father Stahel, our provincial at that time, was most generous in his praise of our decision, though we didn't have the ceremony once common and now frequent, of receiving the "missionary cross." Simplicity probably seemed what was called for, and we liked it that way.

Charles Thibodeaux, one of the four of us who arrived in 1980 and one of the two still privileged to be working there (the other being Don Bahlinger), is surely one of the most beloved Jesuits of the New Orleans and the Paraguay Provinces. While Charlie's Spanish is fairly original, and his Guaraní more so, even his French and English give proof, if proof were needed, that the language of the heart is far more important than any other.

Though Charlie's branch of the family is more closely related to Ben and Clare's branch, I like to insist that we are all cousins. We call one another "cousin," using the French pronunciation. We are all equally proud of our Cajun ancestry. I've been blessed by the opportunity to be closely associated with Cousin Charles, both in Louisiana and in Paraguay. Furthermore, Charlie's sister, a nun, taught in the same school as my mother, and they were good friends even before I first knew Charlie when he entered the Jesuit novitiate at Grand Coteau.

Several years later, when Charlie was studying philosophy in Indiana, I was suddenly called to his mother's deathbed in

Carencro, not far from Grand Coteau where I was teaching at the time. While working with her husband in the fields, she had had a stroke. They both spontaneously said their prayers together; then Mr. Thibodeaux carried her into the house. When I arrived, we gave her the last sacraments, then started the rosary; when we came to the glorious mystery of the Resurrection, Mrs. Thibodeaux died peacefully.

Bishop Jeanmard, who deeply admired the Thibodeaux family and was aware that they had two members in religious orders, said the Mass of the day, appropriately the Feast of the Epiphany, explaining why he felt justified in doing so. Our juniorate choir sang the *Missa Papae Marcelli* by Palestrina, "Gloria" included, in the spirit of the Epiphany, "the manifestation" of Christ—with Bishop Jeanmard's glad approval.

Years later, when Charlie was ordained and planning to celebrate his first Mass in Carencro, he invited me to give the sermon. I realized that it would be appropriate to give it in both French and English, and decided to preach on the gorgeous stained glass windows in the church—celebrating the life of Saint Peter, one of the first priests. When the Mass was over, I was chatting with Charlie's father, hoping for a compliment. He smiled, said he liked the sermon, but was glad that there were only twenty windows! I suppose that's the type of honesty one can expect from one's "cousins."

Don Bahlinger, though not technically a Cajun, belongs to one of those great German families, thoroughly assimilated into Cajun Louisiana, which have given many spiritual leaders to our state. It was a blessing for me to be back from Paraguay in the early 1990s at the time Mrs. Bahlinger (nee Fabacher) went to God. Both she and her husband had received high papal honors. Don arrived in time for the funeral, attended by Bishop Stanley Ott and a host of other priests in Baton Rouge. Bishop Ott insisted that Don be the celebrant and give the homily—though one would have expected the bishop himself to do it. At the end of the Mass, Bishop Ott explained why he felt that the exception was appropriate: this is such an exceptional Catholic family, he understandably stated, with several priests and other religious serving the church in South Louisiana. There was no way that one could disagree with that assessment. The bishop himself was to die just a couple of years later, mourned by everyone.

Don was and is a great leader in Paraguay. One day he asked me to type out a list of his activities (my facility at the typewriter being something of a legend); the list went beyond two pages. Following the ouster of Stroessner, Don could be more and more overt in his criticism of the government—as often appeared in the international press. One of his most important gestures was his fasting until the new government provided needed resources for the hospital in San Ignacio, which had been only a facade with no real facilities. Word got around the country, and even abroad, and in a matter of a few days the hospital was doing what it was supposed to be doing—saving lives.

The fourth "apocalyptic horseman" of the 1980 group of missioners for Paraguay was not a Cajun in any sense at all, much as we'd love to claim him as one. Frank Renfroe had been in the U.S. Navy for a while, before entering the Jesuits. He hailed from Dallas, enjoyed a splendid football career in high school, and was a successful teacher in his old school before volunteering for Paraguay. His first year there was tough, plagued as he was by a reluctant stomach.

Then Frank was sent to the Paraguayan mission in Posadas, Argentina, across the great Paraná River, now linked to Paraguay's Encarnación by a three-kilometer bridge named after Saint Roque González de Santa Cruz, who founded both cities. It was not long before word reached us in Asunción that Frank was himself again. Every time I saw the distinguished senior Jesuit Fernando Maria Moreno, who had held every post of importance in the Society from Spain to Argentina, Father Moreno made no secret of the fact that he regarded Father Renfroe as the finest superior he had ever worked under. This was doubly impressive, given Father Moreno's unimpeachable qualifications as a person of discernment. The rest of us "Cajuns" couldn't have been happier for Frank.

To resume the narrative of our passage to Paraguay, we stopped in Brazil to see our fellow Jesuits from the New Orleans Province—Brother Coco and Father Dougherty in Campinas, Fathers Rahm, Tiblier, and Vessels in São Paulo. I went on to Asunción almost immediately and was met by several fathers and scholastics, who whisked me to the Juniorate House, Colegio Técnico Javier, in the parish of Trinidad, Asunción. It so happened that I was the only one of the four men from the Province who had a definite status in Paraguay (as teacher in the juniorate).The other three, perhaps because of their greater versatility and wider previous experience, were given more time for decision making about their apostolates. Don Bahlinger, for example, had already worked as a missioner in Central America, and Charlie Thibodeaux in several mission-like parishes in South Louisiana. Meantime, there was a good deal of work to be done, papers to be filled out and the like, since Paraguay under Stroessner was hardly a free country.

Several of the juniors I had already met either at Encarnación or later, at San Ignacio, during the making of our film. Hugo Maidana and José Arias stood out in my memory, and that both pleased and surprised them. One of the young men, whose name I can't recall and who has since left the Society, asked me somewhat bluntly: "Why, really, did you come to Paraguay?" I'm not sure what reply he expected. I reflected for a moment and answered honestly:"I came in order to disappear." He looked puzzled, reflected, then smiled as he grasped my meaning. None of us had come in order to gain anything (except the happiness of being of some help to our brothers), but it might have seemed boastful to say that. A line I dimly remembered from Saint Vincent de Paul (in the great movie on his life *Monsieur Vincent*) came to my help.Vincent was telling the young nuns who were going out to do charity:"Sisters, when you do works of charity, do them in such a way that the poor will not hate you for it!"

It took a while for me to get settled and would have taken longer were it not for the initiative and energy of Carlos Benítez, whom we called in Jesuit jargon "the beadle"—sort of a corporal or sergeant in charge of communications between staff and fellows. Some beadles are obviously more generous than others; luckily for me Carlos was what one might call a super-beadle. The building I lived in was comfortable by Paraguayan standards, but with neither fans nor heating nor hot-and-cold water in individual rooms, though such luxuries existed in the showers. From my window I could see a large meadow, green even in winter.

In a nearby room lived Father Salvador Loring, dean of our juniorate, a great Spanish scholar, and the most generous of people. Oddly, to my way of thinking, Salvador spoke not a word of English, though his ancestors had gone from Spain to Boston! Later I asked Bostonian Father Leonard if he had ever heard of Lorings in Boston. "Of course," he replied, "my first teacher was a very fine person named Miss Loring!" Several New England Jesuits had known chaps named Loring at Harvard; their investigations pointed to a Salvador Loring who had become a Jesuit, but they didn't know where he had gone after that. I was able to put them in touch and served as a sort of translator. Something parallel happened with another Paraguayan friend and famed writer, José Appleyard, who had a relative, also in Boston and a Jesuit, named Joseph Appleyard, whom I had known for some thirty years. Such coincidences are always both fascinating and amusing.

Father Loring was more than a great Spanish scholar, he was the most generous of helpers. Realizing that I would improve my Spanish only by writing as much as possible, I asked if he would mind correcting my efforts. Delighted, he replied. Several times a week I imposed on him (though he never seemed to realize that it was an imposition). He went over my trivia carefully but mercifully.

One day he surprised me by suggesting that I ought to submit something to one of the Asunción daily newspapers. It was a whimsical piece about "dogs," in the literal sense. Paraguayans seem to treat dogs less finicky than Anglos often do. They seem to recognize that dogs are dogs, to be neither cruelly nor indulgently treated. My spoofing article, based on fact, was titled "Quiero a los Perros Paraguayos" ("I Like Paraguayan Dogs"). The reaction was sensational, and several newspapers asked for articles on dogs. The next article was titled "Misa del Gallo con Gallo," which means literally "Mass of the Rooster with Rooster," but in idiomatic Spanish means instead "Midnight Mass with Rooster," "Rooster" in this case being the name of the Jesuit community's dog.

But why was our dog called "Gallo" or "Rooster"? Father Loring explained that it was because as a pup the dog lived in a chicken coop, thus ironically meriting the nickname "Rooster." Gallo loved to traipse about the grounds, especially at night. The midnight Mass I was to celebrate was at the nuns' chapel of the large hospital nearby. When Gallo and I arrived there, Gallo entered the sanctuary, sniffed the crib, or *nacimiento,* apparently approved of it, then ensconced himself like a bishop in full panoply. I must admit I was tempted to stress the joke on Gallo's name, but since the nuns didn't know me very well, I was a bit timid about that. Besides, I didn't want to have them laugh just before or during my first attempt at a sermon in Guaraní—which I had laboriously prepared, helped by the Paraguayan juniors.

After the article on Gallo appeared, photographers from several newspapers appeared at Javier (the name of our school, and by extension of our juniorate) to get pictures of our dog and the dog's "biographer." For some weeks, it may be said, Gallo was the most popular dog in Asunción, and for some months people I knew only slightly would ask, "How's Gallo?" as if this were the only possible topic of conversation.

Most of my everyday work was quite unspectacular—the task of teaching seminarians, mainly Jesuits, and also, as word got around, men from other religious orders as well. It was enjoyable and fulfilling, however, much like the years I had spent in Grand Coteau.

Shortly after my arrival in Asunción, it was a particular delight, and a surprise, to see Kanji Takeno again. I last spoke of him when mentioning his wedding to Joyce in New Orleans. He had headed for Ecuador by plane, then, almost running out of money, decided to make the rest of the trip to Asunción by bus even though it was now midwinter. Another interracial surprise visit came from Carl Riley, one of the finest flautists I know of his generation and a most versatile composer. How proud I was to have as a close friend the first African American our scholastics in Paraguay came to know well.

One of the promises that I hoped to follow through on while I was in Paraguay I made to Father Jim Carter, president of Loyola University. Before I left New Orleans, Jim asked me to get in touch with Archbishop Helder Câmara and to invite him to accept an honorary doctorate from the university. Realizing how far Recife was from Asunción, I'm sure I qualified my promise by saying I would if I could. It was an agreeable surprise, then, when I saw Father Ed Dougherty, a fellow Southern Jesuit, while I was making my annual retreat in Campinas, Brazil, and discovered that all the bishops of the country were gathered at the Jesuit retreat house in Itaici, not far from Campinas. Ed was kind enough to offer to drive me there and make sure I met the famed archbishop.

This all seemed too good to be true, but I gladly accepted. As we approached the immense retreat house, I felt twinges of fear, since the church was not in the good graces of the government at that time. "Not to worry," Ed assured me, and without any hesitation he led me into the cathedral-size chapel. Mass was just about over, but with his considerable height Ed was able to spot the archbishop amid the hundreds of other bishops. "We'll catch him when they start moving out," Ed whispered confidently.

No one stopped us, probably because we were dressed in clerical garb, and in any case most of the bishops seemed to know Ed from his apostolic work in the region. He presented me to Archbishop Helder Câmara, who thereupon invited me to join him at supper. I had never (except at Vatican Council II) seen so many bishops together, most of them dressed informally and everyone seeming cordial. I explained to the archbishop what Jim Carter had invited him to do. "Do you think it's worth doing, Father?" the archbishop asked in total humility. "I believe it is, Your Excellency," I replied, "I believe it might edify a lot of our North American bishops to read your message to us." With perfect simplicity, the archbishop then accepted and asked about several details.

Then we chatted with several dozen bishops, including the two Lorscheiders (one the brother, the other the cousin of my Jesuit colleague at Sophia University in Tokyo), all of whom seemed models of apostolic simplicity. When I stepped out to visit the bookshop, a frail-looking young man in blue jeans joined me and spoke cordially. "My name is Casaldáliga," he smilingly explained, "what's yours?" "Mine's McNaspy, from New Orleans," I replied, then asked with a gasp, "Are you the famous Monseñor Casaldáliga?" "Not famous," he corrected me instantly, "Notorious maybe."

Monseñor Casaldáliga was the young bishop of São Felix, a fearless champion of civil rights. On Monday, October 11, 1976, he had gone with Father João Bosco Burnier, Brazilian Jesuit novice master, to police headquarters in Ribeira do Garcas. They wanted to inquire about persons detained by the military police, especially two women prisoners who had, in fact, been tortured without trial. Both Casaldáliga and Burnier were threatened by the police, and Father Burnier was struck by a young policeman and shot in the head. He was dead within a few hours.

I took the occasion to ask Bishop Casaldáliga about Father Burnier's martyrdom. He replied, "I believe the police thought they were killing me when they shot my friend. As an older man he was presumed to be the bishop!" In the funeral ceremony, Bishop Casaldáliga referred to his murdered Jesuit friend as "a martyr for Christ."

I suppose that every missionary or Peace Corps person, however well prepared, still has a lot to learn when entering a new world. I surely did, however ready I thought I was, having visited Paraguay several times and having read a number of books before taking the definitive leap. Nothing prepared me, though, for the day a tiny girl stopped me on the street and asked if she could tickle my double chin. Even before I could say "yes," she had tickled it and exclaimed, "Qué suave!" ("How soft!"). Granted, her older sister seemed mortified, but I don't think she really was. And then the time that a young couple came to see me and offered a new pair of socks, I wondered why. They explained that they needed an old pair of unwashed socks "from a priest" to put on their baby's head to save the baby from God-knows-what ailment. Such interesting instances could be multiplied, like the time a proud Paraguayan tossed his son into the air during the "peace" ceremony at Mass.

Many missioners to Sri Lanka and other countries in the Third World like to share experiences of bizarre events like exorcisms. The most frightening occasion for me was the time a young man asked me to come with him to help his mother, who was convinced she was possessed by the devil. Whether or not it was indeed a case of diabolical possession, the experience is one I'll never forget. It was a dark, stormy night in Asunción; I had tripped over barbed wire on my way to the Church of Trinidad, where I was substituting for the regular pastor. At the end of the Mass I noticed that my knees were hurting (this was probably the beginning of my bout with arthritis), but I was met at the door of the sacristy by a well-dressed young man who asked if I could visit his mother who was near death. "Of course," I replied.

I expected the young man to have a car, but he led me to the public bus instead. We took the one leading to the edge of the city, past the Botanical Gardens. He mentioned, as casually as he could, his mother's conviction that she was possessed. I recalled the prohibition against performing exorcisms without the explicit permission of the bishop and wondered what I should do. I must admit that I began praying with unusual fervor, and my efforts to make small talk met with little success. We reached the end of the bus line and stepped out into the night. It was still drizzling, and no city lights were visible.

We walked in the dark for some minutes, until he announced that we had reached his house. As we entered, we heard shouts of agony and then his mother cried out, "Don't come in here!" "Why not?" her son asked, as we went in. "Because the devil is here and has me in his fists!" shouted the terrified woman, trying to tear her hair out. It was almost as if the poor woman had seen *The Exorcist,* although of course she had seen neither that nor any other film. I was frightened and indeed prayed for help. "I don't believe the devil has you, Señora," I replied. "Why don't you?" she cried. Again a prayer for help, in silence, and I suddenly must have given the right answer: "Because Jesus has overcome the devil, and the devil can't possess you unless you want him to." I seemed myself to be shouting. This calmed the woman down. So I asked her, solemnly, "Do you prefer to go with Jesus or with the devil? Answer me!" "With Jesus," she cried out.

Relieved, I asked the whole family to repeat with her and with me: "I renounce the devil, and all his pomps and all his works. I am sorry for my sins, and I ask Jesus to forgive me and to save me from the devil." Then I recited the Our Father slowly, asking them to say it with me. I asked for some water, blessed it solemnly, and sprinkled it around the room very quietly. She had been baptized, I was informed, but no more. So I helped her to make the act of contrition, with the whole family, and then gave her absolution since she was obviously not far from death. She subsided into what seemed deep peace.

Her son and I left quietly, and he accompanied me to where the last bus would be. Thanking me profusely, he promised to keep in touch. The next morning, in fact, he came to Javier and, sobbing, announced, "Mama died last night, Father, but she was at peace. We all want to thank you." "When do you want the funeral?" I asked. "We're too poor to have a funeral," the young man replied, "we'll just put her in the ground." "Oh, no," I insisted, "Your mother deserves better. Can you come to the church at about three o'clock, and we'll have a fitting funeral? It won't cost a thing, but it'll be most consoling."

Meantime I made it a point to tell my experience to Brother Pedro Herrans, a Jesuit from Spain who worked with the very poor and prayed with them often. "I know the case," Brother Pedro stated. "They would never let me into their house. Thank God you helped her." I invited Brother Pedro to go with me to the church before the designated time. "We'll give her the funeral of an archduchess!" I said smiling. The pastor was away on a visit to Spain, so we were in a position to do as we saw fit.

We brought out all the candles and vestments we could find. When the poor family arrived, we met them, escorted the little wooden box that served as a coffin up to the altar. Brother Pedro read a beautiful epistle, I the Gospel passage, and we did as lovely a ceremony as our gifts allowed. Our scholastics sang and read Holy Scripture, in Guaraní and Spanish. Everyone was at peace, even happy under the circumstances. No one blessed by being there will soon forget that beautiful afternoon in Trinidad parish.

You may be sure that word got around the poor area where the family lived, and I was often asked to give special blessings to the sick. Whether or not this had been an exorcism, as rumor had it, it surely was a benediction at least to me and to the people. Incidentally, as I was writing these recollections, I received a letter from Javier, telling me that Brother Pedro was in the process of building an infirmary for the Jesuits of the Paraguay Province.

It wasn't long before people in nearby barrios, as many perhaps as fourteen, began asking me for frequent Masses in homes or on streets. In fact, the parish priest soon had to intervene to save me, I believe, or at least to prevent certain barrios from becoming overprivileged, thus causing jealousies. I saw his point and tried to cooperate. He wisely allowed some exceptions, especially the Hogar de los Ancianos (roughly "the Old Veterans' Home"). This was something I felt unwittingly prepared for since for some years, in New Orleans, I had been offering Mass every Sunday at an analogous home and have gladly returned to it now that my stint in Paraguay is over. In both homes there were wonderful volunteers as well as professional helpers. Yet, the Hogar was surely very much poorer, at least in appearance, without central heating or air-conditioning (in that respect much like our own Jesuit houses in Asunción). Sunday after Sunday, for at least nine years, I went to the Hogar, coming to know some of the finest people I've ever known, both staff and patients.

A particular instance I should like to mention—the beautiful friendship between Sebastian and Patrocinio (whose surnames I can't recall, since we never used them). Patrocinio had lost both legs during the Chaco War, while Sebastian had been totally blind almost from birth. They seemed inseparable: Patrocinio practically lived in a wheelchair, while Sebastian had the strength to drive him anywhere, provided Patrocinio guided him. In their complementarity, they reminded me of two "ancient" Jesuits I had known at Grand Coteau, Fathers Pat Walsh and Cliff McLaughlin. They, too, were almost inseparable and, on one occasion, while walking in the meadows they became lost. Pat was not too strong mentally while Cliff, though quite blind, never lost his other faculties. Pat announced, "Cliff, I think we're lost." Cliff responded, "Don't worry, Patrick; you tell me what you see, and I'll tell you where we are!"

The experience of trying to teach one's own language to others can be less than easy. When the superior invited me to teach an English course to students in their last year of studies at Colegio Técnico Javier, I leapt to the challenge, only to discover that there were no textbooks and that the students were no more interested in English than in Sanskrit. This promised total disaster; yet refusing to face reality, I tried an experiment—teaching the ABCs of U.S. football and baseball. I was even more surprised to find out how little the students knew about these supremely North American sports, for example, the terms *down* and *strike* with their multiple meanings. Anyone born in the U.S. is at home with these concepts, even one as innocent of athletics as I am. But that made me all the more determined.

Basketball was simpler since it has become something of an international game. Even so, my class was losing games to other classes. So they asked me to be a sort of coach. I agreed, but finding that I had to leave Paraguay for a month or so, I simply wrote down "the" five principles of basketball. When I wrote *the,* I hadn't the slightest idea of what was to follow. Brazenly, however, I did type out "The first principle is to play as 'one' team, not five players." This "radical" idea turned them from a losing to a winning team and enhanced whatever legend I had become.

As sometimes happens, a tragedy galvanized our divided class into a unity. One afternoon, several Jesuit juniors came to my room with the dismal news: "A terrible accident! All your stu-

dents are dead or wounded!" I rushed downstairs and found
Father Mariano, who was principal of the school at the time. He
explained that though all of the students had been hurt, only
Celso Larosa was dead, crushed beyond recognition when the
public bus turned over. Without his wallet, he would have
remained unidentifiable. Mariano had to bear the tragic news to
Celso's widowed mother, who had been pinning all her family
hopes on what Celso would be after his graduation. The whole
class gathered at the wake, and some days later I was able to
offer a Mass for Celso, his family, and all his classmates. For several years, Celso's anniversary occasioned our main class
reunion.

Not long after arriving in Paraguay, I was invited to play
recordings of the Bach cantatas on various radio stations, thus
establishing something of a reputation in Asunción. The "quan-
tum leap," if such it was, came, however, with a visit to Paraguay
from Phil Bourret, Jesuit director of radio missions. Phil and I had
been friends since we met in Taiwan, and he had helped the
Franciscans get started on their Radio Caritas. "Don't you know
C. J. McNaspy?" he asked the Franciscan Brother, who replied
that he had heard of, but never met me. So Phil arranged the
meeting, and from then on I focused most of my radio work on
Radio Caritas, presenting all the Bach cantatas Sunday by
Sunday, with my translations into Spanish.

A great group of laymen did most of the work on Radio
Caritas. Jorge Bajac, a wonderful person with a lovely wife and
children, was the engineer with whom I specially worked. I was
somewhat concerned about his health, since it seemed to be
deteriorating at the time of my departure from Paraguay. One of
the finest services he and other young radio men did their country occurred during the coup that ousted Stroessner in favor of
his son-in-law Rodríguez. The only news medium people trusted
at the time was Radio Caritas, and it was uncanny to hear the
young announcers right in the midst of the coup, telling the
truth as they saw it, regardless of personal risk.

One thing led to another, and my radio programs occasioned
many invitations regarding music. The conservatory, or Ateneo
(Athenaeum), of Asunción did not take long to invite me to
teach music history, or whatever I cared to teach there. For a
while, at least, I found the experience fascinating, especially my

contacts with young Mennonites and other people dedicated to religious music, as well as with some Panamanians and people from other countries who had come to Paraguay to learn the Paraguayan harp. Of course, I couldn't help them with the Paraguayan harp, but I did give them an occasional home-away-from-home at Javier, where we could listen to recordings of great music.

The great Paraguayan guitar composer Agustín Barrios (who often used the Guaraní name "Mangorí"), born May 5, 1855, in San Juan Bautista (Misiones) near San Ignacio Guazú, died in San Salvador in 1944. A group of eager Asuncenos, to whom I gave informal lessons in music appreciation, came up with the idea of a monument to Barrios. "Do we really need a monument?" I protested. "Wouldn't it be better to spend the money promoting Barrios' music, with prizes for young performers?"

Another suggestion was to ask the government to put out a commemorative stamp in Barrios's honor. That wasn't hard to achieve since governments like to make money on stamps. What we hadn't anticipated, however, was that the government would make the stamp prohibitively expensive, missing our point entirely. We received official letters of gratitude, but not a single stamp. Finally, José Fernández and I went to the post office and succeeded in securing a stamp—one stamp—for each of the eleven members of the committee that had organized the entire program. Such parsimony, not to say stinginess, was, to put it mildly, shocking.

I can't recall Oswaldo's surname, but his Christian name is, in fact, as unforgettable as he is. The youngest of a large family, Oswaldo was about ten years old and somewhat slight. It was with me that he made his first trip ever into downtown Asunción. His parents had no objection to my introducing him to the marvels of Asunción, least of all to Radio Caritas. Jorge Bajac, the engineer who did my programs, adopted Oswaldo and introduced him to the marvels of radio. One day I felt it would be good for Oswaldo to see his first movie—*Star Wars*. Imagine, if you can, the impression made by a wide-screen presentation of such an exciting movie, when the nearest thing to a movie Oswaldo had seen previously was something on a black-and-white television set.

Of course, I hadn't adopted him; Oswaldo had adopted me. At the Hogar de los Ancianos, where he dropped in for Mass, he realized that I needed help, whatever that might mean. For several years Oswaldo never missed Sunday, though signs of weariness ultimately began to show. Meantime, of course, there were other compensations. For example, when my friends from the German embassy gave a party presenting Father Blanch's and my new book *Lost Cities of Paraguay,* Oswaldo came, dressed like an ambassador, and solemnly greeted all comers. It was his night of glory.

While hardly gifted in matters academic, young Oswaldo showed remarkable sensitivity toward his elders, especially his grandmother. One evening he came to Javier to express his fear that she might be dying. "What do your parents say?" I asked. "I don't think they understand, but Grandma is surely dying. Can you come and give her the holy oils?" It was hard to resist Oswaldo's urgency. So, I accompanied him to the tiny hut where she lived and found her apparently as feeble as Oswaldo thought. We sang the *"Ore poriahu vereko"* ("Lord, have mercy on us"), and I gave her the sacrament of the sick and viaticum. She seemed very much consoled, and so were we. The next morning Oswaldo arrived again to announce his grandmother's passing from this world.

Oswaldo knew everybody in the barrio, and not least the brothers and sisters of Hector, to whom he introduced me. It occurred to me that Hector probably had never heard of his famous namesake. So I asked him if he knew he was named after a very famous warrior. "No," he replied, hopefully. "Well, then," I ventured, "tomorrow afternoon, at three o'clock, bring your friends to the porch of our library, and I'll read to you all about Hector." That proved the excitement of the month. Imagine, again, a dozen or so young Paraguayans, who had no idea of what a library was, listening to a "Yanqui" declaiming, in Spanish, the marvels of Hector and Andromache and little Astyanax, with whom they identified most fully. Had I been able to sing, I could have imagined myself chanting the sixth book of the *Iliad,* with some of the gusto of ancient Homer singing to barefoot kids of his own century. The experience seemed to prove to me what we classicists so often claim; namely, that the classics enjoy a certain universality and immortality.

Mentioning the German embassy brings happily to mind several of my best friends in Asunción—Clemens von Thuemen and his lovely wife, Gisela. Both friends, noble in every sense of the word, were the soul of generosity. Clemens, a Graf (a German or Austrian count), who had barely escaped Hitler's odium, arrived in South America penniless but, by sheer industriousness, had founded an important plastics factory; Gisela was a direct descendant of a line of Lutheran pastors and bishops going back to Johannes Kepler.

The von Thuemens are among the most cordial and cultured friends I have ever known and certainly among those I most miss in Paraguay. Their friendship was far from exclusive, embracing pastors, nuns, priests, musicians, painters, poets, journalists, and anyone you may think of as interesting and especially good. When their son Florian was preparing for confirmation at the hands of Pastor Ihle, he was spontaneously good enough to come to Javier and personally invite me to be present. Pastor Ihle, a friend of Father Blanch and other Jesuits involved in social work, made something of a fuss over my arrival, wondering aloud, "What would Saint Ignatius think of this?" "I hope he'd approve," I countered, almost giggling.

During the year 1985, a multiple centenary (Bach, Scarlatti, Handel, and the great Lutheran Schuetz), Clemens and Gisela asked me to speak of the big four and offered their home for lectures and receptions. I can't think of how many birthday parties they gave me. I was particularly delighted to be able to celebrate Mass at Clemens's factory, principally for his workmen, almost all of whom were Catholic. He was radiant on that and other occasions. It later was a great joy, too, to receive Gisela in Rome, and to visit the papal gardens together with her and Ernie Burrus. Her obvious veneration for Saint Ignatius kept her meditating at his altar for something like an hour after we had finished Mass.

The celebrations of the anniversary of Domenico Zipoli, 1688–1726, chief musician of the Jesuit Reductions, were climaxed by several presentations of the Mass of Zipoli, in both Paraguay and Argentina, sponsored by the group known as Los Amigos de Zipoli. Friends not only of Zipoli, but of Jesuits and persons of culture generally, they included Maria Alicia Parkerson (wife of the United States Information Service director), Gisela von Thuemen, Carlos Seoane Urioste (important Bolivian choral director), Luis Szarán, Isis de Bárcena, José María Blanch, and representatives of Fundación Alemana Paracuaria,

Embajada de España en el Paraguay, Obispado de Asunción, and Obispado de Encarnación. No wonder that when I met someone leaving Paraguay for Europe and asked him what he had enjoyed most during his stay in Paraguay, he replied instantly, "The Mass of Zipoli."

Alicia and Philip Parkerson, together with their children and Alicia's parents, were all exceptional friends and with the years have become even more so. A great moment in our lives was the First Communion of Alicia's daughter, also named Alicia. Gisela had suggested that I attend. I presented myself to the parish priest, who very kindly invited me to administer Alicia's First Communion and to give communion as well to her mother and her grandmother, another Alicia! Alicia Parkerson arranged a wonderful seventieth birthday celebration for me, having a string quartet directed by Luis Szarán play a special composition written for the occasion. It made me feel almost like an Ester-házy, patron of Haydn. Alicia, being a wizard in the kitchen, made perhaps the finest jambalaya (a Louisiana dish) I've ever eaten, even though it was her first attempt.

I mentioned earlier that after some years of helping me at Sunday Masses, Oswaldo began to show signs of wearying. Meantime, another youngster, Adolfo, not quite as bright as Oswaldo, seemed to want to take over. When I suggested this to Oswaldo, instead of being annoyed he was obviously pleased. He was reaching the age when altar boys often are more inclined to girl watching, whereas Adolfo preferred the dignity of a place of honor at the altar. Moreover, Adolfo enjoyed trying hard to help me from the first moment.

Saturday morning he invariably arrived at Javier looking for "Padre Clemente," though later he began calling me, as did some of the scholastics, "Joven Clemente." In fact, as soon as he appeared in the quadrangle, the word would spread: "Adolfo is here! Tell Joven Clemente!" Adolfo had no problem whatsoever entertaining me. As the first fireflies of the year appeared, he announced their names in Guaraní—*muah,* with a strongly nasalized "ah."

Then before long everyone in the barrio got to know him and show him the respect he felt was his due. They enjoyed it, and he enjoyed it and, of course, so did I. It was a joy to get to know Adolfo's family and friends. His grandmother was especially proud of him, and he more than reciprocated, speaking of her every time I met him. He looked forward to Holy Week as the special opportunity for his grandmother and other relatives to meet his friend "Pa'í Clemente." In fact, he used a term for our annual get-together which he seemed to save for that exclusive event— "an audience with Pa'í Clemente."

All Saints Day is, in some ways, the principal feast in Paraguay, a country where power seems especially important, and God's best friends, the saints, are reckoned most powerful. On particular saints' days, the statue is moved from house to house, followed by a special Mass. The Feast of Our Lady of Caacupé is the biggest Marian day in Paraguay, overshadowing the Feast of the Immaculate Conception, which falls on the same date. I almost had to quarrel with the *ABC-Color* editor to get permission to include Our Lady of Guadalupe with Our Lady of Caacupé, as though they were rivals and not the same person. At my first barrio, Virgin of Fatima, I was privileged to celebrate Mass together with the archbishop, at the insistence of the pastor himself, on the Feast of Our Lady of Fatima. They use a lovely word for blessing a church or a house or whatever—*mongaraí,* which means basically "to baptize."

Good Friday ceremonies last some five hours, especially when the Estacioneros come through—singers with a remarkable repertory of very old unwritten traditional music. And, of course, Easter takes on a special Marian meaning, as everyone celebrates the Tupasy Nuvaiti—the meeting with God's Mother. (In the *Spiritual Exercises,* Saint Ignatius, while admitting that this meeting is not mentioned in the Bible, nonetheless adds, "Are you also without understanding?") Processions and fireworks are all part of popular religion, the more the merrier.

The first week of summer vacation that we Southerners from Brazil and Paraguay managed to spend together was at a retreat house in what used to be called Presidente Stroessner (today renamed "City of the East"). It was a splendid experience indeed, with several unexpected features. One was the privilege to be invited to celebrate Mass with the nuns in their chapel, in Spanish, since we were on the Paraguayan-Spanish side of the river. I noticed one nun, in a somewhat distinct habit, kneeling at a special *prie-dieu.*

Assuming that she was the Mother Superior, I went up after Mass to thank her, introducing myself to her at the same time.

When she replied in English, I asked, "Where did you learn such excellent English, sister?" I asked. "At Georgetown University," she replied with total simplicity. I later discovered that she was the daughter of Marshall Estigarribia, one of Paraguay's best presidents and a man of considerable culture. She was establishing a convent-within-a-convent of Visitation nuns there. A great lady indeed!

It would perhaps be better not to name my most impressive students in Paraguay than to fail to name so many who deserve to be mentioned. (And lest I seem to be guilty of partiality, I shall omit all my Jesuit students.) The first young Paraguayan to overwhelm me with his brilliance and goodness was Carlos Penayo. I got to know him through his grandmother, who lived near the Hogar de los Ancianos and repeatedly invited me to have a cup of coffee after my Sunday morning Mass. Knowing virtually nothing about higher mathematical physics, I can only judge Carlos as the German scientists did who gave him a six-year scholarship, with all expenses paid, including several home trips. Carlos had delayed his confirmation until he had the chance to make an Ignatian retreat. After this, he came to see me and invited me to be his Godfather. It was an honor I shall never forget.

And what a delight it was to know young Berta Rojas. Berta had, in my judgment, come out first in the guitar competition honoring Agustín Barrios (mentioned earlier). There was only one problem: she was a girl! I overheard at least one of the "judges" make this complaint, but felt that as a foreigner I couldn't protest too loudly. Instead, I went to the U.S. cultural attaché, Alan Rogers, registered my complaint and asked what I could do. Alan suggested that we tape some of Berta's performances, certify them, and send them to Washington. Washington responded by giving her a most remarkable scholarship—an entire summer visiting and playing for the finest guitarists in the United States. When she played for a marvelous New Orleans guitarist, a Cuban, he ordered her to do the entire Bach Chaconne by heart, then stated, "Darling, I play the Chaconne like Segovia, but you already play it better than we do!" All of this helped her become, as she is now, internationally famous.

Another outstanding Paraguayan youngster is Jorge Postel, one of the best oboists of his generation, if not of any generation. He is now in Europe, having won various U.S. scholarships.

He was kind enough to play at several of my farewell events and is as modest as he is brilliant. And how do I praise graduate student Juan Godoy, whom Paraguay's leading philosophers referred to as the finest young mind in the country? Since I'm hardly a philosopher, I'm much less fit to make such a judgment.

Although I have omitted my Jesuit students, perhaps I can be permitted the indulgence of mentioning two Jesuit colleagues whose service to the missions in Brazil and Paraguay deserves noting—David Romero and Angel Camiña. All those who know David Romero in South Louisiana—and I pity those who don't—know that he is from New Iberia and that his name isn't pronounced like the English "David" but like the French and Spanish "David," with the accent on the last syllable. His surname suggested that he was very Iberian and this could have caused trouble in Paraguay, since everyone might have assumed that he spoke Spanish as well as they did. Still, David is so charming that it wouldn't really have mattered. The surprising thing is that he has mastered the Spanish of his ancestors as well as the Portuguese of Brazil, now that he is stationed in that giant country, where many of our New Orleans Province Jesuits are hard at work. All of us who have had the experience of working in both Paraguay and Brazil seem to have fallen in love with both Iberian lands and languages.

The other is Angel Camiña, one of the staunchest Basques that I've ever known and one of my closest Jesuit friends. Coincidentally, Angel's family lives in the same apartment house in Bilbao as do the relatives of Father Pedro Arrupe, the beloved Father General who preceded Father Kolvenbach and is certainly one of the outstanding superiors general in Jesuit history. We were very fortunate at Javier when Angel joined us to teach communications and specifically film. When I mentioned to a number of young experts in film that Angel Camiña was coming to teach in Paraguay, they gasped incredulously and asked, "Not *the* Angel Camiña?"

For years Angel had worked as film critic in Madrid, with the prestigious journal *Razón y Fe*. As a master of the Ignatian Spiritual Exercises as well, Angel was the obvious choice for superior of the Centro de Espiritualidad Santos Mártires, while continuing his irreplaceable work with the young religious at Javier. On November 1, 1991, our "Basque Angel" completed ten years as a missioner in Paraguay and has now returned to his beloved homeland.

Several wonderful people participated with me in a journey to Bolivia, in search of Jesuit Reductions there. An extraordinary Jesuit brother, a Swiss, offered to pay my way, using his own vacation money. A Franciscan Bishop, Bösl, did the same for Gregg Servis, a young Californian Jesuit, and the von Thuemens paid T. Frank Kennedy's way. It would be hard to find two better travel companions, not even the two McCowns when we were all younger. We flew from Asunción to Santa Cruz de la Sierra, then into the jungle over impassable rivers and through even less passable bayous (as we say in the South). Our driver, with a macabre sense of humor, frightened us repeatedly until we met Hans Roth, a Swiss theologian and disciple of the incomparable Hans Urs von Balthasar.

Roth guided us through some of the most terrifying parts of Bolivia, where drug barons hold forth and where a blowout could mean one's last moments on earth, to Concepción, perhaps the greatest of the Bolivian Reductions and now restored as the Cathedral of the Bolivian (that is, the Chiquitos Indian) Reductions. Hans Roth continued his superlative work of restoration. When finally he escorted us back to the weekly plane, he cautioned us that the person who entered just ahead of us was the "most wanted" man in South America for his drug connections. This didn't make sleeping on the plane any easier.

T. Frank Kennedy's research, now nearly all published, has established him as a leading authority on Guaraní and Chiquito music, and his more recent publication and presentation of *The Apotheosis or Consecration of Saints Ignatius of Loyola and Francis Xavier,* already mentioned in chapter 12, can hardly be matched for timeliness. I had seen the unpublished text over a year before and tried vainly to persuade T. Frank against attempting it. Fortunately, I was wrong, as I happily admitted in a lengthy article in *America.* As for Gregg Servis, both T. Frank and I would be the first to stress the value of his contributions to the study of the Reductions. We were delighted when his tutor at Santa Clara University allowed him to make the journey with us, for credit, provided that he wrote a paper that proved satisfactory. Apparently it proved far more than satisfactory. Gregg has since returned to South America, where he is now studying theology in Brazil.

Thanks to Don Gelpi, distinguished professor at the Berkeley Theological Union and a member of the New Orleans province, I was invited to attend an important meeting of experts on Bartolomé de Las Casas, including Professor Lewis Hanke, my old friends Ernie Burrus and Frank Sullivan (then a theologian at Boston College), and others. The most important news to me was the announcement made by Father Damian Aloysius Byrne, master general of the Dominican Order, that the chapter general had formally requested of the Holy See the beatification of Las Casas.

Playing "Devil's Advocate," I suggested that black Catholics often held a grudge against the great Dominican for having suggested that if the Spaniards needed slaves, they could more appropriately use blacks, who were accustomed to slavery, rather than Indians who could not survive under such pressure. The master general was delighted, however, when I mentioned having discovered Las Casas's retraction and apology, found in chapters 102 and 129 of *Historia de las Indias III:* "This suggestion [to give permission to bring Black slaves to these lands] Father Las Casas did give, not observing the injustice with which the Portuguese took and made slaves of them, . . . for the same reasons apply to Blacks as to Indians." Unfortunately, far more people are aware of Las Casas's mistake than of his retraction and the reasons given for it.

I had been asked to make a strict translation of Las Casas's great book, composed in difficult Renaissance Latin, *De Unico Modo,* and did so while in Paraguay. To my regret, after handing in my work and believing it accepted, I later discovered that it had been found too literal and the assignment was accordingly given to someone else. Thus my own version will apparently not be published.

I nourish hopes, however, of living to see the great Dominican beatified. One of my special reasons is the fact that Las Casas's books were well known to the Jesuits in Peru, and if Saint Roque González de Santa Cruz's vigorous condemnation of Indian slavery sounds very much like Las Casas's, the reason may be quite simple: Roque, together with Ruiz de Montoya and other Jesuits of the early Paraguay Reductions, had received much of their education in Peru and thus knew Las Casas's works well.

One of the greatest Paraguayans I was privileged to meet, though only most briefly and at that shortly before his death, was

Bishop Angel Acha Duarte (of Carapeguá). He seemed one of those Christ-like bishops who reminded me of Lafayette's Bishop Jeanmard—saintly, modest, hardworking, friendly, democratic, and particularly learned. In fact, it was he whom the other bishops chose to do the history of the church in Paraguay (from 1547 to 1980). He completed it just before his untimely death and was mourned by the entire country. The facts he records are so interesting, I ask my reader's indulgence if I quote at some length.

Bishop Acha speaks of "the first missioners who arrived in Paraguay" as "the twelve Franciscans who reached Asunción. In 1575 Luis de Bolaños and Alonso de S. Buenaventura arrived and founded the towns of Altos, Yaguarón, San Blas de Ita, and several others. Then came Dominicans and Mercedarians." But, the bishop continues,

> those who gave the greatest impulse to the progress of the faith and to the foundation of magnificent Christian towns were the Fathers of the Society of Jesus, who were established in Paraguay in 1588. The first Jesuit missioners to arrive on our shores were Fathers Thomas Fields (Irish) and Manuel Ortega (Portuguese), destined for Guaíra, founding the first Jesuit house in Villarica del Espiritu Santo in 1593. In 1609 there arrived the famous Fathers Simon Masseta and Jose Cataldino, then Father Antonio Ruiz de Montoya and Martin de Ortazun. These missioners founded the Reduction of Loreto. In 1593 Father Romero, superior of the mission, arrived in Paraguay, and Fathers Marcial de Lorenzana, Gaspar Monroy, and Juan Viana.
>
> In 1604 there arrived Father Provincial Diego de Torres and thirteen priests; in 1609 Father Lorenzana founded the first Jesuit Reduction eight leagues from the Tebicuary River— the Reduction of San Ignacio Guazú.
>
> When Father Lorenzana was called away by the provincial, the Asunceno missioner of the same order, Roque González de Santa Cruz, remained to replace him. In less than twenty years these missioners built more than thirty Reductions—eleven on the banks of the Paraná River, the principal ones being Itapua [today Encarnación], Carmen, San Cosme, Trinidad, Santiago, Jesús, Santa Rosa, Santa María de Fe and others. Important Reductions were also founded on the banks of the Uruguay River. All this is the most famous aspect of the church history of Paraguay.

From the founding of Asunción in 1547, to the episco-
pacy of Bishop Juan Sinforiano Bogarín Gonzáles (1900), some
350 years passed during which the church of Asunción was
without a head, *sede vacante* or abandoned for 174 years! Of
the first forty bishops named, only twenty reached Paraguay
and took possession of their see! Even so, the seed sown by
our missioners not only germinated, but "because it fell on
good ground, bore fruit a hundredfold."

The first bishop of Paraguay was Juan de Barrios, O.F.M.,
who died before he reached Paraguay (1548). The sixth
bishop, Alonso de Guerra, O.P., brought the first Jesuits to
Paraguay, especially Villarica del Espíritu Santo. The eighth,
Martín Ignacio de Loyola, O.F.M., nephew or grand nephew of
Saint Ignatius, approved the catechism of Luis de Bolaños.
Reinaldo de Lizárraga, O.P., was the ninth bishop. San Ignacio
Guazu was founded, also Itapua (Encarnación). The 15th
bishop was Cristóbal de Aresti, O.S.B.

The 17th bishop was Bernardino de Cárdenas, O.F.M., of La
Paz. Consecrated before the Bull was expedited, he left in
Paraguay only memories of his extravagant conduct, having to
abandon it to reside in Santa Cruz de la Sierra, where he died.

The 24th bishop, José de Palos, O.F.M., witnessed the
beginnings of independence, captained by Jose de Antequera.
The 28th bishop, López y Espinoza, elected in 1765, never
even got to Paraguay.

In 1768 the Society of Jesus was expelled with 15,000
missioners. With their expulsion the flourishing realm of faith
and progress of thirty-three Paraguayan towns was liquidated.
Dominicans, Mercedarians, and Franciscans and secular clergy
took charge of the Reductions, but there was no way to prevent the towns from collapsing totally.

The 33rd bishop, Pedro García de Panes, O.F.M., was the
last bishop who came from Spain to Paraguay. Dictator Francia
extinguished the Orders of Saint Dominic, Saint Francis, and
Our Lady of Mercy, and their professed fathers were secular-
ized. The 36th bishop was Basilio Antonio López, O.F.M., a
native Paraguayan from The Recolet, first Paraguayan elected
bishop of Asunción.

———

"Whatever happened to the Peace Corps?" was the sort of question in vogue some years ago and the title of at least two articles that I am aware of, one of them mine. I had often thought of the Peace Corps, writing what was one of the first articles back in 1961 when I was working at *America*. Quite frankly, many of us optimists—as we were often insultingly styled— seemed to our less naive colleagues to be indulging in a "Children's Crusade."

Living in New York at the time just a few blocks from the United Nations building, I was brash enough to visit some fifty or so ambassadors and ask for their blunt appraisal of Peace Corps probabilities. "The new volunteers," a young African cautioned me, "must somehow eradicate apprehensions felt by my people." Understandably, they lumped us together with British, Belgian, French, Dutch, and other imperialist powers.

Peace Corps volunteers, some of the ambassadors stated, must be "hardworking, indifferent as to where one sleeps or eats, not emotional, not easily discouraged, determined, rugged, the out-of-door, self-reliant, and even-tempered types." All this seemed obvious enough, but more was needed; for example, "a willingness to work with local people and not appear lords and ladies of the manor." Happily, my travels and activities abroad, especially during the Hong Kong conference, gave me endless opportunities to see Peace Corps personnel at work. I saw them sweating in Southeast Asian refugee camps, working in teams, finding satisfaction in handling desperate needs.

In Paraguay, where the Peace Corps was urgently needed and accepted (while Brazil seemed too proud to admit the need), I found a warmth of acceptance, with no cynical remarks. J. J. Earheart, later a Yale graduate, trained each group of new arrivals, inviting me to give them some background on the Paraguay Reductions and to show the film Bob McCown and I had made. J. J.'s wife, a member of the California Getty family, seemed herself enriched by participating in her husband's work. Both were close friends of Don Bahlinger, who shared their friendship with me.

When the head of the Paraguayan Peace Corps died in a New Year's Eve plane crash in Bolivia, hundreds of members of the Corps gathered for the wake and funeral service. The director's wife invited me to help in the service, in which participants from all over South America did their part. I was especially delighted to see the name LaFarge on the program, wondering whether it could be a relative of Uncle John's. Spotting the person who seemed most to display the family genes, I walked toward him and started to ask if he was a LaFarge, but he beat me to it and said simply: "Yes." He was, in fact, Ted LaFarge, representing the entire Peace Corps from Washington and remembered the fact that we had both been at Uncle John's funeral Mass together, though he was only ten at the time.

After the ceremony I invited Ted over to our Jesuit residence in Asunción and showed him, among other things, the vow crucifix that had belonged to "our" Uncle John. I was even tempted to give it to him, but somehow managed to resist the noble temptation.

Shortly after my seventieth birthday, a number of ailments began to take their modest toll, principally minor nuisances proper to senescence or perhaps senility. During all this time, the superior of Javier community, Father Escobar, proved unfailingly the soul of charitable concern and did more to help my dubious health than could be expected of the most dedicated parent. He knew the best physicians in Asunción, both specialists and generalists, and did not hesitate to ask for their help. Though not fully conscious at the time, I later recalled and will not forget now that, on a Sunday when doctors are hard to find, he drove all the way across the city to find a specialist who would care for my acute hepatitis, with fever 104 degrees Fahrenheit.

Meantime, Father Eddie Gros, a New Orleanian, had arrived in Asunción to work with the scholastics and do spiritual direction in the Colegio Técnico Javier. No finer choice could have been made. I had known Eddie closely for many years, and his presence—not only for the younger men but for his aging friend as well—gave that special sense of security needed when one is seriously ill far from home. He could not have done more even for his own parents, though I should not want to embarrass him by being too specific.

A splendid California Jesuit, Tom Splain, never failed in his concern, nor did the Irish Jesuit, now recently ordained, Brendan Rumley. Several Spanish or Paraguayan Jesuits, like the great communications expert Angel Camiña, of whom I just wrote, and polyfaceted Brother Andrés Martín, the scholastic Filemón, and others, could not have been more amiable, as was U.S. alumnus of St. Peter's (in Jersey City) Vin Fragano, an almost daily visitor when I was ailing, and Gisela and Clemens von Thuemen, Philip and Alicia Parkerson, and Don Celestín (nicknamed Pichín).

While speaking of health, I must mention an incident that turned out far better than I deserved and which happened before Eddie Gros's arrival. It was a beautiful Sunday afternoon, but my cough felt and sounded worse than ever. "Let's go to the hospital right away," insisted Brother Andrés. Without bothering to pack pajamas or other necessities, we hurried to the emergency entrance. I was found to have high fever and dangerous congestion. They rushed me to a vacant bed, in the large ward built to accommodate one hundred patients, with only one public toilet. It was chilly, and I began to wonder how I'd survive the night. Finally a doctor appeared. My only question was: "When can I go home?" His reply: "In the morning if you're feeling better." He hadn't asked for my name or address and obviously had no idea I was a Jesuit from Javier, and I didn't want to ask for special treatment anyway. No one else called.

When darkness became total, I tried to go to sleep, but the groans and shrieks of people suffering from weekend accidents made it unthinkable. I had begun the long vigil of an endless night when into the bed next to mine stumbled an elderly man, moaning. I rashly thought he was drunk. His son then appeared and helped him get settled. The young man spoke to me, explaining that his father had been robbed and beaten by hoodlums. He was obviously telling the truth. Without asking who I was, he showed great care for me and made sure that my IV tubes didn't get entangled. I remained anonymous, while he, his father, and everyone else in the ward seemed asleep. After what seemed like dozens of hours, dawn finally began to break.

Taking the doctor's only word literally, I felt I could escape legitimately, delighting in "the rosy-fingered dawn." Not a soul saw me, nor was there any alarm. Once I was out, however, I felt there was no return possible. Yet in the early morning the temperature was at least twenty degrees below what it had been when I had entered. I have to admit that I was as frightened as I've ever been.

Suddenly I heard what sounded like a cry of horror. It was Father Tormo, octogenarian chaplain of the hospital, discovering me shivering in the morning cold. As well as anyone can explain the inexplicable, I tried to tell him that I was obeying the doctor, quite literally. He pointed to a shelter and ordered me to wait there, admitting no possibility of argument. Soon a doctor arrived in a car; he drove me home to Javier, where nobody, except Father Tormo, seemed up. I tiptoed to my room and went to bed. I'm not sure how many people learned of my folly, but quite likely I would never have been readmitted to that hospital again had I stayed on in Paraguay. At least I was alive, and once in my own bed, I was able to sleep for hours.

The thrill of a lifetime came on May 16, 1988, when Pope John Paul II, just after he landed, canonized Roque González de Santa Cruz in Asunción's "Ñu Guazú" (Guaraní for "Big Field"), which was between the city limits and the airport. I would have been even happier had I been able to attend the ceremony, but a chilling rain and a little common sense helped me realize that, thanks to TV, I could watch it more safely and comfortably and almost as thrillingly from a distance. What made Roque so special was that he was the first martyr of South America's southern cone as well as of Brazil. Further, he was a native-born South American, a Creole, unlike many other important saints associated with the continent, such as Peter Claver, or such giant missioners as Bartolomé de Las Casas, José de Anchieta, Manuel da Nóbrega, not to mention the northern continent's Jean de Brébeuf, Eusebio Kino, Isaac Jogues, and Junípero Serra. No wonder that, despite rain all day, over half a million South Americans hailed Roque's canonization, including a number of his own surviving relatives.

Six months later, when back in New Orleans, I was invited to give a homily on Saint Roque, which I did with immense gusto. After Mass, Mrs. Collens Curtis, a lovely lady, came back to say hello and to share a memento with me. It was a lengthy clipping from the Fall River, Massachusetts, *Labor Standard* for November 15, 1879, that would have thrilled Roque as much as it did me. It announced the death of the Hon. T. Wharton Collens, the lady's great grandfather and an eminent jurist of New Orleans.

The editorial explained,

> It is not as a lawyer that we in this part of the country will treasure his memory, but as a wise, judicious and efficient friend of humanity, especially with reference to the great

industrial problems of our time. Judge Collens was a Christian Labor Reformer; a true reformer, but not a revolutionist. He had been led by the study of the remarkable Communities called "Reductions" in Paraguay, South America, to have altogether deeper and truer views of the real nature of Christianity as a system of practical life, than Christians of any church on this continent generally hold. . . . So good, so true, so eager for the welfare of humanity, so full of the spirit of Jesus; so self-forgetful, so courteous, so ready to act with and through others, so clear of mind and firm of heart, so truly a Christian and so nobly a man, when shall we who are called Labor Reformers see his like among us again. (Signed) Jesse H. Jones, Protestant Clergyman.

———

The nine years or so that I spent largely in Paraguay were already more than anyone had anticipated. At least nowadays, we tend to think of five years as a sort of norm for missionaries-to-be, not absolute or strictly normative, but a handy round number. Few of my friends believed I would go at all and fewer still that I would last the more or less usual five years. Personally, after the decision was made to go to Paraguay, I felt that I should leave the time open, relying on hints from providence and directives from superiors.

The first five years were almost continuous, with a few major journeys (one for my fiftieth jubilee as a Jesuit, another for an honorary doctorate, several to meetings about the Reductions in Brazil or Argentina). I was further invited to meetings in Korea and Japan, with stopovers in Berkeley and in New Orleans. Since our Paraguay Province had few financial resources, it was understood that any travel I did would be paid for by the host countries.

The next four years were broken by various assignments. I remember especially the six months spent in Rome at the Jesuit House of Writers, working with Charlie O'Neill, Joe Tylenda, and Bob Gerlich on the bilingual dictionary-encyclopedia on Jesuits and their history. Before leaving for Rome I had done some fifty articles, absentmindedly written in Spanish (later I had to translate them into English). Some fifty other articles, most of them dealing with aspects of the Paraguay Reductions, were also done, this time in English, with a translation into Spanish to be done by someone else. It is increasingly obvious that the two principal languages of the Society of Jesus, now that Latin has lost most of its usefulness as an international instrument of communication, are English and Spanish. The present superior general has been urging everyone to achieve a speaking skill in one language or the other, or better yet, in both.

During the period of my involvement with the Paraguayan Province, my publications (individually unimportant to be sure) gradually became composed mainly in Spanish, save for things explicitly translated into English, such as Montoya's *Conquista Espiritual,* and were *Porqué Ser Católico?, De Unico Modo, Conquistador Sin Espada, Las Ciudades Perdidas del Paraguay, Texto Explicativo de la Misa de Zipoli, Una Visita a las Ruinas Jesuíticas,* and a plethora of articles in daily newspapers, Sunday supplements, and *Educar, Acción, Radio So'o, Dimension,* and *Estudios Paraguayos.*

Shortly before returning definitively to the United States, I received a most unusual invitation from the University of Oklahoma to participate in a five-day, nine-session, twenty-seven-hour seminar known as the Scholar Leadership Enrichment Program (SLEP). It was impossible to turn down for a variety of reasons—the quality of participants, the hundreds of eminent predecessors, and the very generous stipend, plus the fact that the topic was left entirely to me. I chose, in fact, "Discovery of the Americas: Conflicting Ideologies."

During my stay on the campus, I had as a resource person the eminent Latin American historian, Lowell Gudmundson. While not mere echoes of one another, we found it easy to dialogue. The "conquest" of America took on unexpected meaning for me because the students were carefully chosen, allowed though not obliged to participate, and they came from all the important colleges and universities of Oklahoma, sectarian and nonsectarian. There seemed an atmosphere of total ecumenism, no one trying to practice one-upmanship. Though the majority of the participants were not Catholic, it got so that one couldn't tell who was and who wasn't. We became united in the belief that the conquest was one of the supreme moments of world history and was from the Christian viewpoint the beginning of the evangelization of the Native Americans.

It was good for me to be in Oklahoma (my first time ever, in fact) and to learn about the work of Oklahoma missioner Father Ramon Carlin in converting the Tzutuhil language to a written form so that the people of Santiago Atitlán could hear Mass celebrated in their own tongue—the sort of thing the best missionaries have been doing since the beginning.

The most moving moment for me was at the final public lecture, when all the students stood in an applause that seemed thunderous. I was moved if possible even more, a few days later, when cards of condolence came from many students because of the assassination of my brother Jesuits in San Salvador. I was particularly touched, too, by the comments of a participant who, when asked by the press about her reactions, replied, "It's fascinating. We spend all day and all evening with him. You can see his mind is about ten sentences down the road. Sometimes it's difficult for him to get his mind back where his tongue is! He is quiet-spoken. So many wonderful anecdotes. Such wide-ranging knowledge. Everyone is impressed by his gentle manner. They are more than satisfied. They smile at the mention of his name."

Among previous visiting SLEP scholars were Peter Berger, Joseph Campbell, Bruno Bettelheim, Kenneth Clarke, Norman Cousins, Buckminster Fuller, Douglas Hofstadter, Elisabeth Kübler-Ross, Martin Marty, Leonard Meyer, Vance Packard, Charles Rosen, Bayard Rustin, Huston Smith, and Alvin Toffler. Surely it isn't hard to understand why I should feel honored to join such company.

Chapter Seventeen

Autographing copies of Lost Cities
of Paraguay *and related works.*

"Jesuits in the Missions"

The Nash Lecture, 1987

Early in 1986, Father Joseph Gavin, the Jesuit president of
Campion College in Regina, Saskatchewan, Canada, wrote me in
Asunción, inviting me to give the ninth Nash Lecture later that
year. Father Gavin added a special "lagniappe"—the widest
option for the lecture's theme. I wrote in reply, thanking him for
the honor and promising to propose a topic as soon as possible.
After some thought it occurred to me that "Conquest or Inculturation: Ways of Ministry in the Early Jesuit Missions" would be
both timely and otherwise appropriate, given my previous study
of the subject in French Canada and my present work on the
Jesuit missions of Paraguay, very much in the news because of
Robert Bolt's exceptional screenplay for Roland Joffe's film *The
Mission,* then at its peak of popularity.

I began by saying something about the great Jesuit pioneer,
the Italian Alessandro Valignano, who twenty-one years after
Xavier's death (1552), was appointed director of all Jesuit missions in the Far East, and who devised a new, enlightened
approach. Knowing something of the heights of Chinese and
other Far Eastern cultures, he realized better than most of his
contemporaries that it was not enough simply to preach, that a
more appropriate approach in Asia should be horizontal rather
than vertical—not looking down on the Asians but honestly
treating them as equals.

The first and best things for prospective missioners to do
would be to master the difficult Asian languages and dig deep
into their ancient classics. This was a radically new idea, exceed-
ingly hard for smug Europeans to cope with, then flushed as
they were with a sense of Renaissance glory and perhaps more
ethnocentric than ever. We recall that Michelangelo was still

alive when Valignano was born, and Titian was to die three years after Valignano's appointment as religious superior of all Jesuits in the Far East.

This was hardly a moment for Europeans to treat other cultures as equal. If Georgio Vasari was then enlightening the West as to the superiority of the Italian Renaissance to the art of the belittled medieval Gothic, what would he have thought of Chinese or other oriental art? One of the most astonishing intercultural achievements of the epoch was the compilation and printing of the very first Japanese dictionary ever to be published, the work of a committee of Japanese and European Jesuits, the *Vocabulario da Lingoa de Iapam* (1604). This was followed four years later by Father João Rodrigues's volume *Arte da Lingoa de Iapam,* again the first grammar of that language ever done. This was all part of the mammoth process of what we would call today inculturation or acculturation. The Jesuits had already become professionally interested in astronomy. Valignano encouraged this interest in Japan, especially since he himself had been a student of Christopher Clavius, the renowned German Jesuit astronomer, who did most to devise our present "Gregorian" calendar.

Another student of Clavius was Carlo Spinola, who established an academy of sciences and together with his colleague Giulio Aleni made the first scientific observation of a lunar eclipse ever studied in Japan; Spinola would later become famous as a martyr.

At the same time, another Italian, Matteo Ricci, was serving as Valignano's first emissary. He had also adopted a Chinese name, Li Ma-tou, and learned to wear the robes of a Buddhist bonze to suggest that he was "a man of God." Later he switched to Mandarin dress, on discovering that the bonzes were not always in good repute, whereas the Mandarin status was that of a scholar. Ricci discovered in contemporary Confucianism, as in the forms of Buddhism he encountered, what he judged to be superstitious elements. Accordingly he worked to restore the earlier, "pure" Confucianism. Like Valignano, Ricci had studied under the celebrated Clavius and was sometimes dubbed "The Euclid of the East." According to Jonathan Spense's remarkable book *The Memory Palace of Matteo Ricci,* when Ricci died, there were in China some fifty thousand Christians, many of them intellectuals.

Still, during the entire period of the Jesuit Chinese mission, roughly 1590–1680, more than six hundred Jesuits started from Lisbon toward China, but only one hundred actually made it—the rest succumbed to shipwreck, illness, or murder. Even so, the volunteers came. Ricci's best known associates, Ferdinand Verbiest and Adam Schall, competent scientists and missioners, carried on his work, upholding the orthodoxy of "the Chinese Rites," as that method of cultural accommodation was called.

Verbiest also published twenty volumes on astronomy, and his observatory still stands high on the only part of the Beijing wall not torn down by the present government. At this point of the Nash Lecture, I included a good deal of Sebes's book on the Treaty of Nerchinsk and on the great work of Giuseppe Castiglione (Lang Shi-ning), a Jesuit brother elevated to the rank of court painter, whose works are well studied in Cecile and Michel Beurdelay's recent monograph *A Jesuit at the Court of the Chinese Emperors.* Another Jesuit painter, Wu Li Yu-shan, was a native, a Chinese who coincidentally was ordained priest in 1688, the very year of Castiglione's birth. One may thank God that phrases from various documents of Vatican Council II almost read as if Ricci himself had written them. Recently, too, when Pope John Paul II formally addressed Jesuit leaders assembled in Rome, one of the two points he especially singled out for praise in Jesuit history was the work of Ricci.

In July 1580, the very month when Ricci was ordained a priest near Goa on his way to China, three of his confreres were engaged in serious intercultural discussions with another famous emperor. Jahal-ud-din Muhammad Akbar (known more simply as Akbar) was head of what is today all northern India, Pakistan, and large parts of Afghanistan. Moreover, they had been invited by Akbar to be his guests in his newly constructed capital Fatehpur-Sikri, not far from where his grandson Shah Jehan would build the Taj Mahal.

Wandering about these two jewels of Mogul architecture, I nostalgically recalled my spiritual ancestors' bittersweet experience here. These were Rodolfo Acquaviva, Ricci's close friend, who had traveled with him from Lisbon to Portuguese Goa, and two interesting companions—Antonio Monserrate, a Spaniard, and Francis Henriques, born a Muslim in Persia, who first converted to Christianity and then became a Jesuit. Acquaviva returned to Goa in February 1583, carrying a letter to his superior from the emperor himself. "Regarding Father Rodolfo, since I like very much the book of the heavenly Jesus and desire to discover the truth of it, and with the aid of his skill to find out the meanings of those who have written in the past, therefore I have much love for the Father and desire to have him every hour in conversation with me, and for this reason I refused him permission to leave my court. But as you asked it of me by several letters, I did so and give him permission."

Rudolfo did go back to Goa only to learn of the martyrdom of Edmund Campion at Tyburn and to lament his own unworthiness of a similar blessing. His hope for martyrdom, however, was about to be fulfilled, for only five months later he was killed at Cuncolimin on the Peninsula of Salcete, by a mob enraged against the missionaries.

Yet another Italian, Roberto de Nobili, a man of almost Riccian stature, began what one historian calls "one of the major breakthroughs in western mission history." Though only twenty-eight years old when he arrived in India, he quickly discovered that a new approach was needed, that of adaptation to concepts of the great subcontinent. For example, he dressed as a *sannyasi* ("man of God"), in red ochre, with a triangular mark on his forehead and using high wooden sandals. To master the Vedas he had to master Sanskrit and in fact became the first European ever to do so, memorizing whole passages of the Vedas to plumb their religious depths. Another missioner to India especially worth mentioning here was Father Thomas Stephens, a close friend of Edmund Campion, who also knew Ricci during their stay in Goa. Stephens quickly mastered Konkani, the native language; in fact, his Konkani grammar was the first of an Indian tongue to be published (save for Panini's classic Sanskrit grammar). But it was Stephen's *Christian Purana* completed in 1616 in the Marathi language that gave him immortality—a long poem, relating the story of both Hebrew and Christian Scriptures. For centuries it remained part of the cultural heritage of Indian Christians. Both missionaries would be happy to know that today native Jesuits of India are more numerous than those of any European country, running a close second to those of the United States.

Here in America first contacts between Europeans and Native Americans were entirely different. Because in Asia missionaries encountered civilizations comparable to and in some ways more sophisticated than their own, it was comparatively easy to recognize their greatness and thus start missionary work with becoming modesty.

In America, on the other hand, the European found much to feed his arrogance. Understandably the proudest country in Europe, Spain had just emerged united after centuries of the *Reconquista,* finally expelling Moors and Jews just as the *Conquista* of America was about to get under way. Its self image, according to Enrique Dussel, was that of a nation uniquely elected by God to be the instrument for the salvation of the world. Others, not least the English, of course relished a similar myth, even if not precisely for the same reasons. Portugal's vision of its own position in the world is rather analogous to both Spain and England and can be seen at its eloquent best in Luis de Camoens's incomparably proud epic, *Os Lusiadas.*

Among the conquistadors, then, especially after the massive but fragile Aztec and Inca empires had been shattered, there could be little thought of adaptation or acculturation toward native cultures. Thus religious conversion or any other kind of contact was inevitably envisioned as vertical, from the top down. Such arrogance, as it seems to us, complacent as we are with easy hindsight, must have been inevitable. Indeed, for a time missionaries were even troubled by the question whether the American "Indians" were fully human and thus capable of becoming Christians at all.

Yet it was not the envious English, French, or Dutch who first proclaimed "the Black Legend," often, to be sure, for sectarian or chauvinistic motives. Rather, as I believe, it was the intrepid Spanish Dominican priest Antonio de Montesinos, who seeing the hideousness of his compatriots' behavior toward the Indians, vigorously excoriated them in an Advent sermon in December 1511, using words redolent of the liturgical text citing John the Baptist: "You are all living in mortal sin, and you will live and die in sin because of the cruelty and tyranny with which you abuse these innocent people!"

The even more famous Dominican Bartolomé de Las Casas, mentioned earlier in these pages, arrived in Santo Domingo three years later as a typical colonist. Within four months, however, he recognized his own injustice, turned in his new wealth and became a Dominican friar. The following year he preached an even more passionate sermon than had Montesinos and shortly afterward sailed to Spain to labor for the Indians' human rights.

After many efforts, finally at the end of 1519, he was ready to defend the Indian cause at court against Juan de Quevedo, bishop of Panama. Las Casas won his case, then returned to America, where again he failed and had to go back to Spain. It was here that he wrote his most important works, among them *De Unico Modo.* Then he returned to America, becoming one of fourteen bishops (all but three of them Dominicans) whom Dussel calls "the Latin American Fathers of the Church." All were valiant men, some suffering martyrdom at the hands of their own compatriots for their defense of native rights.

In the Portuguese half of South America, Brazil, the Jesuits were pioneers, some of them as early as 1549, during Saint Ignatius's lifetime, arriving with the first colonists and participating in the founding of Salvador (Bahía) and São Paulo. Today, all along the coast of Brazil one finds towns, bridges, schools, and superhighways named after such pioneer Jesuits as Manuel da Nóbrega and especially José de Anchieta. Dussel states, "The Jesuits in Brazil, as they did in Mexico, organized the Indians into villages or *reducciones.*" The method used by the Jesuits was that of the tabula rasa ("clean slate"), as it were "starting from scratch," for in Brazil no vestige of high civilization existed. Studying the Tupí language, Jesuit Juan de Azpilcuera Navarro produced a dictionary, while Anchieta developed the first grammar. The Spaniards, unable to understand the ultimate bases of the Indian culture and civilization (according to Dussel), sought to obliterate every vestige of the pre-Hispanic American civilization. Tragically, there was no adult interlocutor such as Matteo Ricci encountered in China or Roberto de Nobili in India. The indigenous American peoples lacked the philosophers and theologians who could have acted as bridges between the Hispanic and the American "ethico-mythical nucleus."

Moreover, the multiplicity of languages and cultures impeded the conquerors from absorbing the cultural wealth of the vanquished tribes and peoples. The pioneer founders of the Jesuit Reductions, men like Antonio Ruiz de Montoya and Roque González de Santa Cruz, had read Bartolomé de Las Casas's works and surely were in agreement with him. Indeed, Montoya's greatest book, *Conquista Espiritual* (which I have recently published as principal translator), makes the same point again and again, as he was struggling to get permission for the Reduction Indians to bear arms in defense of themselves against the Portuguese and other invaders. And some of Roque's published letters are at least as eloquent as Las Casas's in defense of the Indians, especially against his fellow Spanish creoles and even his own family. Granted, the South American Indians, even in the highly developed Andean civilizations, were not book people, unlike the Asian civilizations. Yet they were eminently people of the spoken word.

Further, as the Jesuits were quick to discover, these languages were every bit as sophisticated as any that they had left behind in Europe. Every one of the missionaries who touched on Guaraní wrote eulogistically about it. Ignace Chome, esteemed as a polyglot, had this to say: "I confess that I was amazed to find in Guaraní such a combination of majesty and energy. I never could have imagined that here, in this barbarous region, such a language could be spoken, one which for nobility and harmony is in no way inferior to European languages I have learned." And this from one who had grown up on Racine and Bossuet!

Pedro Lozano, a Spaniard, concurs, "Without doubt Guaraní is one of the richest and most eloquent languages in the world. Men who know well both it and Greek find it little if any inferior to Greek and superior to other famous languages." They also pointed out, as did Francisco Jarque, that "Guaraní is even more difficult than Greek, Hebrew, Arabic, and other languages that I have studied." Ruiz de Montoya wrote a Guaraní grammar and dictionary still recognized by Guaraní scholars as the standard for that language's classical form, and more recent dictionaries regularly prove a point by placing "M" (for Montoya) after terms that may be controverted. The copy I used in Paraguay contained more than eight hundred pages, including pronunciations and all possible uses of a given word during Montoya's epoch. His achievement seems as incomprehensible to me as was the Japanese dictionary of Jesuit João Rodrigues and his collaborators a generation earlier.

Roque González's mastery of Guaraní and prodigious skill as a preacher is somewhat less astonishing. For Roque was born in Asunción and picked up Guaraní "on the streets." Even today Asunción is an almost uniquely bilingual city, where virtually every native-born Paraguayan is equally at home in two languages. Roque insisted that anyone who wanted to work among the Guaranís should not only speak it, but speak it with complete mastery. Here, in fact, he was echoing the first instructions given prospective missionaries by the founder of the Paraguay Province of Jesuits, Diego de Torres Bollo, a man in many ways comparable to Valignano in Asia. While the son of a conquistador, Roque was as conscious of the evil endemic in the system as Bartolomé de Las Casas had been, and fought it as vigorously. Not surprisingly, Roque was to die a violent death. His murderers were, however, not Spaniards but, rather ironically, Indians who neither lived in the Reductions nor knew Roque at all.

Despite their struggle for Indians' rights, the Jesuits often had to allay suspicions that they were secret Spanish agents being used by the Spanish authorities. In a piquant story Father Dobrizhoffer tells us: "The cacique and his tribe have no trust in any Portuguese or Spaniard and wouldn't believe a word they said. I had to assure him again and again that I was neither a Portuguese nor a Spaniard. I explained that between my country and Spain and Portugual there lay many lands and that my parents, grandparents, and great grandparents knew not a word of Spanish or Portuguese, and that I had made a very hard journey over the ocean, many months long, just to bring them the word of God and show them the way to salvation. This went a long way toward making us friends."

Father Dobrizhoffer's remarkable work has a strange name: *History of the Abipons* or, in the original Latin, *Historia de Abiponibus,* the Abipons being a tribe in Paraguay. Dobrizhoffer was born in Frymburk (Bohemia, Czechoslovakia, September 15, 1718). We know a good deal about his life, as we know a good deal about the lives of many Jesuits who worked in the missions of Paraguay, thanks to the careful research of Father Hugo Storni, librarian of the Jesuit House of Writers in Rome, who published in 1980 his *Catalogue of the Jesuits of Paraguay.*

Dobrizhoffer's history strikes me as one of the most valuable studies ever to come out of the Jesuit missions of Paraguay, perhaps even the most valuable in terms of quantity and the level of historiography. It was edited some years ago by the great Argentinian Jesuit with the unlikely name of Guillermo Cardiff Furlong (his parents actually came from Ireland). Much of the preliminary editorial work on Dobrizhoffer's masterpiece was done by Dr. Ernest Maeder, dean of humanities in Argentina's National University of the Northeast, in Resistencia, and a close friend of Father Furlong, whom I am honored to have known well. Dr. Maeder had made the entire Spiritual Exercises of Saint Ignatius under Father Furlong's direction and had the greatest esteem for him.

A more voguish accusation against the Reductions' Jesuits today is that they kept the Indians in *statu pupillari,* like innocent docile children. In this respect I find the answer in Robert Bolt's script of *The Mission* closer to history. We have a number of letters composed by the caciques of the seven cabildos ordered evacuated by the Treaty of Limits in 1750. The letters are preserved in the National Archives in Madrid and are addressed to José Andonaegui, the Spanish governor in whose jurisdiction the seven "rebellious" Reductions lay. Here are several typical and compelling sentences:

> Lord Governor: We have received your letter but cannot believe that these are the words of our King. For they go against what King Philip V promised us, that if we were faithful vassals and defended his land, he would never surrender it to another king. The king, our king, cannot break his promise made to our forefathers and to us. We are all creatures of one and the same God. Can it be that He loves Spaniards more than us Indians? Why then would He want to deprive us of our lands and homes. Even wild animals love their dens and attack anyone that threatens them. How much more do we Christians love the town God has given us and our great, beautiful church, all built out of stone by our own hands and sweat! In this land of ours have died our holy teachers, priests who wore themselves out for us and who suffered so much for God and His love. Surely if the present king understood all this he would not want us to leave our land but would be full of anger against those who do. We do not want war. But if war comes, trusting in Jesus Christ we say: Let's save our lives, our lands, all our property! If God wills that we die, then this is the land where we were born and baptized and where we grew up. Only here do we wish to die. And you, Lord Governor, will pay for this eternally in hell!

Hardly the sentiments of innocent, docile children, victims of paternalism!

Basically, this description was the substance of the lecture written in 1986 and delivered on January 14, 1987. Joseph Schner, who was then the Jesuit president of Campion College, had invited at least a hundred scholars, most of them not Catholic, and their response seemed most cordial. The official response was given by a leading Lutheran theologian, who had been a missionary in China for some twenty years. He could not have been more generous, expressing himself in total agreement with my thesis. Much of this same material I have used in my SLEP seminar at Oklahoma University, and in various lectures at Fordham University, the University of San Francisco, Boston College, and the Americas Society in New York, as well as in my contribution to Kenneth Keulman's book, *Critical Moments in Religious History*.

Chapter Eighteen

*A cold, clear day by the icy shore of
Lake Michigan on Loyola University
Chicago's campus.*

Homecoming and
Sweet Remembrances

Loyola University, New Orleans, 1989–95

When a decline in health led my superiors to decide in 1989 that it was time for me to return to Louisiana, one of the voids I deeply felt was that left by the death of Colonel Rousseau Van Voorhies, who had died December 5, 1983. In the opinion of all who knew him, Rousseau was one of humanity's most original and witty treasures. His mother, Alice Mouton, was Cajun through and through, while his father, Edward, was one of those happy blends of French and Dutch that provide the *joie de vivre* that Cajun Louisiana is famous for.

While it was 1950 or so before I met Rousseau personally, in our native Lafayette, I had long felt that I knew him, at least as long ago as 1925. His nephew Henry (later Dr. Henry Voorhies), my classmate, delighted in nothing so much as mail from Rousseau, signed "Rousseau, Jr." (though there never was such a person), addressed somewhere in Paris, where his imaginary father consorted with Gertrude Stein, Matisse, Picasso, Virgil Thompson, and a host of other creative eccentrics. Rousseau, in fact, was involved at the time in the production of the Stein-Thompson masterpiece *Four Saints in Three Acts.* We youngsters in Acadiana felt, thanks to Rousseau, that we were part of that incredible generation. Little did I dream that the real Rousseau (Sr.) would prove even more delightful than the imaginary character he had created.

The meeting took place at the home of Ben and Louise Voorhies, Ben being Rousseau's lawyer brother and Louise my former babysitter, two of whose sons are today Roman-trained priests of the Lafayette diocese. It was then and there that I learned of Rousseau's later exploits—his work with the *Encyclopaedia Britannica* and his friendship with the great

philosopher Mortimer Adler of the University of Chicago and
with Robert Maynard Hutchins, the university's distinguished
president, with whom he founded the Boswell Institute, whose
motto was "Culture for Chicago!"

The Boswell Institute upheld standards for more than
Chicago, awarding honorary Doctorates of Frustration (F.D.) and
Worldly Wisdom (S.M.D.). The latter degree, as literary scholars
will quickly recognize, refers to the title of one of the masterpieces of the Spanish Jesuit prose writer Baltasar Gracián, one of
the wittiest if not most cynical masters of the language of
Cervantes and Quevedo. The only award transcending these two
doctorates was that of the Order of Gracián (O.G.), comparable
in Rousseau's eyes to the British Order of Merit.

Rousseau was kind, or quixotic, enough to present several of
these titles to friends like me on less than objective grounds. At
the same time, I cannot gainsay the joy of being elevated to such
honors together with Spike Jones, USL's former coach Bob Brown,
Representative Lindy Boggs, four-time Governor Edwin Edwards,
and the great constitutional lawyer Brendan Brown, who had
much to do with modernizing Japan's post-war constitution.

But my oldest nephews, Clement and Henry, will be the first
to stress Rousseau's democratic tastes. In 1966, when Clement
graduated from Loyola, Rousseau planned a great feast for
Clement, Henry, and me, which he served in his third-order
Franciscan habit, the entire menu consisting of hard-boiled eggs,
vodka, and crackers in abundance. Observing how charmed we
were by this original set of recipes, Rousseau invited us again, in
1972, to celebrate the conferral of Clement's law degree, explicitly repeating the exact menu precisely, as he said, "Because you
enjoyed it so much the last time!"

How wonderful it will be to celebrate the celestial festivities
together with that ultimate Cajun chef extraordinaire, authentic
spiritual son of Francis of Assisi, and doctor of all wisdom, both
worldly and unworldly.

The Ignatian Year began officially on September 27, 1990,
the 450th anniversary of Pope Paul III's approval of the Society
of Jesus, and ended on July 31, 1991, recalling that day in 1556,
when, in Father Kolvenbach's words, Ignatius "could at last con-
template face to face his Creator and Lord." For Jesuits, the

Ignatian year had no other goal than renewal in the Spirit of their apostolic life, individual and communitarian. The Jubilee will be useful and fruitful, we were instructed, to the degree it succeeds in deepening "the Society's fidelity to its mission." We don't know exactly when Saint Ignatius was born, but scholars agree the year was 1491, and my classmates and I were delighted beyond words to commemorate in 1991 the sixtieth anniversary of our entry into the Society that Ignatius had founded and named after Jesus. In so many ways, the Ignatian Year provided marvelous opportunities for Jesuits the world over to celebrate their bond of community, their spiritual family.

At Loyola University, I was especially happy to observe the Ignatian Year by giving two courses in Ignatian spirituality. For one I used the recent life of Ignatius by Father Dalmases, and for the other the even more recent life by Philip Caraman (author also of *The Lost Paradise,* about the Jesuit Reductions). It was a special joy also to be able to invite Fathers David Stanley, John O'Malley, and Don Gelpi to participate in an important seminar on Ignatius and to be able to hear two of the three speak. Regrettably, David was prevented by ill health from flying to New Orleans from Toronto.

———

Yet another world of teaching is now part of my recent life— teaching adults in night school (or City College as it is called at Loyola with great dignity). We try to alternate music and other fine arts, from semester to semester, with some effort at demonstrating the similarities between, say, baroque music and baroque architecture, poetry, painting, and sculpture. Another of my favorite programs is called "The Bridge"—for students who have merited to enter Loyola, but who would do even better with some intensive coaching in English composition or whatever. The program that Hacker Fagot and Sara Smith initiated several years ago has grown in both quantity and success, and I have found it an honor to be allowed to participate. I have worked with many international students, and because I had some ten years of experience in writing in Spanish and believe strongly in the value of constant writing in one's second language, I could point to my own experience as proof.

One aspect of my life at Loyola during these years, and even earlier at the Music School, that I must not fail to mention, was my work with the aged and infirm at the New Orleans Home and Center for Rehabilitation. It took some time for the long established Home for the Incurables to change its name in 1979 into something more optimistic and really closer to the truth. But under whatever name, truly great work is going on there, a work made possible by the cooperation of a large number of volunteers, many of them members of the Legion of Mary of Holy Name of Jesus Parish and of the St. Roch Circle of Saint Margaret's Daughters. Personnel over the years have included such wonderful people as Rita Odenheimer Huntsinger, Louis and Jan Gaudet, Nick and Betty Gordon, Larry and Ernestine Springer, Ben and Betty Lockett, Vincent Arena, Isabelle Murphy, Alice Salomon, Father Larry O'Neill of Holy Name Parish, and Brothers Brenden and Leo of De La Salle High School, as well as several student volunteers from Rummel and Chapelle High Schools. If I mention that within a few months recently we celebrated the sixteenth birthday of Vincent Arena, a leader of our student volunteers, the awarding of a medal for fifty years of service to Isabelle Murphy, and the wedding of Rita Odenheimer, a widow of twenty years, to Merle Huntsinger, this may give some hint of the rich diversity of our group.

When I had to be out of town my fellow Jesuits, such as Larry Moore, Ted Arroyo, Leo Nicoll, Jerry Fagin, Tom Barberito, the late John MacFarland, and Roland Lesseps and John Stacer, both now doing mission work in Africa, were not only willing but eager to take over for me. So attractive was the opportunity to work with lay volunteers such as those I have mentioned that replacements could easily be found for me whenever I left New Orleans on my frequent travels.

———

On August 23, 1991, the news broke in the media that "poor" *Pravda* was dead, slain by Comrade Yeltsin. On such occasions one recalls the ancient bromides about "No truth in *Pravda,* and no news in *Isvestia,*" a case where the joke was literally true. It's been years, now, since I've read *Pravda,* though back in the 1950s and 1960s, for something like fifteen years I read at least some of it every day. Moreover, my reading led to several articles in *America* and had a great deal to do, I'm sure, with Thurston Davis's inviting me to join the staff.

His point was not that this made me an expert in Soviet studies, but more simply that a weekly journal of opinion should have at least one editor who could read Russian in case of necessity. The proverbial "gentle reader" will perhaps wonder why I bothered with *Pravda* at all. The answer is simpler than one may have expected: a good friend secured a daily subscription to the Soviet official newspaper, which came daily by air from Moscow to Grand Coteau, Louisiana, where I was teaching at the time, and later to New Orleans and still later to New York. How could anyone, even a good friend, afford such a gift, and why?

The friend was a former student from my Spring Hill days, Harry Alexander of Rahway, New Jersey, a person richly endowed with both intelligence and humor, and later with a wonderful wife and family, whom I often visited when I was stationed in New York. The sad news recently reached me that Harry was dying, and the next day his wife phoned that he had passed on. It was a comfort to be able to celebrate Mass for him that very day. Reading at least a few minutes of *Pravda* a day, starting especially during the Cold War period of Sputnik and the like, was a greater experience than most people could imagine. There was just enough of the unexpected to provide some interest and at least enough of the repetitious to give me a strong basic vocabulary.

I found it particularly interesting to discover what the Communist Party was telling the Soviet people and how they interpreted bits and pieces from the United States. Curiously, the first column I read every day for all those years was sports. Why, that hardly being my principal interest? Mainly because the vocabulary was so easy—almost all very close to English, since most of the world's sports vocabulary is based on the sports of English-speaking countries. Everyone who has studied a difficult foreign language realizes the wonderful advantages that a daily dose of *Pravda* provided. (The article mentioned above is titled "The Two Faces of *Pravda*," *America,* 8 November 1958.)

———

From October 10, 1990, to December 29, 1991, the glory of Mexican arts was splendidly exhibited in New York, San Antonio, and

Los Angeles successively—some four hundred pieces, all of exceptional importance, from sites, museums, churches, and private collections. It was an unprecedented collaboration between institutions in Mexico, the United States, and seven other countries.

I was fortunate to be in New York for the inaugural opening, which happened to be on the very day that Octavio Paz, master of Mexican culture, received the Nobel Prize. In a magisterial essay, some thirty-five pages in length, Señor Paz demonstrates, in word and image, the complexity of Mexican art. He shows how, for some, the Indians were Egyptians; in the seventeenth century this was vigorously sustained by the famous Athanasius Kircher, while other Jesuits believed that the god Quetzalcoatl was Saint Thomas the apostle.

We can think of Mesoamerica as a constellation of nations, different languages and conflicting concerns, but similar political institutions, analogous social organization, and related cosmogonies—a world that recalls the Greek polis or the republics of the Italian renaissance for its cultural homogeneity and intense, ferocious rivalries. As for the missionaries, Alfonso Reyes has defined them concisely as "lambs with the hearts of lions." Most were Spanish, but they were also from the south of France, Flanders, and northern Europe. Many were influenced by Erasmian doctrines, such as Bishop Vasco de Quiroga, who also drew ideas from Sir Thomas More. These priests defended the Indians against the evils of the *encomenderos,* taught them new arts and skills, won their hearts, recorded their stories and traditions, baptized them, and finally effected a true revolution.

Like all conversions, that of the Mexican Indians entailed not only a change of their beliefs but the transformation of the beliefs they adopted. In the words of Johanna Hecht:

> The Jesuits, the teachers and the moral and aesthetic con-
> science of the aristocracy of New Spain, skillful collectors of
> funds and great builders, were the intelligent and efficient
> beneficiaries of *criollo largesse.* The coming together of the
> native aristocracy and the Society of Jesus was the origin of
> the "second great moment" in New Spain's art. The Jesuits,
> among other contributions to the spiritual life of the country,

distinguished themselves through their promotion of the cult of the Virgin of Guadalupe; some have even seen their expulsion as one of the actions of the Bourbon kings that created great disaffection in their New World possessions and helped set the stage for Independence. The depiction of Ignatius of Loyola, who died in 1556 and was canonized in 1625, was a firmly established convention based on the many contemporary portraits attesting to his appearance. Still, the expression on this figure's face seems particularly benign; it may perhaps be a sign of the instant nostalgia felt at the loss of the Jesuits, perceived by many Mexicans as their special protectors against the regalist power wielded by the episcopal hierarchy.

————

With the Bible's allotted lifespan already securely in place, I consider myself, as I began by saying, more than abundantly blessed. At this stage in my journey, I think often and gratefully of my family as well as my friends, and of the place that came over the years to be the liturgical center of my family—Our Lady of Wisdom Chapel at Southwestern (USL). Appropriately and repeatedly, it has been the site of important moments in my family's life.

I say "appropriately" since the entire Newman Club movement was launched in the South by my dad, and a chalice in the chapel includes a dedication to him.

Father Al Sigur, who succeeded Father Irving DeBlanc and preceded Bishop Jude Speyrer as head chaplain at Southwestern, was kind enough to preach at my jubilee celebration, at Mama's funeral Mass, and at other significant family events; and our special friend Father Amos Vincent provided organ music of comparable quality. Southwestern's eminent musicologist and professor of organ George Brown, while a devout Baptist, has trained many a Catholic organist and can hardly be matched for his musical help and guidance to me personally and to a number of other Jesuits. When our novitiate at Grand Coteau finally managed to acquire a modest pipe organ in the 1950s, George inaugurated it, having already guided us in matters of style and taste.

If I was my dad's *"tocayo"* and he mine, this marvelous Spanish word *tocayo* must mean something more than "namesake"—

like "special friend" or "buddy" or "pal"—since it goes both ways. I have three wonderful nephews and two marvelous nieces, but only one tocayo now in the family, my nephew Clem Kennington. Kitty, his wife, and most of his friends call him "Clem," though most of the relatives use the abbreviation of his middle name, simply "Mac." I call him, unhesitatingly, "Tocayo."

I feel very fortunate in having such a tocayo. When hurricane Betsy wrecked New Orleans, and I was in far-away New York, my tocayo was there to give security to Mama and Nenaine Alyce. He was still an undergraduate at Loyola, but just the man two aging ladies needed to have around. When he was to receive his diploma as a law graduate at Loyola, Dean Marcel Garsaud invited my tocayo to receive his diploma from his tocayo. The term is so egalitarian, making us feel equal.

Since I have returned to New Orleans from Paraguay, it has been a repeated treat to be so close to my tocayo once again, but apparently a treat for just about everyone in the Jesuit community here. A very learned philosopher here at Loyola always seems reassured when he sees my tocayo, realizing that it must be Sunday. I feel reassured, too.

The wisest thing my tocayo ever did, though, was marrying Kitty Moore, a charming and highly competent kindergarten teacher. I recall vividly Mama's sage evaluation of her colleague, spoken unequivocally to her: "I like you, Kitty; you have good sense!" The ultimate compliment of one great teacher to another.

After some years of happy married life, however, Kitty and Clem realized that more was needed. They succeeded in adopting, and allowed me to baptize, a robust, bouncing baby named "McRae" (Kitty's father's name). As this is being written, McRae has just celebrated his first birthday, or rather we are celebrating his first birthday, that of the first new member of the Kennington clan. The first boy, that is.

Years ago while I was visiting my sister's family in St. Louis, the youngest boy, Joe, woke me up earnestly one morning, just at dawn, with a pressing question: "Uncle C. J., do you like me?" "Of course, I do, Joe." "I don't mean that. What I mean is: do you like me as much as you do Kenny and Mac?" (Kenny was the nickname for my nephew Henry Kennington.) I didn't have to be thoroughly awake to realize that this was a serious matter.

Joe was too bright to be taken in by a facile lie; further, I didn't want to lie to him in any case.

I offered a quick prayer to the Holy Spirit, asking for much-needed Solomonic wisdom—at least a tiny bit of it. The answer that seemed best at the moment came out about like this: "Now, Joe, please remember that I've known both your brothers a lot longer than I have known you—about seven years longer, in fact." Joe knitted his brows and finally accepted my mathematics. "I see what you mean, Uncle C. J." I went on, to make sure. "You see, Joe, it wouldn't be true to say I know you as well as I know Kenny and Mac. But I can tell you truthfully that I do like you as much as I liked them when they were your age, and I feel sure that I'll like you as much as I like them when you're as old as they are now. O.K., Joe?" "O.K., Uncle."

When his father, Henry Kennington, was dying of cancer, Joe, then a successful physician, was the soul of concern. At the wake, Joe came to summon me: "C. J., I want you to see something." (By that time I was plain C. J. to him, of course.) I went with him to see Henry laid out in the casket. It was all done very tastefully, and I congratulated Joe. "Do you see what he has in his hand?" I saw a rosary, which seemed appropriate, given Henry's devotion to Mary. And I said so. "No, the other hand," Joe insisted. Very discreetly, and observable only to someone who knew, Joe had placed there the handle of Henry's favorite golf club. "I thought Pop might like this with him. It might improve his game in heaven," Joe added.

My two charming nieces are Alyce and Anne. Alyce was certainly named after our Aunt Alyce, our mother's only sister and my godmother (or as I loved to call her, "Nenaine"). Everyone who knew Aunt Alyce was sure to love her: no one could have been more generous, energetic, unselfish. Alyce's godmother, Kate Stokes Borne, was very much like Aunt Alyce. Little wonder that Alyce is so great! Anne also reminds my sister of Aunt Alyce, with her wonderful generosity, and she too reminds both of us of her godmother, Sudie Carroll, one of Southwestern's stellar English teachers and like a sister to Flo and Ruby Landry, intimate friends of the family. We all hope that someone writes Sudie's biography; the only problem would be to find a writer worthy of such a superlative person as Sudie Carroll. Sudie, incidentally, was a descendant of the famous Carrolls of Maryland. Her branch of the family had become Baptist, but Sudie herself had, as the phrase goes, returned to the faith of her ancestors.

———

Somehow I always called my mother, at least to her face, simply "Mama." My sister, Mary Agnes, grew up faster than I did, anyway calling her "Mother" and (oh, horrors!) "Agnes" even before she was in college. Her students called her, very phonetically, "Miss Smack" (that is, Mrs. Mac), while our favorite maid referred to her and to Miss Edith Dupre, perhaps Mama's closet friend, as "The Fast Birds of the Air." Even Miss Dupre, however, never found out her exact age, receiving this reply: "Old Father Time, when questioned, with a twinkle in his eye, said, 'Not now, I may tell you bye and bye'!"

Some of this I remember, and some I just read in a tribute to Mama done at least forty years ago, when she was still going strong but had to face tributes. One tribute, in particular, was done by Mabel Leftwich Pelletier, our wonderful neighbor's second wife, and stepmother of Louise Voorhies, my own babysitter. A very literary person, Mabel (a loyal Virginian) didn't hesitate to quote eighteenth century French writer Madame de Staël, when describing Mama: "Sow good services; sweet remembrances will grow from them." How right they both were! No wonder that when Mama died, the first person whose name appeared in the guest book was the mayor of Lafayette, who had been her grateful pupil over the years. In her own way, though limiting her teaching to second grade (my sister and I always teased her about never getting promoted), she was as beloved as our dad had been forty years earlier. It's one of the great joys of having been a teacher: those sweet remembrances.

It may seem negative when I say that the last word I heard her say was "No." But one must know the context. I had just asked her: "Are you suffering, Mama?" This, too, is a sweet remembrance, perhaps the sweetest of them all—the one time I genuinely welcomed a "No" from her.

Chapter Nineteen

Reflections on a Ministry

When Father Joseph Downey, editorial director of Loyola Press, sent his much hoped-for acceptance of an earlier draft of these memoirs, he said that he felt I ought to add a final chapter reflecting back on the meaning of such a variegated story. "I would suggest," he wrote, "that you sit down with some friends and helpers and figure out how that might be developed." At this point Father Louis Poché, who is my present religious superior, sensing how very reluctant I was to write such a chapter, suggested that we invite several of my old friends each to contribute his own personal reflections. My fear that this might look like a premature collection of obituaries was overcome by the realization that the results would probably be more amusing than eulogistic and that I would thereby be relieved of a task that I was not at all eager to perform.

Here, then, are the reflections of several of my friends, uninhibited either by decorum on my part or by objectivity on theirs.

ONE SATURDAY I MARCHED into C. J.'s room in the Jesuit residence at Loyola—his door was always open—and told him that I had to perform a mixed Catholic-Jewish wedding in our chapel in a few hours. A large number of Jewish people were coming from New York for the wedding, I said, and I wondered if there were not something special I might do liturgically? Ten minutes later I was practicing a prayer in Hebrew that C. J. took the trouble to type out and teach me, and which I inserted into the ceremony. The guests told me afterward how special they had been made to feel by my recitation of that familiar prayer. Some days later I received a letter from the groom's father in New York thanking me again, but it was the goodness and super-availability of C. J. that had helped me to add that creative component.

One fellow Jesuit, a graduate student at Tulane, was in danger of not having his dissertation approved for lack of a particular medieval Latin text. No library in this country had the book, and the director of the thesis was being difficult. C. J., who had to travel to England on business then, went early one day to the Bodleian Library and convinced the librarian to allow him, a former Oxford student, to read for a few hours. (His reading card, C. J. explained, would have been "a bit faded" by then.) The rare text, a drama in Medieval Latin, was located, and C. J. spent the next three hours reading and taking notes. Later on, in New Orleans, the dissertation was approved, to the amazement of a not-too-happy thesis director.

Such stories of C. J.'s benevolence could be multiplied. I took him with me once to a struggling inner-city parish in New Orleans to hear a program of Advent and Christmas music. The result of that evening was a review in *America* that helped the choir to gain the recognition locally it deserved. The "Golden Voices," as the St. Francis de Sales Choir is known even twenty-five years later, went on to make several recordings, and soon they began to attract worshippers and other voices from outside the parish to their Sunday liturgies.

It always amazed me that C. J.'s writing never seemed to need revision. He seldom had to revise anything. Still, it does not surprise me that his autobiography stopped where it did, short of the sentences and paragraphs that might have revealed a more personal side to himself. Many of us who lived and worked and laughed with C. J. over the years understand today a perhaps unique meaning of the expression "a man for others."

Louis A. Poché, S.J.
Ignatius Residence, New Orleans

✉

IF C. J. MCNASPY WERE A BOOK, critics would dispute forever whether to class him among the epics or the ballads. Spirits kindred to Matthew Arnold would argue passionately for the former, alleging his unmistakable *spoudaiates* or high serious-ness, while neo-Chestertonians would insist that his *eutrapelia* or winsome frivolity plainly required the latter genre.

Deconstructionists would angrily refuse to read him, con-vinced that his text was an elaborate hoax, composed in cipher.

Among the learned there would be unanimity that he was certainly not the work of any single author, ancient or mod-ern. Heated controversy, exacerbated by nationalism, would rage over the ingenious Tubingen thesis that he was a lost *Bildungsroman* of Goethe, reinterpreted as a cosmic allegory by Teilhard de Chardin, only to be whimsically revised by a one-time collaboration of Umberto Eco and P. G. Wodehouse.

As for the illustrations, traces of what appear to be Doré originals are discernible beneath the overlay of Dali and Thurber.

Claims that he had been set to music, for virginal and Jew's harp, by Sir Arthur Sullivan, although plausible, would remain unconfirmed. Plans for a movie, however, would not survive the refusal of Sir Alec Guinness and Woody Allen to combine in the single role.

Catholic opinion would oscillate between the *Wanderer* review, speculating ominously over his lack of an *imprimatur* and that of the *National Catholic Reporter,* demonstrating how easily he might have been done in gender-inclusive language.

Perhaps the sole point of agreement would be that, once having taken him up, it was scarcely possible to put him down!

But of course C. J. McNaspy is not a book.

There are no copies.

There never will be.

Only this marvelous original!

Tolle lege.

James Gaffney
Loyola University, New Orleans

PERHAPS THE MOST DAUNTING REQUEST that has come my way of late is that I do "a few words" about C. J. McNaspy. Easier to get Ken Burns to do *Baseball* in one "inning." Even so, here goes.

Friends and mere acquaintances of C. J.'s have given testimony over the years to his many gifts, talents, and achievements—and there are many such. He is all of the following and more: bright, witty, caring, dedicated, unobtrusively holy, generous to a fault, genuinely self-effacing and, impossible as it seems, truly unaware of how extraordinary he is.

Father Tom Culley delights in telling about the time someone asked J. S. Bach, that most talented of composers, how he accomplished works of such genius. Bach responded: "I work very hard." C. J., blessed with intellectual gifts that many have classified as in the genius category, and spiritual gifts of equal magnitude, "works very hard" developing and using his gifts for the greater glory of God, thereby returning them fully developed to that most generous of Givers.

What makes C. J. unique among the few so gifted by God is the easy manner he maintains while living out his day-to-day Jesuit commitment to love and serve God, so clearly manifest in his personal dealings with all who enter his life. He is equally at ease in the presence of the "mighty" as well as those of more humble repute. Neatest of all, he always puts people at ease when they are in his presence.

Possibly most remarkable of all is his pervading equanimity and balance, clearly evidenced by a sense of humor that is at once self-deprecating, gentle, and, invariably, dead center. Freed thereby of all the baggage which weighs down the self-important, he meets the world with a beautiful lightness of touch (even in "weighty" matters) that is profoundly well-informed and thoughtful. In short, he is a rare repository of enormous gifts that, with humility, grace, and admirable moral fiber, he has honed to near perfection.

Vince MacDonnell
The Smithsonian

✉

I HAVE KNOWN C. J. FOR MANY YEARS, ever since, when he was dean of Loyola University's College of Music, I registered for an extension course in Piano Literature. I was already a wife and the mother of two children, but with C. J.'s encouragement and inspiration, I soon decided to become a full-time student and eventually managed to graduate in 1964. When he left to become an editor of *America,* we remained close friends, and we have kept in touch ever since.

Whenever I have spoken to him after his move to Ignatius Residence, he is characteristically much more concerned about my health than he is about his own. As C. J. continues work on his memoirs, one of his editorial assistants has asked me, in his name, to contribute a few words to this final chapter. But as much as C. J. means to me, I could not find the right words. I could not, that is, until one day at Loyola I overheard a lady introduce herself to someone as the wife of C. J. McNaspy's "best friend." She was not boasting, or asking for any special recognition. She was simply stating something that is true of an incredible number of us. Each of us is truly his best friend. Whenever he is with any of us, we have his undivided attention. We love him well; he has loved us better, and he treats each of us as if we are every bit as extraordinary as he is. We are not, of course; but in a very true sense that does not matter either to him or to us.

Joan Underhill May
New Orleans

IT HAS BEEN MY GOOD FORTUNE, like so many before and after me, to be a student of C. J. McNaspy. But unlike most, I have managed to keep in touch with him for all of my adult life and to witness the growth of his career. My first encounter with C. J. was as an undergraduate in music at Loyola in New Orleans. Later, on his return there from New York, I worked with him as a younger faculty colleague, giving various lectures in his hugely popular "Music-in-Humanities" seminars. Still later, on his return from Paraguay, I counted him as an old friend. With each renewed acquaintance, I have been reminded afresh of C. J.'s remarkable personality. It is the sort of personality that makes an impression—that attracts and delights people and leaves them flattered to have known him. The list of C. J.'s devotees is endless, and it crosses effortlessly all human boundaries—

social, racial, religious, generational, political, linguistic. What accounts for this special charisma that has served him so well in his vocation as teacher, counselor, and mentor? Many would say it's his formidable and far-ranging knowledge that makes its mark; others would say it's his exuberant and infectious optimism. Still others would say it's his simplicity of spirit, so essentially Christlike and all the more attractive in one so accomplished. Surely, it is the sum of all these that go to define C. J.'s unique impact, but to these I would add a smaller, more personal attribute: a whimsical, even impish sense of humor. Perhaps this is best illustrated by an anecdote.

Some years ago, when I was in Florence on a Fulbright grant, C. J. came up from Rome for a visit. One morning, as we were preparing to leave my flat for a look at some Donatello sculptures at the Bargello Museum, C. J., on an impulse, sat at my piano and tore into a gusty rendition of "Sweet Georgia Brown"—hardly the sort of piece for the occasion, but as delightful as it was unexpected. As we stepped out of the flat, I congratulated him on his unerring instinct for the incongruous. On leaving the museum, inspired by the glories of Florentine statuary, we stopped in a tiny camera shop for some film when, to my astonishment, there drifted out of the ceiling speakers a related and equally unlikely tune, "Georgia on My Mind"! The expression on C. J.'s face—the faintest hint of a mischievous smile that rivaled the Mona Lisa's—was as if he had planned the deliciously ridiculous coincidence, a kind of coda to his absurd prelude. It fixed the whole day in my memory.

I cite this episode not merely to draw a chuckle but because of the insight it offers into the man. This inclination to punctuate the sublime with the ridiculous is a quintessential McNaspyism and an inseparable part of his charm. It bespeaks a gentle refusal to take himself more seriously than his subject and is surely a key to his resounding success as a teacher. With McNaspy, the most exalted discourse falls ready prey to the excruciating pun or the pious aside that, far from trivializing his subject, robs it of all pretentiousness and disarms even the most elementary and indisposed audience. Thus have I seen him deftly guide a class of skeptical jazz majors into the arcane splendors of a Palestrina mass or the expressive subtleties of a Schubert *lied*. Or direct the gaze of zealous piano majors beyond the keyboard to the architectural and aesthetic dimensions of a late Beethoven sonata. Or instill in a casual public audience an awakened sense of the spiritual depths of the Bach B-minor Mass or the Fauré Requiem. These are the achievements of a great teacher: to open the minds of students to the intellectual and spiritual dimensions of art. By demonstrating that profundity is not incompatible with wit, he has taught generations of devoted followers the "joy" of music.

It is clear that C. J. McNaspy's has been a life of consequence. If he has had a "calling," it is surely to be an influencer of people. In this, he is a true son of Ignatius, an exemplar of the Jesuit Order. And if his preoccupation as music educator has been to broaden the vision of his students, to help them see their discipline in the fuller perspective of the Western intellectual tradition, to discover the aesthetic link between music and her sister arts, he is a genuine humanist, a perfect practitioner of Cardinal Newman's idea of a liberal education. Father McNaspy's versatile intellect was God's own gift . . . the dedicated manner in which he developed it and the tireless manner in which he shared it is his gift to all who have known him. I count myself lucky to be among them.

John Joyce
Tulane University

THERE IS A VIRTUE in what might first appear as dilettantism: to know when the senses have had enough. C. J. taught me a remarkable lesson one early winter evening in Manhattan in 1968. What was to have been the typical liturgy of the American concert hall—a serious composition by Mahler, a glittery intermission, then something cacophonic but brief from the twentieth century and, finally, to heal the damaged nerves, a melodic concerto—suddenly stopped. In a sudden and almost instinctual act—not in one of those moments of recognition when everything congeals—C. J. asked in that thin, impatient voice that supplants his musically rumbling tones, "Have you heard enough?" At that breakaway moment before the down-beat of the second movement, I was up, and in minutes we were out in front of Alice Tully Hall.

Did I feel like a doctor paged for some heroic surgery? I could then have enjoyed the mix of disdain and curiosity at our exit. But I felt a dizzy kind of release. I think I know that cavalier joy when one tosses off a bauble. There's a duplicate in reserve. No, that wasn't it. Nor, conversely, was it a flash of delicious guilt about missing the second half. How often had I genuflected at every icon in the Whitney—long after the passion of my devotion to Edward Hopper had worn away—and left regretting my thoroughness.

Here was a master aesthete giving me an adult lesson that I thought I had learned long ago as a sculptor: "Don't over-work your art." But now he was applying it to the rules of perception. "Don't inundate your ears." Forget how much you paid for the tickets. Leave when your ears are full of music.

Eugene M. Geinzer, S.J.
Loyola University, Chicago

✉

EVEN IN A SOCIETY THAT IS RENOWNED for producing fine educators, C. J. McNaspy stands out as extraordinary in his ability to teach in the only truly successful way—by inspiring learning in others. I am, to say the least, a grateful former student.

A. Ransom Marlow, S.J.
Loyola University, New Orleans

✉

SOMEWHAT AMBIVALENTLY, I recall my initiatory years (1949–53) at Grand Coteau, Louisiana, as a foretaste of "cyberspace"! At the very least, I surely had my first encounter with a master helmsman who shared his extraordinary navigational skills in the exploration of all the vast dimensions of reality. C. J. McNaspy, in that "primordial" clime and time, did not have access to "electronic imaging" or "computer enhancement"—but he really didn't need it. His pedagogical, androgogical, and mysta-gogical talents were enough to transport us into whatever space-time coordinates he chose; and when we "visited" these exciting realms, with him as guide, we saw vistas and heard melodies and tasted flavors and smelled aromas and felt tex-tures that touched our hearts as well as our minds.

When we staged Christopher Fry's *First Born* with only the most rudimentary resources, we did not settle for mini-malist theatrics; we designed and hand-painted our own hiero-glyphs, we set the Voice of God to an authentic Hebraic psalmodic melody, we made the whole thing a palpable "Hag-gadah"—and thus we experienced the Paschal Mystery in a fresh and engaging way. Whenever C. J. returned from some exotic travel, he did not bring us some trifling souvenirs. He enabled us to enter the places, to encounter the persons, to participate in the events that he had experienced, almost as if we had been there ourselves. His classes were always imagi-native, memorable, and delightful. Even when he had to drill us, drudgingly, through Latin declensions and conjugations, it was not too farfetched to visualize Iñigo de Loyola, an adult amid schoolboys, going through the same—and thus to empathize with him.

Maybe C. J.'s gifts were hereditary; perhaps they were infused. I can't help believing that whatever their origin they were singularly enhanced by his own experience of the *Spiritual Exercises* of Ignatius Loyola. Ignatian insights and guidelines for personal prayer include such characteristic ele-ments as composition of place, envisioning of persons, eaves-dropping on dialogues, watching carefully the unfolding of events, entering personally into the reality of the mystery, and giving ample vent to the affections that are aroused—prayer such as this is a readiness for the Divine Reality to interact with us. Once you get a taste of that, the rest of the universe and our lives within it take on a whole new meaning and value. C.J.(and Ignatius) would revel in "cyberspace"—because it is just the newest of a long line of navigational aids to steer us through all the swells and troughs of life.

Had I studied at MIT, rather than St. Charles College dur-ing those early years, I might have encountered the "father of cybernetics," Norman Wiener, who was just then at the top of the charts. He might have tried to convince me that the Jesuit Order (not unlike the Communist Party!) was a typical embodiment of the "voices of rigidity." If Norman Wiener had known C. J. McNaspy (as I suspect that Wiener *was* known by McNaspy!), his own rigid views of Jesuits might have been attenuated by the style of Ignatian helmsmanship that C. J. practiced with real virtuosity. He steered us down the languid flow of the bayous, onto the reckless currents of mighty rivers, and out into the turbulent gulfs and seas and oceans of our world. Thanks to him, the Odyssey continues!

Donald J. Martin, S.J.
Notre Dame Seminary, New Orleans

IN 1950, I REMEMBER how eagerly I looked forward to getting to the other side of that big building in Grand Coteau, Louisiana, known as St. Charles College because Father McNaspy was there. I had met him, felt his charm, his enthusiasm, and was eager to learn from him. When I arrived at that "other side," I marveled at this "Pied Piper." He introduced us to the masters of history, literature, and music, the classics of Greece and Rome. We not only read these, we experienced them. Learning a polyphonic motet by Vittoria or a Gregorian Graduale, singing and acting in a Gilbert and Sullivan production were enriching then, and that enrichment endures today in all those he touched.

Linguist, writer, historian, musician, priest, Jesuit. A dilettante, some would say, in an effort to disparage the legend he has become. Those who know him, however, appreciate the depth of his knowledge of so many areas. But, more importantly, we remember him not as a list of stunning accomplishments but rather as an abiding friend, warm and good-humored.

His sense of humor is memorable and could be biting at times. A friend recalls how once, in mimicking the contrapuntal sounds of a polyphonic composition that the choir under C. J.'s direction had just performed, he had provoked C. J. to retort: "I always wondered what that sounded like to an idiot."

Another good memory I recall when C. J. visited his ancestral homeland, Ireland. He sent me a postcard suggesting in the address some unlikely Irish identity on my part. The card was addressed to one "Servand O'Mendez."

Proof of his humor and of his acceptance of bantering was the occasion on which he and three young Jesuit musicians would gather around the piano in search of new polyphonic motets for the choir's use. The high-pitched falsetto sounds that emanated from that quartet were, to say the least, weird, if not eerie. This led me to describe the group as the "Agony Sisters," a description that amused him considerably enough to recall it many times.

Gratefully, I recall this giant of a man, not only for the learning gleaned from his teaching, but, more importantly, for his enduring friendship over the years.

Servando Mendez
New Orleans

"Gentlemen," said Gus Coyle, the dean of our Juniorate at Grand Coteau, to us novices, "when you come to the juniorate, you will study with C. J. McNaspy, and then your education will begin." He never spoke truer words. C. J. seemed to us to embody a breadth of learning that we nobodies hadn't even begun to imagine. While other Jesuit novices in other provinces parsed Greek and Latin nouns and verbs, C. J. made the classics come alive for us as literature, as life, as humanity. He opened up for us the world of art, of literature, of astronomy, of music, of history, of culture.

He had set himself the task of learning all the Romance languages, and during my time at Grand Coteau had mastered Spanish and Portuguese, and was moving on to Russian. As Lee Phillips, a Jesuit brother who spoke in malapropisms, put it, "That C. J., you never know if he will be speaking Hingdorian or Porkachese." C. J. taught his enthusiasms, and his interests seemed unlimited. Andy Whitman, a fellow novice who had taught mathematics for years before entering, tried C. J. out in math and declared himself impressed.

After he left Grand Coteau, C. J. pursued an impressive number of careers: art critic, journalist, liturgist, art historian, teacher, missionary, hagiographer. He finally did learn all the

Romance languages, Rumanian last of all, I believe. One would have thought that a person of C. J.'s genius would have had an ego to match; but C. J. never did. John Haughey spoke the truth when in a homily celebrating C. J.'s jubilee he said, "C. J. is a great and gifted Jesuit who spent his life praising the accomplishments of other people." C. J. is always celebrating something, but always the accomplishments of people other than himself. About his own accomplishments, he has shown only self-deprecation and self-effacement. Born and raised in Cajun country, C. J. never lost the down-to-earth warmth and humanity of his Cajun roots. He has always loved the little people, the *anawim* of the Bible. He has always championed the underdog, the marginal. His love for the humanities is exceeded only by his love for people, both the gifted and the ordinary.

C. J. opened the door for me to the classics, to the humanities, to the arts, and to human culture. When I left Grand Coteau, I wanted to be like him in every way. I should have known I would never succeed; but C. J. inspired that kind of vision, enthusiasm, and admiration. C. J. also pointed me down the path that I eventually walked. Once John Courtney Murray visited our novitiate at Grand Coteau. C. J. remarked, "Someone will have to continue his work after he's gone." I felt at the time that I would like to try. I never became another Murray either, but I have tried to advance his project, thanks to C. J., the most gifted, human, and humane teacher and friend I have ever had the grace to know.

Donald L. Gelpi, S. J.
Berkeley Theological Union

✉

C. J. McNaspy has been for me over the years a man of surprises. In 1966, when he was an editor of *America,* C. J. was giving us Jesuit scholastics our annual retreat. At that time, I had just met the first Jesuit I didn't like. With aggrieved woe I betook myself to C. J.'s room to ask his advice. He responded by telling me of his own current difficulty in this line—a tale of humanity and vulnerability, but altogether so amiable and surprising that I never forgot it. It was his story, and not advice, that I needed, and he gave it.

In 1980, C. J. was a university professor at Loyola in New Orleans. Because I was responsible for trying to put together a team of Jesuits to send to Paraguay, I approached him with the improbable request that he, at age sixty-five, consider going. He responded immediately that he was scheduled for a medical exam in the next day or so and that if he got a green light from the doctor we could count on him. "You must think this a romantic request, C. J.," I said naively. "No," said C. J., "I've been to Paraguay; it's not romantic." So off he went to Paraguay a few months later, lighthearted and surprising.

In the mid-1980s, as part of his work in Paraguay, C. J. transmitted weekly over Paraguayan radio a classical music program in which he introduced the selections and discussed their merits—in Spanish, of course. That was not so surprising for those who knew of C. J.'s linguistic and musicological sophistication. More startling was his weekly ministering to the poor of Asunción's barrios. A retarded boy whom C. J. had befriended would accompany him. Once a barrio dog bit C. J., and he had to submit to rabies shots. For C. J. none of this was especially noteworthy. It was just his surprising way.

Who would have predicted that an accomplished editor would be so open with a needy scholastic? Or that a chaired professor would so nonchalantly ship out to Paraguay? Or that a polyglot musicologist would put himself in the way of being bitten by a barrio dog? This is the man who once greeted a solemn assemblage of rabbis in Moscow, not in Russian (that would have been easy), but in Hebrew. The same surprising man who celebrated Mass for Paraguayan novices—in Guaraní! And not only that, but singing it, as he told the novices, according to an old Hebrew chant he had picked up in the Middle East.

Heaven will be full of surprises, they say.

Thomas H. Stahel, S.J.
Georgetown University

✉

BEING C. J.'S NURSE during the first serious illness of his life, in a foreign country five thousand miles away from home, at a time when his age made him very vulnerable—were all stars that lined-up just right for our twenty-year acquaintance to grow into a strong friendship. I was with him for many months, as I began my mission in Paraguay, and as he came to face the twilight of his.

C. J. is a true extrovert who generates his energy through relationships. The young Jesuits sought his wise counsel; superiors called upon him to teach and to write; the cultural community of Paraguay gave him countless citations for his research and writing on the history of the Jesuit Reductions; elderly shut-ins were nurtured by his weekly liturgies; and his name lives on as a legend among the simple, uneducated people who live in squalor in the flood basin of the Paraguay River—people to whom *Pa'i Clemente* (Father Clement) also ministered on a weekly basis. And what was most amazing to the Paraguayans is that C. J. learned to communicate with them in their native Guaraní, a most difficult indigenous language of Paraguay that bewildered most veteran Spanish missionaries, but which C. J. learned when he began to study it at age sixty-five.

C. J. enjoys all of his relationships and makes us all feel important. It is this unpretentiousness and simplicity, coupled with such powerful intellectual gifts, that make C. J. who he is. Before all else, C. J. McNaspy is a Jesuit and a priest who has always used his gifts in the service of God's reign. That is what C. J. McNaspy's life is ultimately all about.

Eddie Gros, S.J.
Loyola University, New Orleans

THROUGH OUR YOUNG LIVES we seek out those teachers and individuals who inspire us to grow mentally and spiritually. Father C. J. McNaspy has been that person for so many, and he continues to challenge and astonish his students with his generous and unique spirit. It has been my good fortune to know C. J. in the past few years during his "retirement" and my middle age. And who says the middle-aged don't need models for life and inspiring individuals to point the way, too? C. J. has certainly been that person to me.

As a professor of voice and active professional singer, my life is full of one-on-one contact hours—sometimes upwards of thirty a week. So it is particularly welcome to hear a polite knock at my door asking me to lunch and conversation, real conversation, at the refectory in Thomas Hall. Sometimes we are alone, and it is at these times when I begin to glimpse the amazing breadth of his intellect and experience. I remember an anecdote about a dinner in Greece where C. J. recited in Greek a poem by Sappho to a table of appreciative guests. And all of this is recounted with such sweet nature and beguiling lack of pretension. Other times we dine with members of the community. C. J. has an unfailing instinct for bringing people of like mind together, and often I have discovered, through him, that colleagues I have known only by sight or reputation share the same interests as I. As for C. J. himself, I have never entered into a discussion with him on any topic, either in music or out of it, on which he was not conversant.

Among C. J.'s spiritual gifts is one that I have found very touching—the gift of encouragement. A particularly talented student of mine wondered whether he should sing the Evangelist in Bach's *St. John Passion.* After talking with C. J., he accepted the challenge and went on to perform the role gloriously. My wife Ellen was nervous about her first performance of the soprano solos in the Beethoven *Missa Solemnis* to be performed in Lafayette. He said with empowering confidence, "I know you will be wonderful in it; I only wish I could be there to hear it." "How could I argue with that?" she said, and I knew exactly what she meant.

As I write this, Father McNaspy is recovering from a mild stroke. I don't think my motives are completely selfish in wishing him back on campus as soon as possible; of course I want my friend near me. Like Emily Dickinson who wished just a "little more time for such a curious earth," I wish more time with this generous man of God, this enlightened presence in our lives.

Philip Frohnmayer
Loyola University, New Orleans

✉

C. J. McNaspy is important to me for every one of the thousands of encounters with him that have enriched my life over the past twenty-seven years. He is a person who has formed me and, in fact, been the model for me during all of my Jesuit life. My relationship with him has been exhilarating and fresh, always new and creative—the way that great art is. I am convinced that the artist continually and very naturally makes new statements about our human identity and that the process involves both a continuous gathering and an apprehension of the preceding creative tradition as well as a fresh expression of that tradition revealing some new aspect of who we are. C. J. has been the instance par excellence for me of this paradigm of creativity. How many times over the years have we discussed our favorite pieces by our most-loved composers, usually Bach and Mozart, but also Bernstein and Corigliano, to mention just a few? Each and every time we listen again to these works, a new awareness, however slight, dawns in us, "Yes, that is you who are, because you are hearing your life pass by, knowing that you are a part of what has been, yet always discovering more about yourself in what is newly created."

This paradigm of creativity that my relationship with C. J. typifies for me is anchored in two convictions. The first is that C. J. is a gift to anyone who has the fortune to meet him, but especially a gift to the whole Society of Jesus. Any Jesuit who comes to know C. J. for any length of time will experience him as a person who invites us to make connections not only, simply, with one another, but also, more profoundly, with the depths of our own hearts. I do not know any Jesuit who is as immediately and personally known and loved as C. J. McNaspy. The second has to do with the characteristic way that C. J. unwaveringly responds to the need that we all have for companionship rooted in laughter. Of all of the things he has taught me and shared with me over the years, and they are legion, each is framed by delightful tales embroidered with laughter and sparkling with a zest for life—from reading Horace together on Saturday mornings when I was a young graduate student in music at Tulane Univerity, to discovering with him the only known manuscript collection of music by the eighteenth-century Jesuit composer Domenico Zipoli in a remote corner of Bolivia in 1986, or to the production in 1991 by Jesuits and students of Boston College of an opera first performed by Jesuits and students of the Roman College in 1622. An encounter with C. J. McNaspy, no matter how long, is never to be forgotten, always to be savored; it is an encounter with the best that we are.

T. Frank Kennedy, S.J.
Boston College

N0 DOUBT C. J. McNASPY AGREES with the assertion of Johann Sebastian Bach that "all music should have no other aim than the glory of God and the re-creation of the human spirit." Music brought into being by such as Bach is a strong and eloquent testimony to the godliness inherent in humanity. When God and humanity come together—most supremely in the person of Jesus Christ—the distinctions between "sacred" and "profane" or "divine" and "human" give way to an all-encompassing view of creation as infused with the presence of God.

To me, the essence of C. J.'s life and work lies in his own profound experience of the reality of this "holy humanism," and his subsequent setting out, with a kind of Erasmian brilliance and wit, to share this good news with all kinds of people. As a teacher, C. J. has the rare knack of taking lofty, seemingly complex realms and making them accessible and palpable to readers, listeners, and students. The simplicity and grace with which he leads us into great works of art and music open them up for us and make them come alive. Sometimes it is only later on that we realize what has resulted from this ushering of our minds and hearts: a taste of the transcendent itself.

It is no accident, I feel, that a common appreciation of Bach, bordering on fanaticism, was the initial catalyst in the friendship between "old C. J." and myself in the days when he could justifiably call me "young Brett." *The Well-tempered Clavier* provided our meeting ground, the D-Minor Clavier

Concerto a taking-off point, and the cantatas and passions a grand journey of discovery and delight mutually undertaken. Through this journey, with C. J. as both companion and guide, other worlds of art, literature, and theology gradually unfolded before me in a grand synthesis; connections between Bach and Schubert, Michelangelo and Shakespeare, Francis of Assisi and Ignatius of Loyola became ever more apparent.

I think that during my college years C. J. may have nurtured a secret hope that I might, like him, enter the Society of Jesus. When I finally decided to become a Benedictine, however, he didn't seem to be too disappointed. He said that the Order of Saint Benedict would have been his second choice. Since C. J. has always been for me one of the best examples of religious life well-lived, I like to think that he has a Benedictine corner in his multi-faceted Jesuit heart and that he would see this as no contradiction. After all, Benedict and Ignatius were pointing in the same direction, hundreds of years apart.

Perhaps the increasing popularity of Bach as a kind of prophet to our own overly-secularized era is indicative of our thirst for "ties that bind." This is the same thirst that C. J. the man, the musician, and the minister has been able to help quench for so many of us. The glory of God is the true "re-creation of the human spirit," or, as Irenaeus put it, "humanity fully alive." C. J. has helped countless people to know this. Thank God for such as he.

Sean Brett Duggan, O.S.B.
St. Joseph Seminary College
Saint Benedict, Louisiana

✉

IN THE MIDDLE OF AUGUST 1993, I returned to Ponape Agriculture and Trade School in the Caroline Islands, after having experienced one of the very best years, perhaps the most enjoyable, of my life. At breakfast, shortly after my return, Father Paul Horgan, a fellow Jesuit missionary, asked me how I had liked my sabbatical. I remarked casually that C. J. McNaspy had been a major reason for the success of my year.

As I reflected more later about why I had so spontaneously mentioned C. J., I realized that it was because he had given me what he had obviously given so many of his former students and young Jesuits for decades—namely, a heavy dose of enthusiasm, not only for the arts and humanities but also for life itself. His greatest trait is his uncanny ability—surely a special grace—to animate and propel others into areas they would not go on their own.

We did a lot together during that year. The activities varied, but there was always excitement in the air as we did them. I felt as if we were two kids on an Easter egg hunt. Sometimes we would visit the sick in hospitals, sometimes friends of C. J.'s at their homes. Or C. J. would give me a tour of some of the famous homes in New Orleans' Garden District, houses that I had grown up seeing; with C. J., it was like seeing them for the first time. Frequently, we would go out to movies, and just as frequently stay at Loyola, watching some highly praised classic under Alexis Gonzales' expert direction (and with the benefit of his extraordinary audiovisual equipment). All little things, but savored in a unique way—because of C. J.

Sometime late in my sabbatical year, C. J. told me that I couldn't return to the islands until I had seen the purple martins, birds that come to the Crescent City in the latter part of June and stay for about a month. John Audubon himself recorded their passage, he emphasized. I was less than enthusiastic, but agreed to go with him. When the day for our expedition arrived, we parked near the south-end of the Lake Pontchartrain Causeway—and waited. The sun was going down, but the sky remained clear. Then the symphony of flight began. At first a few clusters of martins appeared, then enough to fill the sky, as if dancing to some measured music we could not hear—then finally the crescendo as thousands danced about us. I told C. J. it was everything he promised and more; in fact, it was one of New Orleans' best kept secrets.

To tell others about the purple martins is, with C. J., to get them excited *about life*.

Terry Todd, S.J.
Ponape, Caroline Islands

✉

C. J.'s APPROACH TO LIFE, it seems me, grows out of his funda-
mental conviction that the vision of beauty and goodness is
not merely a lovelier but a stronger motive for heroic human
effort and heroic generosity to others than is guilt or fear on
the one hand or on the other hand a desire for any of the partial human satisfactions, such as wealth or power or sensuality
or prestige—all of which can and do move us, but never far
enough in the direction in which we most need and most
want to go.

Some people who do not know C. J. very well may have
the impression that he has flitted from flower to flower, that
he is a dilettante. Perhaps he is a dilettante, in the authentic
sense that he always or nearly always finds joy in what he is
doing. But a thoroughly aesthetic approach to life, as C. J. has
demonstrated, and as he has, without putting the matter into
words, helped so many of us to understand, contains its own
rigorous interior discipline.

Living by what is accurately called inspiration can result
in a life full of surprises, odd fragments, and strange juxtaposi-
tions; but it will be a life coherent in ways profound and
organic rather than superficial and imposed.

The old spiritual writers had several good names for this.
One is "purity of intention." Another is "the sacrament of the
present moment."

C. J., ever the artist who prefers to let his work speak for
itself, would never say this sort of thing. And that is one of the
reasons why I feel so strongly impelled to say it.

Hervé Racivitch, S. J.
Ignatius Residence, New Orleans

✉

WHAT NO DOUBT MADE the quotations from Shakespeare and
Keats seem immediately appropriate as an epigraph for C. J.
McNaspy's memoirs were the references to music, which has
been at the heart of C. J.'s apostolate from the beginning.
Anyone who had, as I did, the extraordinary grace of hearing

a McNaspy-trained juniorate choir sing Gregorian chant or classic polyphony on feast days at Grand Coteau knows that, in a variation on Shakespeare, such music does indeed nourish love, the divine initiative remembered in the liturgy. And if unheard melodies are, as Keats suggests, sweeter than heard ones, it is, I would guess, because they invite the imagination to experience timeless beauty.

Ours though is a broader inquiry. How, we wonder, have art, literature, language, and music coalesced in C. J.'s life and in his work? They are all of course the products of and inspirers of the imagination. More than any other teacher I have had, C. J. showed me, by indirection of course, the limitless potential of the human imagination. Without imagination, there is no real freedom—no contemplation, no ritual, no celebration, indeed no play. It is play, I propose, the other shared image from Shakespeare and Keats, that suggests a unifying principle for C. J.'s apostolic endeavors. True, there is a manifest dimension of play in the arts and humanities that are C. J.'s actual subject matter. Language is play, art and literature are play, music is play, liturgy is play, and so forth, even if for the writer, the artist, the musician, the liturgist, they are also often painfully difficult work. But C. J. always transcended the obvious and inspired us to attend to unheard melodies—to experience through play, what William Faulkner called, the eternal verities of the human spirit.

C. J.'s genius as a teacher is, quite simply, to have made study seem like fun, work like play. For his students over the years as well as his friends (and I have been blessed with his friendship too for over four decades now), he has always been the *magister ludi* par excellence. (The Latin word *ludus* means both school and play.) It was C. J. who convinced me early on that art, music, and literature, maybe precisely because they are inherently playful, are also profoundly religious, radically spiritual. They bind us together; they open us up to the divine. One cannot believe without the freedom to imagine greater beauty, better worlds, fuller possibilities.

Hugo Rahner in his classic work *Man at Play* described briefly, yet precisely what C. J.'s pedagogical grace in action was like for us, linking the profoundly human with eschatological hope through the pleasure of play. "There is a sacral secret at the root and in the flowering of all play," Rahner wrote, "it is man's hope for another life taking visible form in gesture."

Jack May
Louisiana State University

It was presumptuous enough for me to attempt a sort of auto-biography or self-exposé, regardless of how many disclaimers of self-glorification. But for me to print evaluations of my own life as seen by such friends as these—this would seem to be a new summit of audacity, a truly reckless disregard for the truth of Pascal's dictum that *"le moi est haïssable."*

When I first mentioned my misgivings to one of these friends, his reply pleased me so much that I am going to print it here: "True, *le moi est haïssable.* But *le moi* refers to the self as an object of interest apart from or even to the exclusion of others. People are, and ought to be, interested in themselves, to love themselves as they love others—no more, and no less. To fail to notice and to delight in what is interesting in one's self is to diminish one's alertness to what is interesting in others. The 'new summit of audacity' to which you refer is completely in character, one more instance of a special kind of audacity, a joie de vivre, which is closer to humility than it is to self-conceit."

If this seems redolent of C. S. Lewis, it may be because for both my friend and me C. S. Lewis has been for many years a constant influence, beginning in my case even before I studied under and with him at Oxford.

Let me not protest too much. Is it any wonder that some of the friends who have contributed to this final chapter have more than once laughed about my being a sort of male equivalent of Auntie Mame? Surely, one quality of Auntie Mame's that I would most happily avow is the great pleasure—shall we say the "litur-gical" pleasure?—I have always found in bringing together peo-ple of all sorts and conditions and talents and backgrounds and seeing them enjoy and appreciate one another. As another friend was kind enough to say, I helped him to understand "that art, music, and literature, maybe precisely because they are inher-ently playful, are also profoundly religious, radically spiritual."

Play on!

Postscript

Liturgy of Christian Resurrection, 1995

Homily at the Vigil of the
Liturgy of Christian Resurrection

by Father Louis A. Poché
Holy Name of Jesus Church, Loyola University
New Orleans, Louisiana
6 February 1995

In Franco Zeffirelli's remarkable film, *Jesus of Nazareth,* there is a scene in which Jesus and his friends one night are all asleep out in an open field, except for two of the disciples. They are having a discussion. It had been a long and exhausting day, and their eyes had seen marvelous things and they had heard extraordinary words. One of the two who could not sleep wondered wearily if he would ever see his family again. "No," his companion answered, "you will never go back. You will never see Capernaum again. We are following HIM now," he said, nodding in the direction where Jesus was asleep, "and our lives will never be the same. And neither will all the world."

C. J. McNaspy affected the lives of many people, as all of us know. Those of us who sat at his feet as students can truly say that our lives have not been the same. As for changing the world, well, if traveling to all parts of the world is a way of changing it, we know that C. J. tried that too. He surely took to heart that part of the Jesuit rule that states, "It is our vocation to travel to any part of the world where there is hope of God's greater glory." C. J. was a great traveler. Whether on the back of a camel in Egypt or as an easy rider clinging to the seat of a motorbike in the barrios of Asunción, he was always just C. J., living in the present moment, living for the present moment, and never allowing himself to be impressed more by the learned than by the lowly. His students who needed him more, in fact, received more. He made many friends and he counted many very close friends, but the friends never formed a fraternity or club around him, and C. J. never closed the circle.

"Blessed are the eyes that see what you see, the ears that hear what you hear." C. J.'s approach to life was certainly an aesthetic one. Yet the inner vision of beauty that inspired him clearly grew out of a faith that led him early in life to concentrate his skills on the sacred liturgy. In 1945 at Grand Coteau, he was telling us things about life and worship that were realized in some modest measure more than twenty years later with the promulgation of Vatican II's Constitution on the Sacred Liturgy. He tried, through liturgy, music, and the fine arts, to share with us what his own eyes had seen and his ears had heard—a vision of life, of beauty, of God; a vision that acquired its Jesuit shape through his formation in the Ignatian school of the *Spiritual Exercises.* Because of that vision, music for C. J. was never just music, and people—all people—were never just people.

A native of Lafayette, Louisiana, C. J. made perhaps the shortest trip of his life when he entered the Jesuit novitiate at Grand Coteau in 1931 at the age of sixteen. His father had been an athlete and was a college professor of physics and athletic coach at Southwestern. He died young, suddenly, when C. J. was just eighteen and still a very young Jesuit at Grand Coteau. C. J.'s mother, who lived a long and beautiful life, once said near the end that if she were to write a life of her son, librarians would not know whether to catalogue it as fact or fiction. Mary Agnes Kennington, C. J.'s only sister (there were no brothers), lives in retirement in St. Louis. She and her late husband, and their five children and their families, have remained close to their brother and uncle through the years.

C. J.'s first book was about astronomy. He wrote it when he was twelve. Twenty-nine books later, and written when he was seventy-nine, his last book—memoirs entitled *Play On!*—was fortunately finished just before he died, fortunate for us because this evening even the broadest and most sweeping allusions to his published works and other enormous achievements would surely take us beyond appropriate limits of time. The books, the many hundreds of articles and lectures, the broadcasts and telecasts in many countries and in the many languages he mastered and taught, not to mention the numerous interesting persons he met in his travels, overwhelm our minds. We can only anticipate the publication soon of *Play On!* It will, at the very least, be much fun to read.

C. J. McNaspy never permitted his intellectual work to keep him from direct pastoral contact with people. At the age of sixty-five, he left for the mission in Paraguay where he labored for nine years. Though most of his activity there was in the classroom and in studios and lecture halls, he nonetheless went on many occasions to minister to the poor, directly and in their own tongue. Back in New Orleans, it was C. J. who went every Sunday to offer Mass and speak words of comfort and hope to the residents at the New Orleans Home and Center for Rehabilitation. The people whose lives he touched through the years of pastoral ministry will long remember Father McNaspy.

Father Hervé Racivitch and C. J. spent long hours together during these last months and days at Ignatius Residence. They were great friends. Together they worked daily on the memoirs, read books and articles, and listened to music. At 10:25 this past Friday morning, they were listening to an early Beethoven String Quartet when suddenly C. J., who apparently had suffered another stroke the day before, drew his last breath and spoke the words, "Yes . . . yes!" It was February 3, 1995, the feast of Saint Blaise, patron of Paraguay.

Blessed are the eyes that C. J. McNaspy helped to see what he saw and the ears that he trained to hear what he heard. Prophets and kings were never so lucky.

Homily at the Liturgy of Christian Resurrection

by Father Eddie Gros
Holy Name of Jesus Church,
7 February 1995

The question "Why me?" has come to mind often since I was asked to preach this homily. There are certainly those who are much more capable, those who have known him much longer than I. Why me? Why anyone? Can anyone capture the life of C. J. McNaspy in a homily? I'll speak to you out of my experience of him, because that's probably why I was asked to do this.

I was assigned to Asunción, Paraguay, in August of 1986, and arrived on the scene while C. J. was enjoying great health and success there. In November, he got hepatitis and came very near death. I was his nurse and constant companion in this illness, the first serious illness of his life, and this more than anything forged the relationship which I had begun with him some twenty years earlier. This illness marked the twilight of his career, for he soon returned to the States. He came back to Paraguay for only two other short periods in subsequent years.

To have seen C. J. in operation in Paraguay was a genuine inspiration, but to see C. J. in one place is to have seen him every place. That's basically the theme of this homily.

You must start with his room, just as he does in his memoirs. Music, tapes, and slides were everywhere as well as books on art, music, Jesuitica, and many other subjects—Scripture, literature, history. Seasoning this academic gumbo was a generous sprinkling of your letters to him—letters that he always answered promptly and knew where to find in the organized chaos that was his room.

Nothing thrilled C. J. more than a person's discovering something of fascination in his room. There was no doubt he would lend it to you.

In Paraguay, his room included many scientific curiosities—binoculars, optical illusions, magnets, and the like. The binoculars were the basis of his astronomy classes when he took the Paraguayan scholastics out at night into the cow pasture to observe the heavens. His star chart still adorns the reading room at Javier in Asunción. His French *Jerusalem Bible* was used for teaching the scholastics to read French because they need to pass a language proficiency exam before going on to study theology.

His humble hand-held electronic keyboard assisted him in his music appreciation classes. The promised piano never arrived, but he happily made do without it.

Javier had one slide projector which he used successfully to create magic in the classroom as he showed his slides of art and travel. The music tapes were played on a simple boom box sort of apparatus, which he always had to fish out of some scholastic's room when he wanted to use it. All of this illustrates that C. J.'s magic could never be restrained *por falta de recursos.* The dream was brought to life there, perhaps with more gusto than ever. And much of the magic can be indexed simply by looking at his room.

Another way to talk about C. J.'s magic is by telling "C. J. Believe It or Nots." We all have "C. J. stories" and pass on tales of his feats in that way. Here are a few of mine.

At age sixty-five, C. J. started studying Guaraní, a most difficult indigenous language of Paraguay. He managed to work through the entire Christian Scriptures, parsing every word. He learned the Canon of the Mass in Guaraní and many expressions and sayings. Just two weeks ago, when he met Nery Gomez, a Paraguayan scholastic here today, C. J. greeted him in Guaraní and charmed him with many phrases still remembered.

In his later years, C. J. published in Spanish. By the time I got to Paraguay, his Spanish was so polished that he did not have to pass his articles before native speakers before submitting them. He published books on many subjects in Spanish—a biography of Saint Roque González, a guide to visiting the Reductions, and even a catechetical guide in which he tried to answer questions about the faith that he had most frequently been asked. Of course, he continued to write in English, and all of his publications were hammered out at incredibly high rates of speed on a manual typewriter, either in sweltering heat or in chilly winters, long after most of us were ushered into the computer age.

As for his influence on the cultural community of Paraguay, these memories stand out. C. J. managed to get the Asunción symphony orchestra to travel to the site of the Trinidad Reduction—a six-hour bus ride from Asunción—to perform the music of Domenico Zipoli, the Italian Jesuit composer who was among the earliest missionaries to South America, an artist whose works C. J. researched and wrote about. Indeed, C. J.'s contribution to our appreciation of the Reductions—research, writing, commentaries, even a documentary film—will stand out for years to come.

The Gospel reading today prompts me to reflect: did not our hearts burn within us as he talked to us on the road, as he explored the Reductions with us, explained musical compositions to us, and wrote letters to us? All of these "feats," as I have called them, were done to help our hearts to burn, to help manifest the reign of God in our world. Let no one be fooled. C. J. McNaspy was above and over all a Jesuit and a priest. More important by far than his feats were his friends.

In Asunción, there is a young man named Adolfo, seriously challenged mentally, who was like an adopted son to C. J. Adolfo still comes to Javier to ask about him. C. J. spent hours patiently talking to Adolfo. Poor people who live in the squalor of the Paraguay River basin were ministered to by C. J. on a weekly basis. For them, C. J. was a great friend. They still ask about him too. He celebrated Mass in three different poverty-stricken communities every weekend, in addition to his liturgy at the local retirement home.

C. J. had friends, too, from high stations of Paraguayan society—from the American Embassy, the Paraguayan Cultural Center, and the University of Asunción. The finest minds in the country consulted him and sought his counsel and friendship.

The young Jesuits there loved him so much they gave him the name *Joven Clemente*—"Young Clement." They loved him, and he loved them. He used to go out to cheer them on at the volleyball court, which came to be named Estadio McNaspy, because they had heard the story of the stadium in Lafayette named after his father. He frequently reminded the scholastics that the only three surviving Jesuits from his novitiate class (at that time Youree Watson, Ed Sheridan, and himself) were the nonathletes, who watched from the sidelines!

Those who want a chronology of his life, 1915 to 1995, will find it in his memoirs, from his Lafayette youth, through his studies at Grand Coteau, St. Louis, Canada, and Oxford, to his varied apostolic ministry—regency at Spring Hill, juniorate professor at Grand Coteau, music dean at Loyola, associate editor of *Amer-*

ica, visiting professor at Sophia University in Tokyo, missioner in Paraguay, and finally teacher again at Loyola. *Play On!* will be published by Loyola Press. It is the story of his life, but it is also, to a really great extent, a story about us, the people in his life.

We will all miss him, but the magic lives on, and we will continue to recognize him in the breaking of the bread. His whole life was lived for that purpose: that people discover the wonders and glory of God in the marvels of the universe and in the artistic creations of the greatest hearts and minds of human history.

Last night, I broke into a smile as I remembered that the date of C. J.'s heavenly birth, February 3, marked the sixth anniversary of the military coup that overthrew Paraguayan dictator Alfredo Stroessner—the longest ruling dictator in Latin America and one of the cruelest. By comparison, what a silent revolution C. J. effected, the aesthetic revolution! The title of his book on Roque González is *Conquistador sin Espada,* the conqueror without a sword. The ultimate "state of siege," so to speak.

To this revolution we all say, "Yes . . . yes," the very last words C. J. uttered as he listened to a Beethoven quartet. The words do indeed end on an affirmative note, as we should this noon. For me, personally, *el cruz del sur* or the Southern Cross will always remind me of C. J., the one who taught me how to find it in the sky. Those stars guide me back south to Paraguay and will forever be a sign of God and of C. J. watching out for me.

Reflections at the Conclusion of the Liturgy of Christian Resurrection

by Father John A. Armstrong,
Acting Provincial of the New Orleans Province

C. J. loved nothing more than being surrounded by his friends. I first met him when I was an awkward and confused twenty-year-old. I soon found that to know C. J. was to know all of his friends. Nothing delighted him more than to introduce people he loved to one another. His love for others and his enduring friendships with them were deeply rooted in his faith. We knew that what we entrusted to him was safe with him because he treasured it, whatever it was.

An instance from my own life comes immediately to mind. When I had known him for a while, I felt that I wanted to tell him what his friendship had meant to me. Anyone who knew C. J. well is aware that this kind of conversation was one that he had little patience with. If you tried to speak that directly about such matters, he quickly changed the subject to something else. In wondering how to express my feelings, I happened on this plan. When a Jesuit pronounces his vows of commitment, he makes three handwritten copies—two for official files, one for himself. It occurred to me that I could give him my own copy of my profession of vows. The moment I gave it to him was one of the very rare occasions when I ever saw him at a loss for words. The incident illustrates perfectly the kind of trust that he inspired. People of widely varying philosophies and points of view found C. J. to be someone they could trust totally. It was that trust that moved me to give him what was in my then young life as a Jesuit my more treasured possession. It is a gift I never regretted.

More than anyone I have known, C. J. lived the mystery of the Incarnation. It was truly his life. He lived and breathed the reality that God is revealed in everything that is good. Great art, great music, the classics of literature—these are all revelations of God among us. C. J. reminded us that God is also alive in each of us; he helped us to believe in the presence of Jesus in each of our hearts because he himself believed it so strongly. He helped us to believe that each of us could communicate the Jesus in our hearts by letting us know that he experienced Him there. C. J. quietly reminded us of what we can and must be for one another. That was surely his greatest gift.

Index